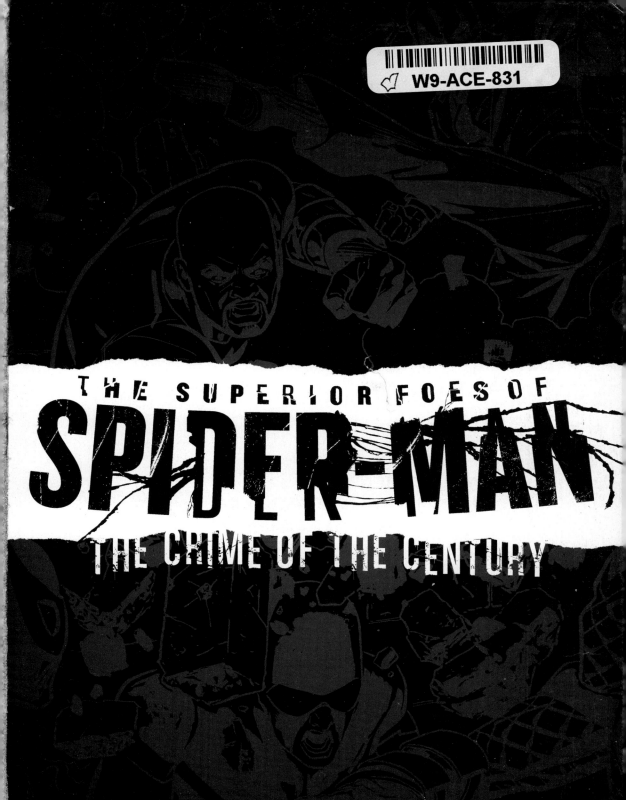

THE SUPERIOR FOES OF
SPIDER-MAN
THE CRIME OF THE CENTURY

#7
WRITER
NICK SPENCER
ARTIST
RICH ELLIS
COLOR ARTIST
LEE LOUGHRIDGE
COVER ARTIST
IN-HYUK LEE

#8
WRITER
NICK SPENCER
ARTIST
STEVE LIEBER
COLOR ARTIST
RACHELLE ROSENBERG
COVER ARTIST
IN-HYUK LEE

#9
WRITER
NICK SPENCER
ARTIST
STEVE LIEBER
ADDITIONAL ART
RICH ELLIS
COLOR ARTISTS
RACHELLE ROSENBERG WITH
RUTH REDMOND &
RICHARD ELLIS
COVER ARTISTS
STEVE LIEBER &
RACHELLE ROSENBERG

#10
WRITER
JAMES ASMUS
RECAP ART
GERARDO SANDOVAL &
ANDRES MOSSA
COVER ARTIST
JOE QUINONES

"FILLING IN"
PENCILER
CARMEN NUNEZ CARNERO
INKER
TERRY PALLOT
COLORIST
ANDRES MOSSA

"DRIVEN"
ARTIST
NUNO PLATI

"TRIAL AND TERROR"
ARTIST
SIYA OUM

"THE ADVENTURES OF THE SPEED DEMON"
ARTIST
PEPE LARRAZ
COLOR ARTIST
ANDRES MOSSA

#11
"DON'T FEEL BAD, YOU CAN BE GOOD"
WRITER
TOM PEYER
ARTIST
WILLIAM SLINEY
COLOR ARTIST
CHRIS SOTOMAYOR
COVER ARTISTS
AL BARRIONUEVO &
CHRIS SOTOMAYOR

"A GRIZZLY SITUATION"
WRITER
TOM PEYER
PENCILER
CARMEN CARNERO
INKER
TERRY PALLOT
COLORIST
CHRIS SOTOMAYOR

"THE SUPERIOR LOOTER"
WRITER
ELLIOTT KALAN
ARTIST
NUNO PLATI
COLORIST
JOHN RAUCH

LETTERERS
VC'S JOE CARAMAGNA &
CLAYTON COWLES

EDITOR
TOM BRENNAN

SENIOR EDITOR
STEPHEN WACKER

Special Thanks to Zach Fischer

Collection Editor: **Alex Starbuck** • Assistant Editor: **Sarah Brunstad**
Editors, Special Projects: **Jennifer Grünwald & Mark D. Beazley** • Senior Editor, Special Projects: **Jeff Youngquist**
SVP Print, Sales & Marketing: **David Gabriel** • Book Design: **Nelson Ribeiro**

Editor in Chief: **Axel Alonso** • Chief Creative Officer: **Joe Quesada** • Publisher: **Dan Buckley** • Executive Producer: **Alan Fine**

THE SUPERIOR FOES OF SPIDER-MAN VOL. 2: THE CRIME OF THE CENTURY. Contains material originally published in magazine form as THE SUPERIOR FOES OF SPIDER-MAN #7-11. First printing 2014. ISBN# 978-0-7851-8495-9. Published by MARVEL WORLDWIDE, INC., a subsidiary of MARVEL ENTERTAINMENT, LLC. OFFICE OF PUBLICATION: 135 West 50th Street, New York, NY 10020. **Printed in Canada**. ALAN FINE, EVP - Office of the President, Marvel Worldwide, Inc. and EVP & CMO Marvel Characters B.V.; DAN BUCKLEY, Publisher & President - Print, Animation & Digital Divisions; JOE QUESADA, Chief Creative Officer; TOM BREVOORT, SVP of Publishing; DAVID BOGART, SVP of Operations & Procurement, Publishing; C.B. CEBULSKI, SVP of Creator & Content Development; DAVID GABRIEL, SVP Print, Sales & Marketing; JIM O'KEEFE, VP of Operations & Logistics; DAN CARR, Executive Director of Publishing Technology; SUSAN CRESPI, Editorial Operations Manager; ALEX MORALES, Publishing Operations Manager; STAN LEE, Chairman Emeritus. For [redacted]

BOOMERANG, SHOCKER, OVERDRIVE, SPEED DEMON, AND BEETLE ARE NOT HEROES. THEY'RE NOT LOVEABLE ROGUES, AND THEY'RE NOT REBELS WITH A CAUSE. MAKE NO MISTAKE, THE NEW SINISTER SIX ARE VILLAINS, PLAIN AND SIMPLE. THEY'RE LIARS, CHEATERS AND THIEVES. THEY DON'T LIKE YOU. THEY DON'T EVEN LIKE EACH OTHER THAT MUCH. THE ONE THING THEY HAVE IN COMMON IS A SHARED HATRED FOR THEIR NEMESIS, THE SUPERIOR SPIDER-MAN – EVEN IF HE'S POSSESSED BY THEIR OLD BOSS DOCTOR OCTOPUS AT THE MOMENT. SOMETIMES THAT MUTUAL DISDAIN FORCES THEM TO SUCK IT UP AND JOIN FORCES.

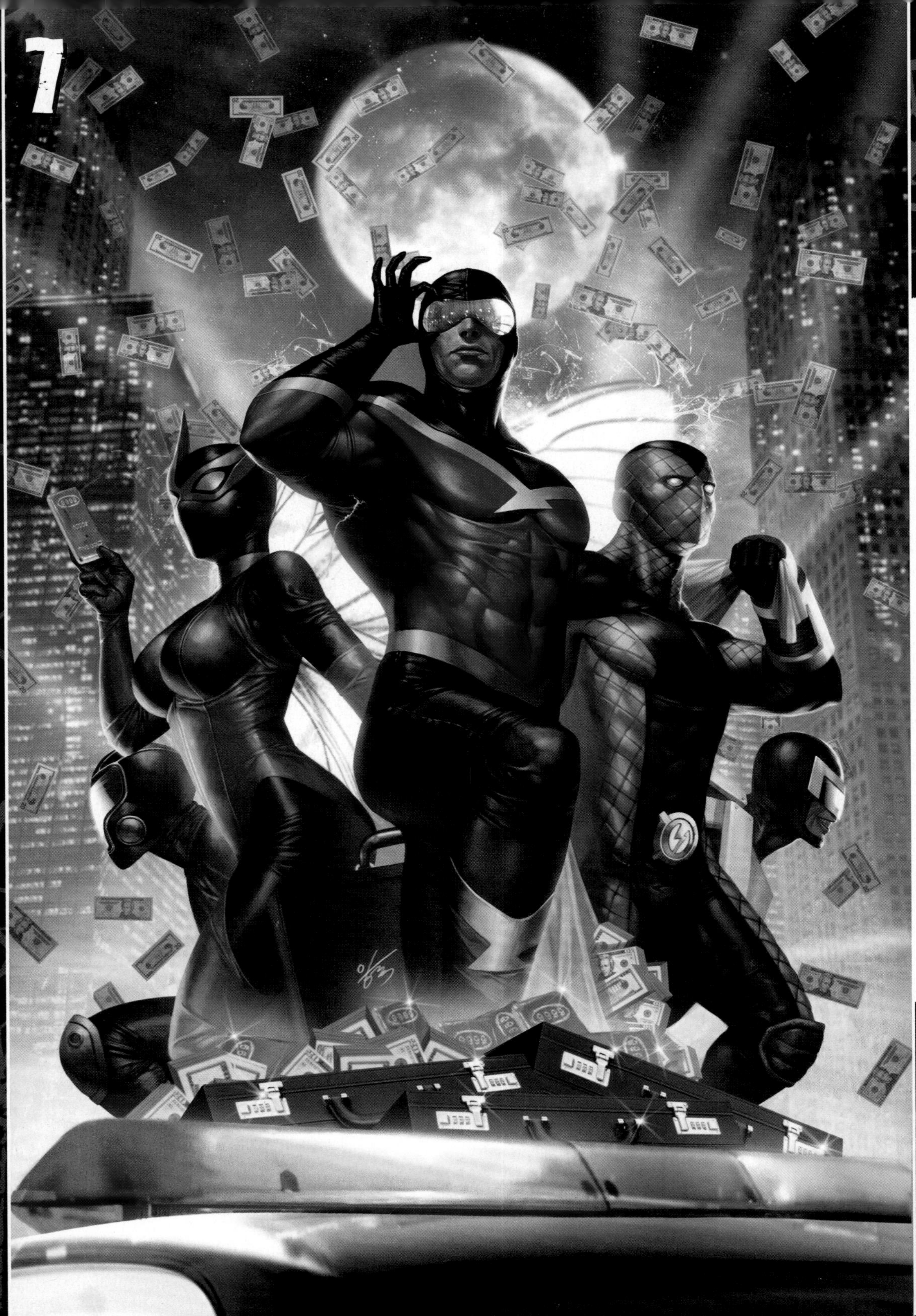
7

DAILY BUGLE

NEW YORK'S FINEST DAILY NEWSPAPER

SINCE 1897

$1.00 (in NYC)
$1.50 (outside city)

INSIDE: S.H.I.E.L.D. ATTACKS THE JEAN GREY SCHOOL IN WESTCHESTER – WHY? RUMOR HAS IT THE SCHOOL'S HEADMASTER, LOGAN, IS "KILLABLE"; THE FOUR SEASONS HOTEL IN HOUSTON EXPLODES – WAS A SPIDER-MAN ON THE SCENE?

BEETLEMANIA!

Little is known about the new Beetle – she first hopped on the scene in battle with Captain America and The Black Widow. After an inauspicious debut, she joined with Boomerang's new Sinister Six – but who is she? And how did she end up in a life of crime?

IT'S TOMBSTONE

Super crime boss Tombstone is back on the scene – the seemingly unkillable, superstrong mobster was spotted at Owl's headquarters on "family matters."

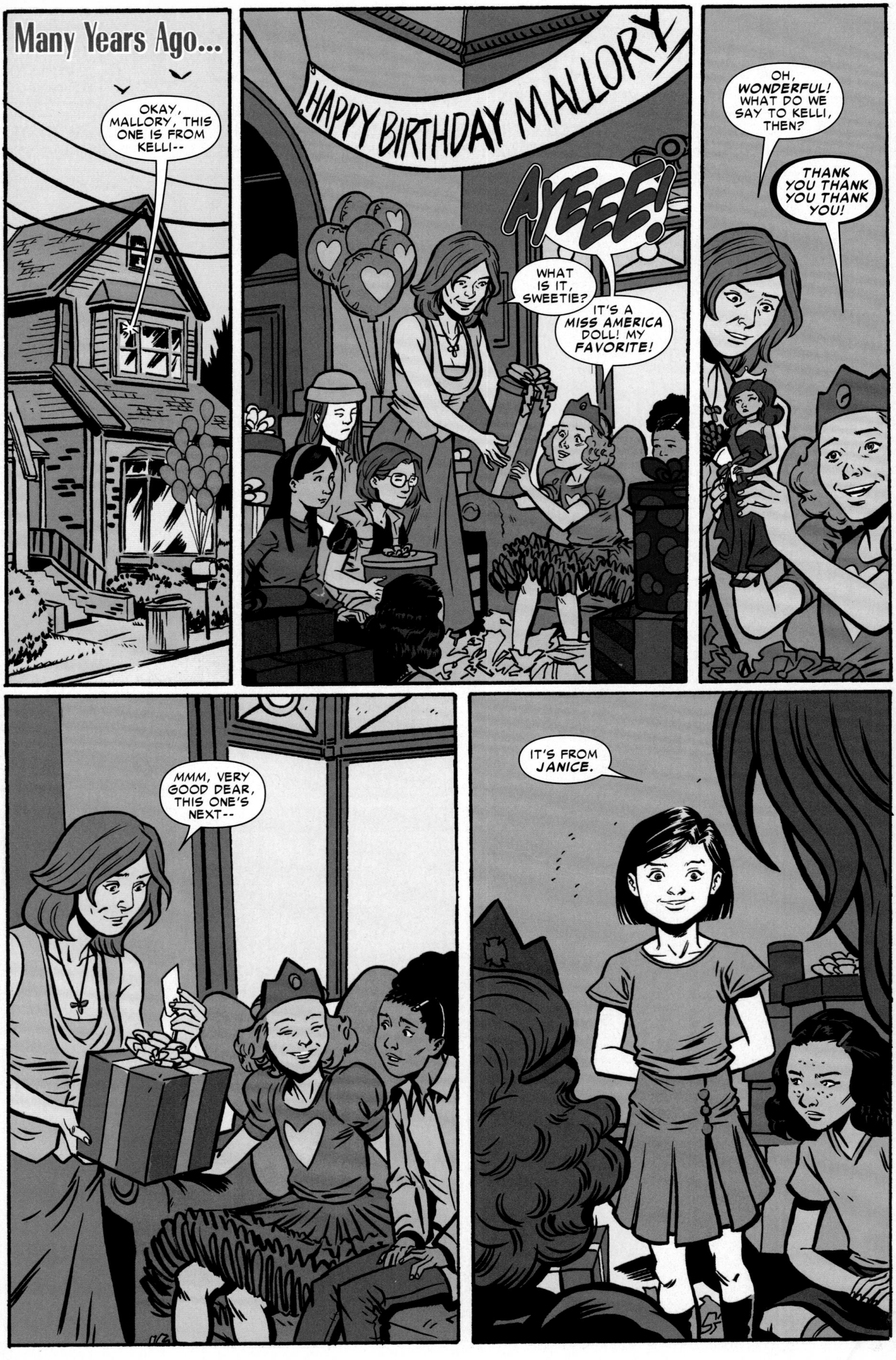
Many Years Ago...
OKAY, MALLORY, THIS ONE IS FROM KELLI--
HAPPY BIRTHDAY MALLORY
AYEEE!
WHAT IS IT, SWEETIE?
IT'S A MISS AMERICA DOLL! MY FAVORITE!
OH, WONDERFUL! WHAT DO WE SAY TO KELLI, THEN?
THANK YOU THANK YOU THANK YOU!
MMM, VERY GOOD DEAR, THIS ONE'S NEXT--
IT'S FROM JANICE.

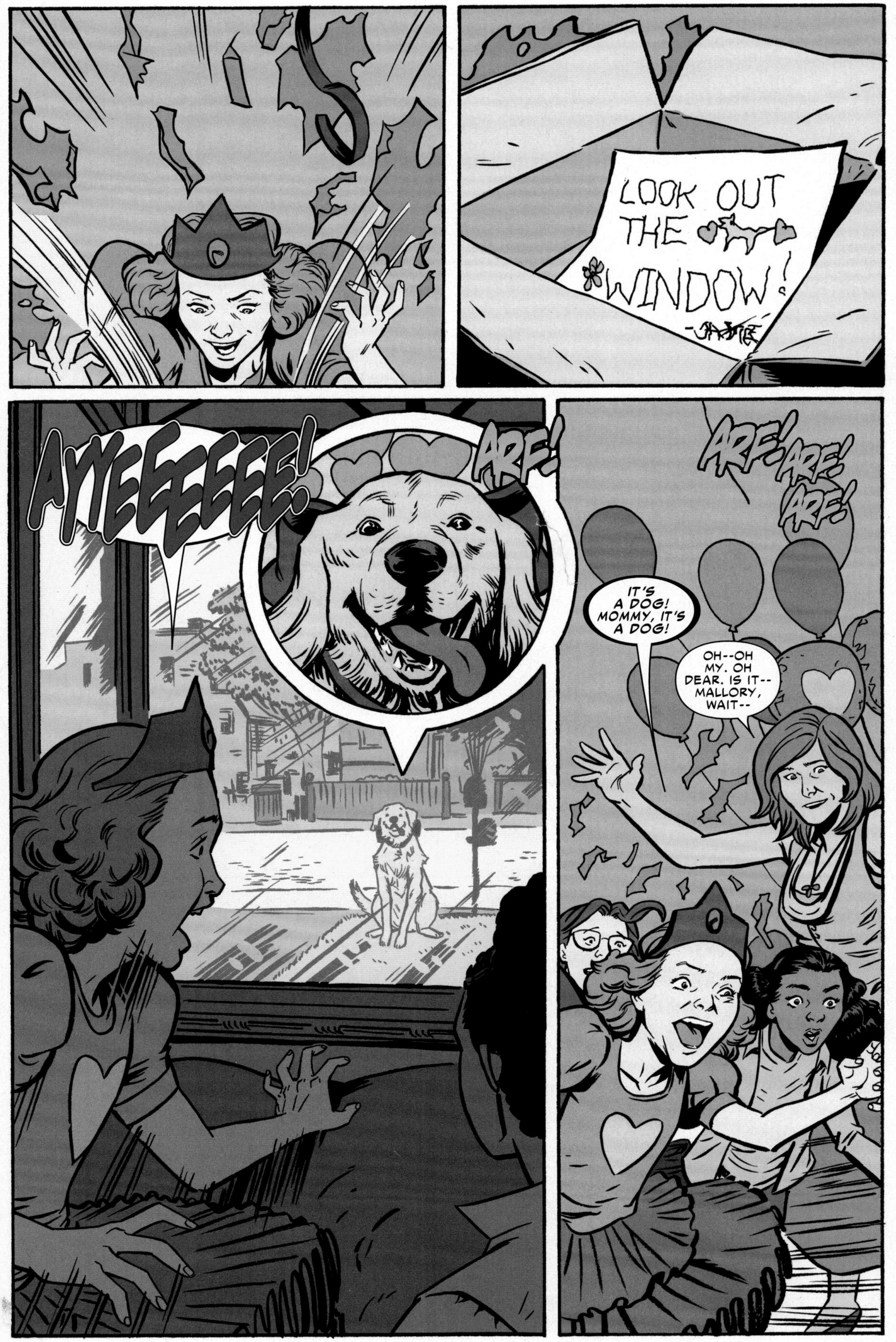
LOOK OUT THE WINDOW!
AYYEEEEEE!
ARF!
ARF! ARF! ARF!
IT'S A DOG! MOMMY, IT'S A DOG!
OH--OH MY. OH DEAR. IS IT-- MALLORY, WAIT--

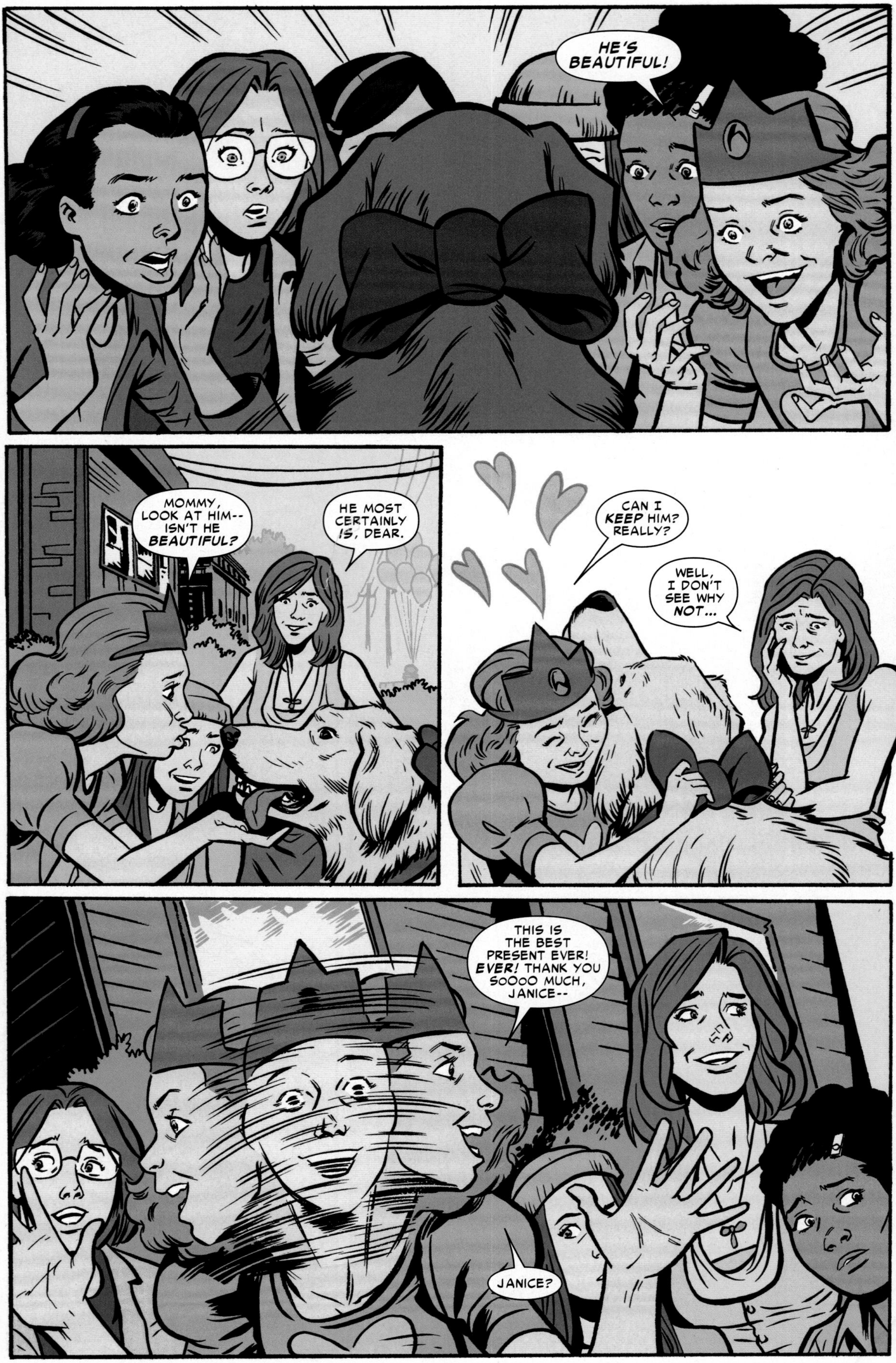
HE'S BEAUTIFUL!
MOMMY, LOOK AT HIM-- ISN'T HE BEAUTIFUL?
HE MOST CERTAINLY IS, DEAR.
CAN I KEEP HIM? REALLY?
WELL, I DON'T SEE WHY NOT...
THIS IS THE BEST PRESENT EVER! EVER! THANK YOU SOOOO MUCH, JANICE--
JANICE?

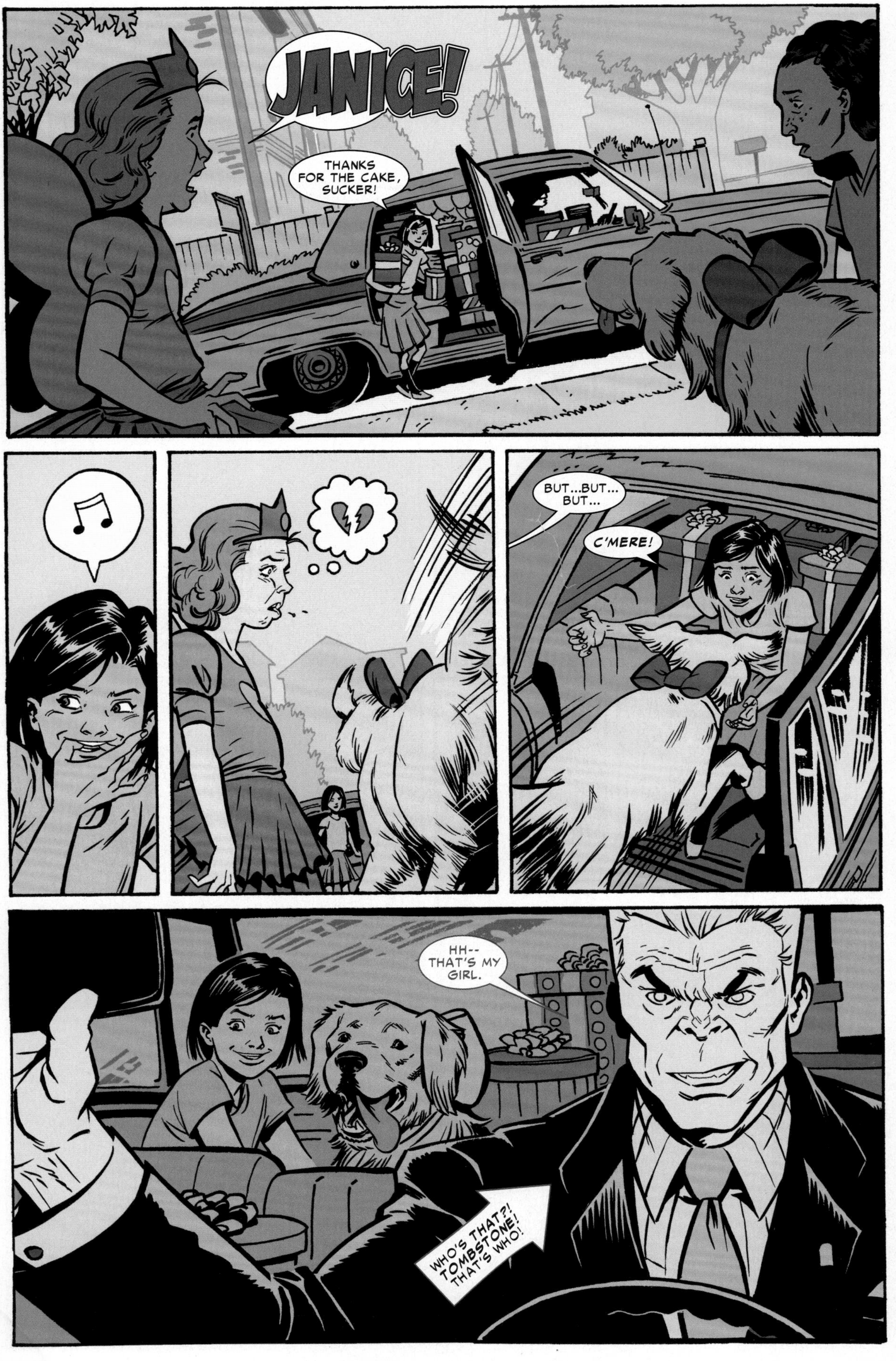

JANICE!
THANKS FOR THE CAKE, SUCKER!
BUT...BUT... BUT...
C'MERE!
HH-- THAT'S MY GIRL.
WHO'S THAT?! TOMBSTONE! THAT'S WHO!

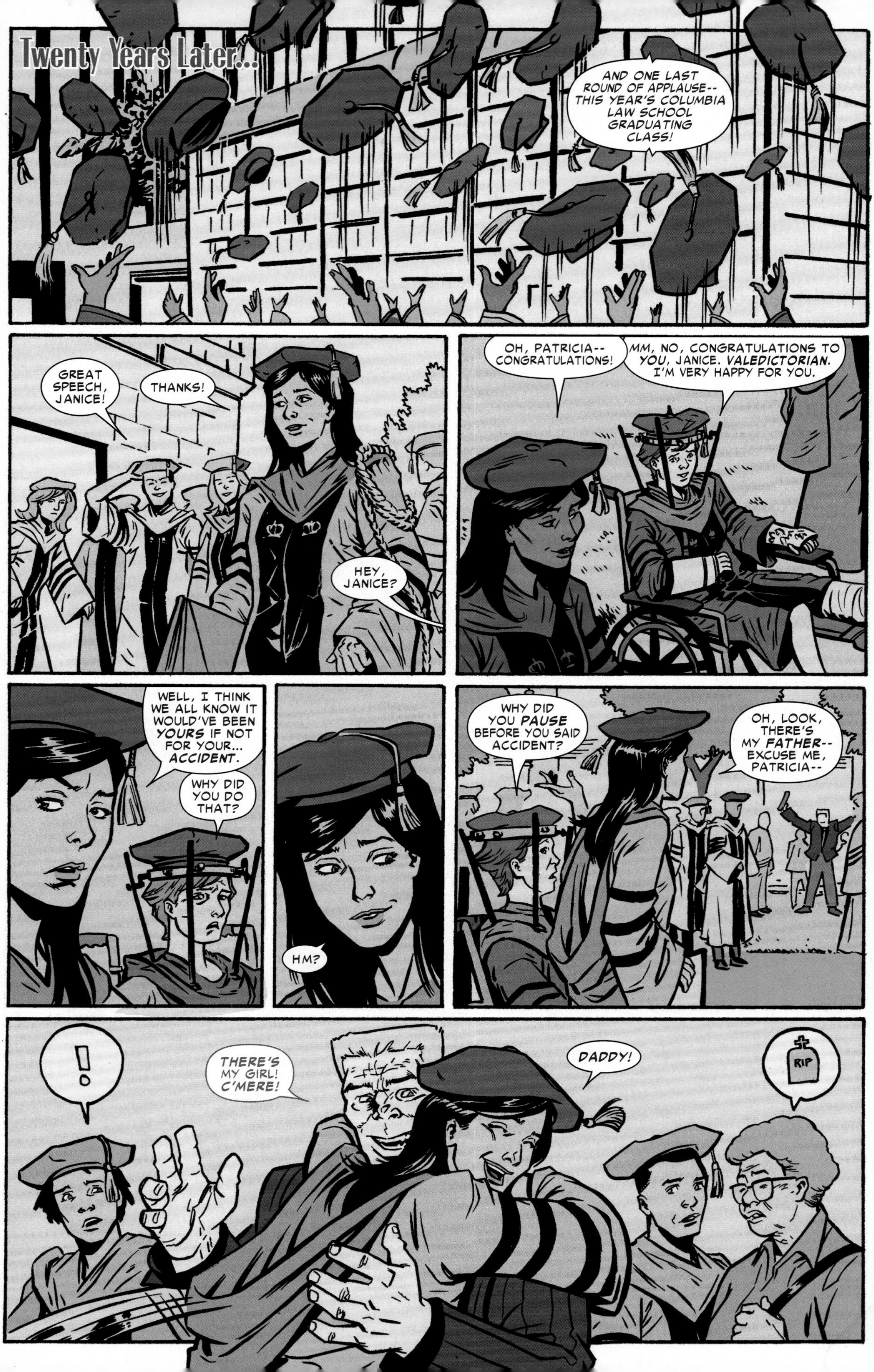
Twenty Years Later...
AND ONE LAST ROUND OF APPLAUSE-- THIS YEAR'S COLUMBIA LAW SCHOOL GRADUATING CLASS!
GREAT SPEECH, JANICE!
THANKS!
HEY, JANICE?
OH, PATRICIA-- CONGRATULATIONS!
MM, NO, CONGRATULATIONS TO YOU, JANICE. VALEDICTORIAN. I'M VERY HAPPY FOR YOU.
WELL, I THINK WE ALL KNOW IT WOULD'VE BEEN YOURS IF NOT FOR YOUR... ACCIDENT.
WHY DID YOU DO THAT?
HM?
WHY DID YOU PAUSE BEFORE YOU SAID ACCIDENT?
OH, LOOK, THERE'S MY FATHER-- EXCUSE ME, PATRICIA--
!
THERE'S MY GIRL! C'MERE!
DADDY!
RIP

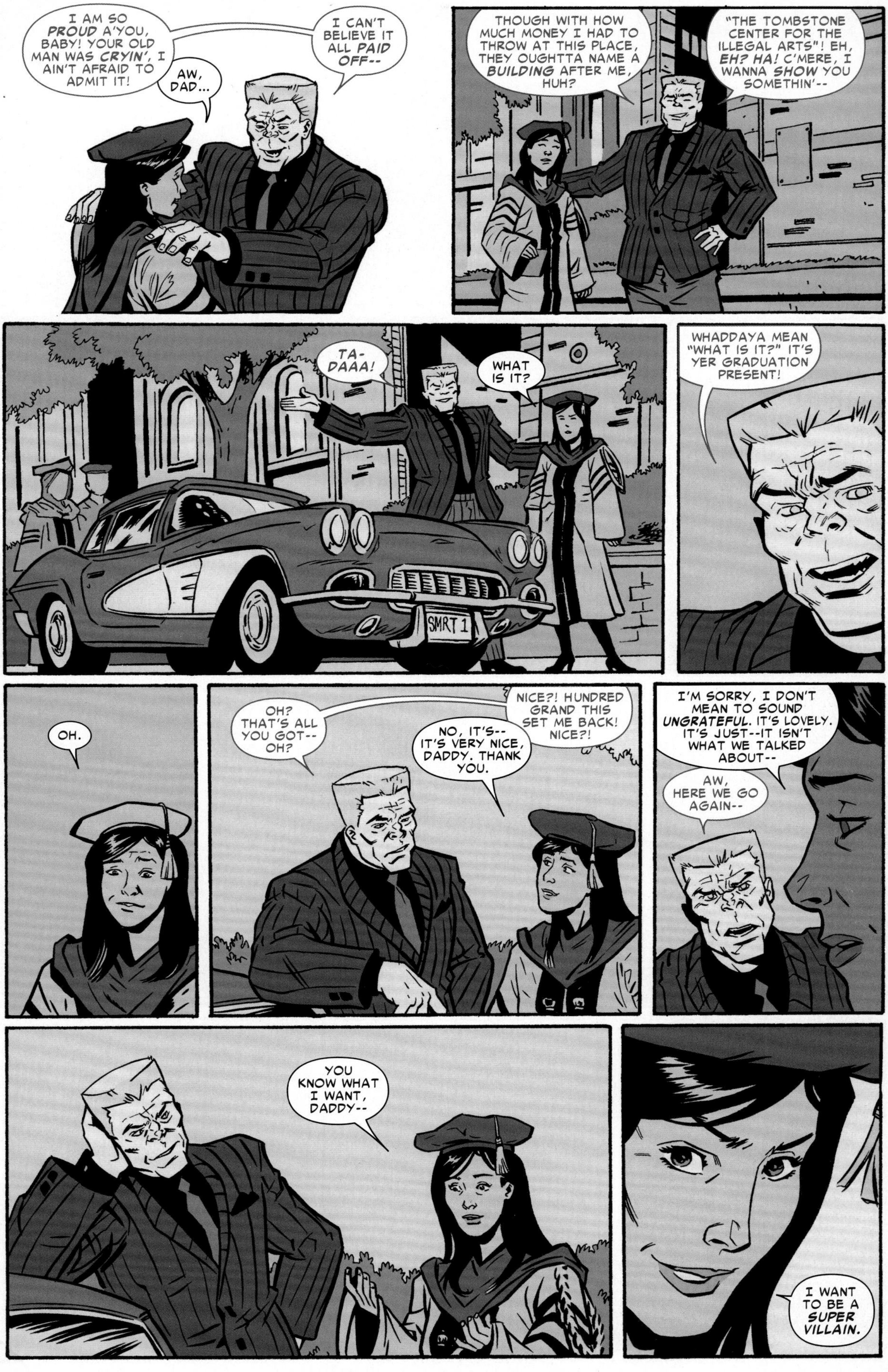
I AM SO PROUD A'YOU, BABY! YOUR OLD MAN WAS CRYIN', I AIN'T AFRAID TO ADMIT IT!
I CAN'T BELIEVE IT ALL PAID OFF--
AW, DAD...
THOUGH WITH HOW MUCH MONEY I HAD TO THROW AT THIS PLACE, THEY OUGHTTA NAME A BUILDING AFTER ME, HUH?
"THE TOMBSTONE CENTER FOR THE ILLEGAL ARTS"! EH, EH? HA! C'MERE, I WANNA SHOW YOU SOMETHIN'--
TA-DAAA!
WHAT IS IT?
SMRT 1
WHADDAYA MEAN "WHAT IS IT?" IT'S YER GRADUATION PRESENT!
OH.
OH? THAT'S ALL YOU GOT-- OH?
NICE?! HUNDRED GRAND THIS SET ME BACK! NICE?!
NO, IT'S-- IT'S VERY NICE, DADDY. THANK YOU.
I'M SORRY, I DON'T MEAN TO SOUND UNGRATEFUL. IT'S LOVELY. IT'S JUST--IT ISN'T WHAT WE TALKED ABOUT--
AW, HERE WE GO AGAIN--
YOU KNOW WHAT I WANT, DADDY--
I WANT TO BE A SUPER VILLAIN.

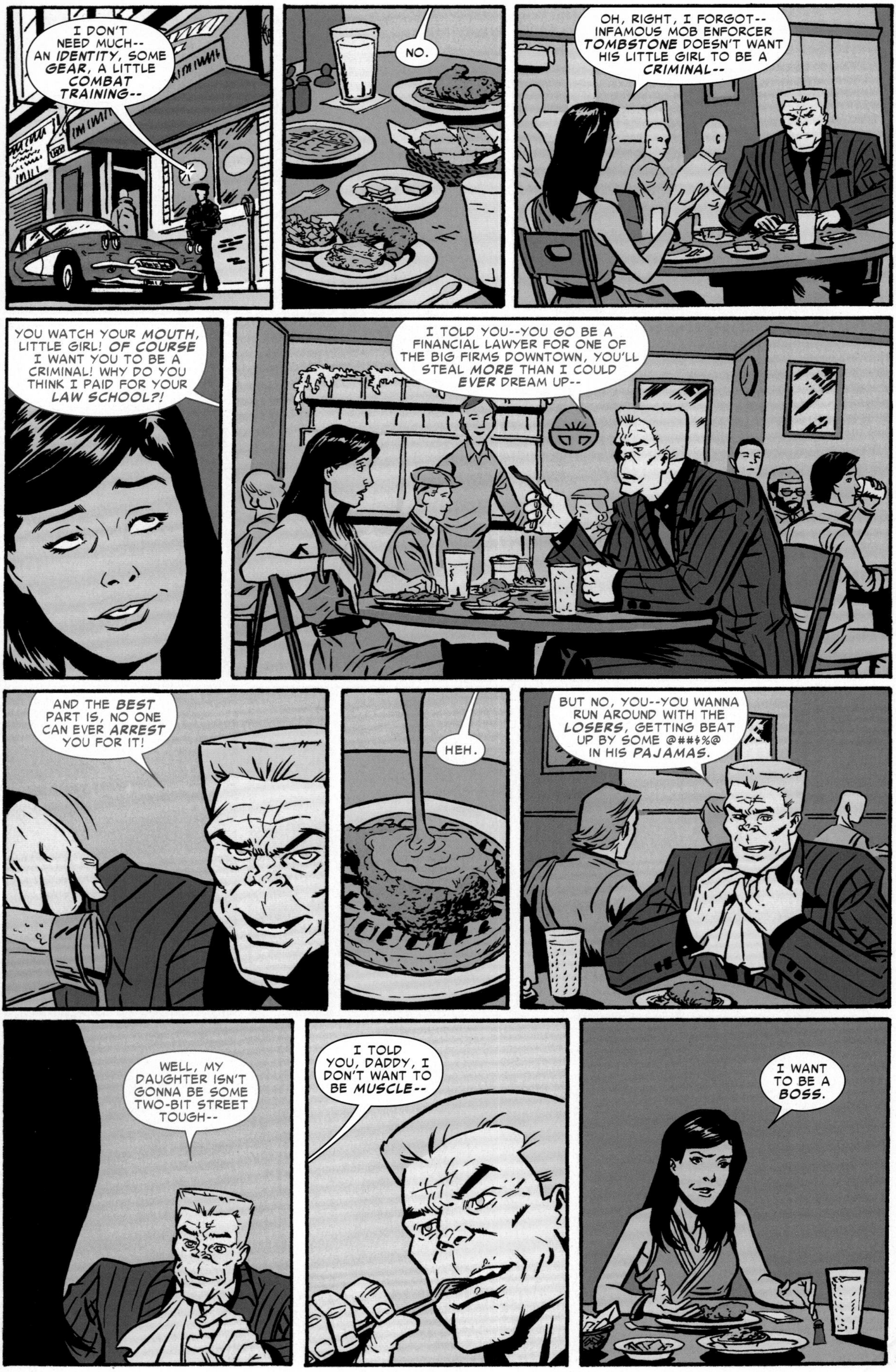
I DON'T NEED MUCH-- AN IDENTITY, SOME GEAR, A LITTLE COMBAT TRAINING--
NO.
OH, RIGHT, I FORGOT-- INFAMOUS MOB ENFORCER TOMBSTONE DOESN'T WANT HIS LITTLE GIRL TO BE A CRIMINAL--
YOU WATCH YOUR MOUTH, LITTLE GIRL! OF COURSE I WANT YOU TO BE A CRIMINAL! WHY DO YOU THINK I PAID FOR YOUR LAW SCHOOL?!
I TOLD YOU--YOU GO BE A FINANCIAL LAWYER FOR ONE OF THE BIG FIRMS DOWNTOWN, YOU'LL STEAL MORE THAN I COULD EVER DREAM UP--
AND THE BEST PART IS, NO ONE CAN EVER ARREST YOU FOR IT!
HEH.
BUT NO, YOU--YOU WANNA RUN AROUND WITH THE LOSERS, GETTING BEAT UP BY SOME @##$%@ IN HIS PAJAMAS.
WELL, MY DAUGHTER ISN'T GONNA BE SOME TWO-BIT STREET TOUGH--
I TOLD YOU, DADDY, I DON'T WANT TO BE MUSCLE--
I WANT TO BE A BOSS.

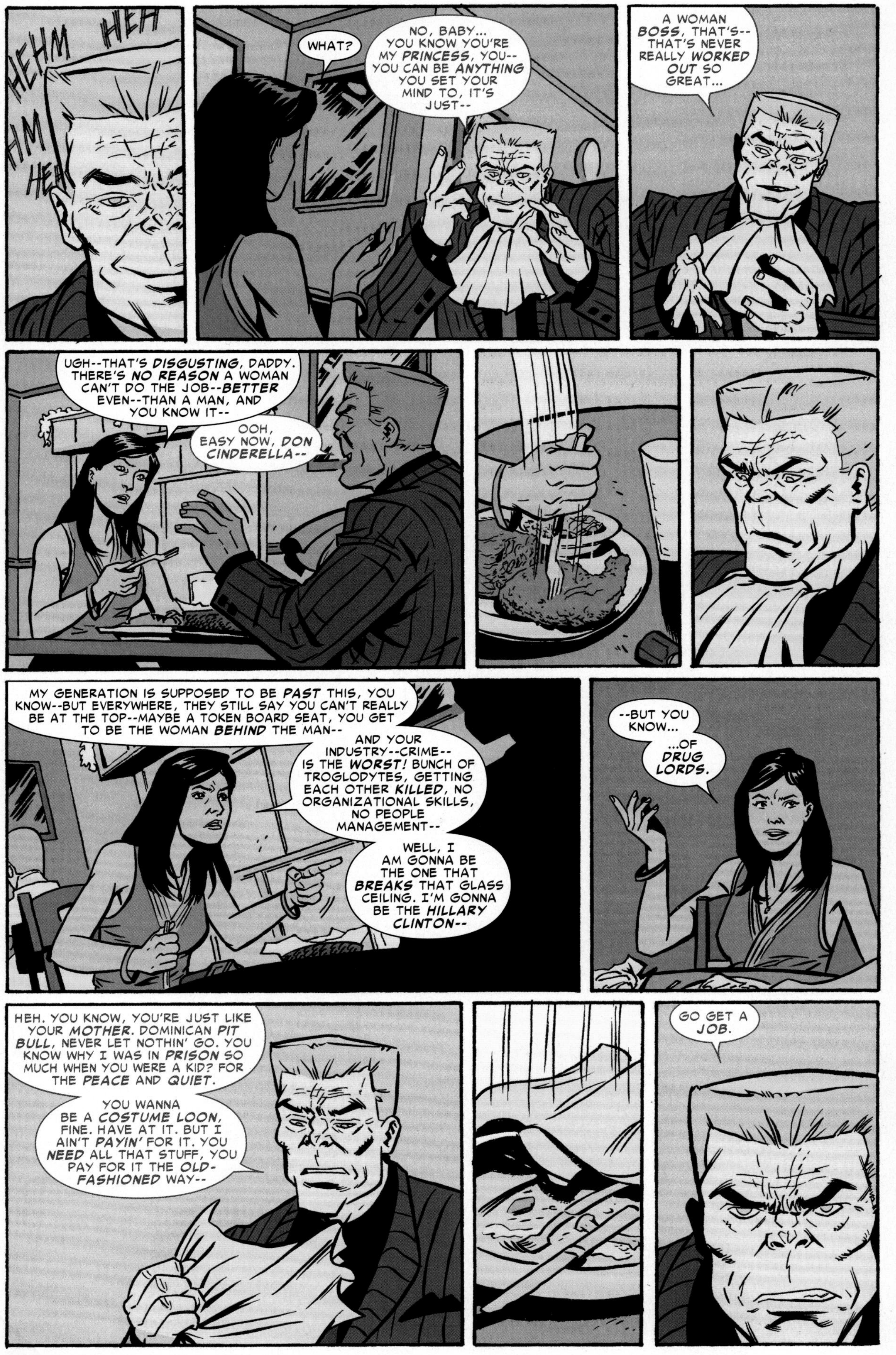
HEHM HEH
HM HEH
WHAT?
NO, BABY... YOU KNOW YOU'RE MY *PRINCESS*, YOU-- YOU CAN BE *ANYTHING* YOU SET YOUR MIND TO, IT'S JUST--
A WOMAN *BOSS*, THAT'S-- THAT'S NEVER REALLY *WORKED OUT* SO GREAT...
UGH--THAT'S *DISGUSTING*, DADDY. THERE'S *NO REASON* A WOMAN CAN'T DO THE JOB--*BETTER* EVEN--THAN A MAN, AND YOU KNOW IT--
OOH, EASY NOW, *DON CINDERELLA*--
MY GENERATION IS SUPPOSED TO BE *PAST* THIS, YOU KNOW--BUT EVERYWHERE, THEY STILL SAY YOU CAN'T REALLY BE AT THE TOP--MAYBE A TOKEN BOARD SEAT, YOU GET TO BE THE WOMAN *BEHIND* THE MAN--
AND YOUR INDUSTRY--CRIME-- IS THE *WORST!* BUNCH OF TROGLODYTES, GETTING EACH OTHER *KILLED*, NO ORGANIZATIONAL SKILLS, NO PEOPLE MANAGEMENT--
WELL, I AM GONNA BE THE ONE THAT *BREAKS* THAT GLASS CEILING. I'M GONNA BE THE *HILLARY CLINTON*--
--BUT YOU KNOW...
...OF *DRUG LORDS*.
HEH. YOU KNOW, YOU'RE JUST LIKE YOUR *MOTHER*. DOMINICAN *PIT BULL*, NEVER LET NOTHIN' GO. YOU KNOW WHY I WAS IN *PRISON* SO MUCH WHEN YOU WERE A KID? FOR THE *PEACE* AND *QUIET*.
YOU WANNA BE A *COSTUME LOON*, FINE. HAVE AT IT. BUT I AIN'T *PAYIN'* FOR IT. YOU *NEED* ALL THAT STUFF, YOU PAY FOR IT THE *OLD-FASHIONED* WAY--
GO GET A *JOB*.

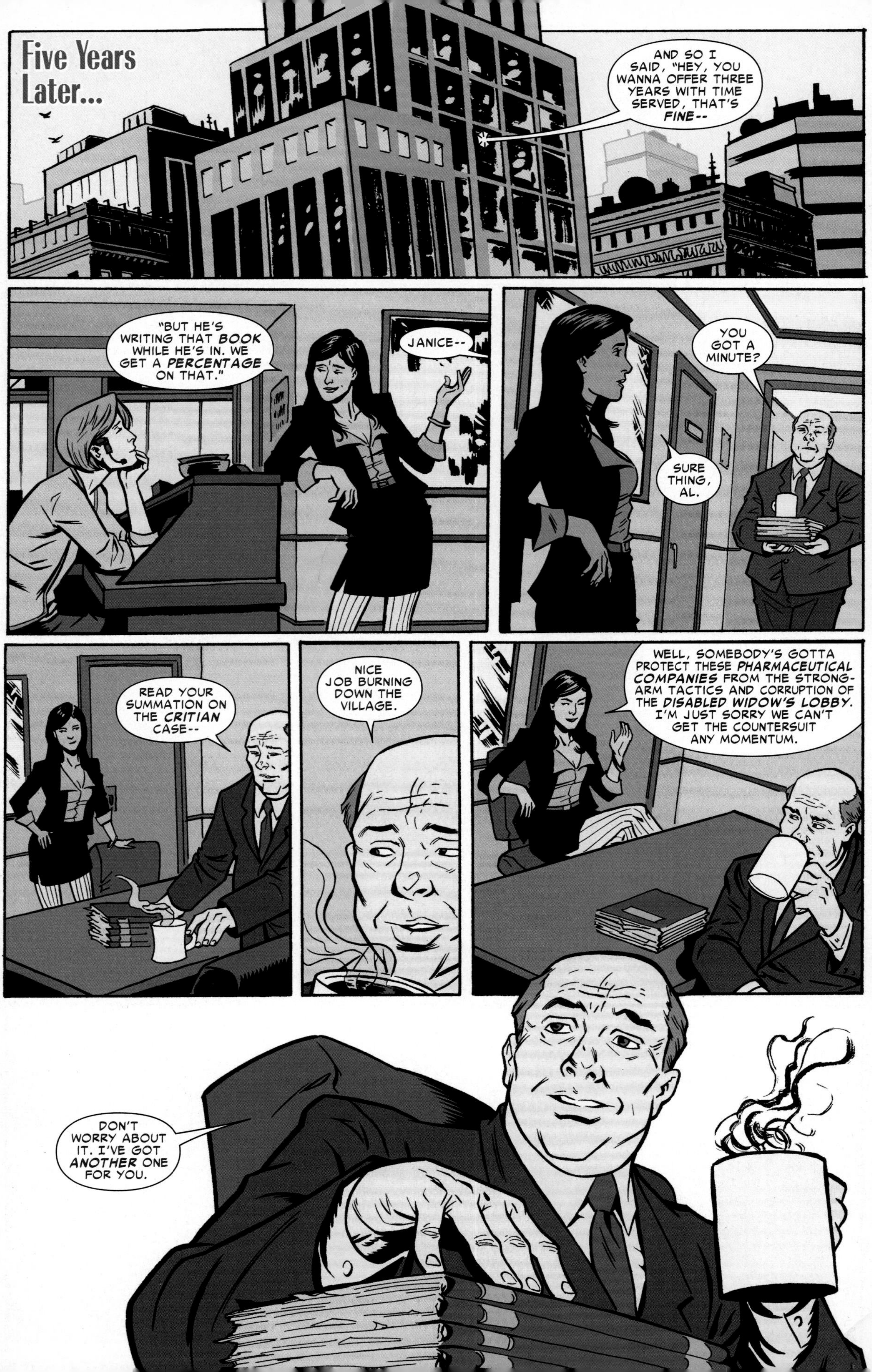
Five Years Later...
AND SO I SAID, "HEY, YOU WANNA OFFER THREE YEARS WITH TIME SERVED, THAT'S FINE--
"BUT HE'S WRITING THAT BOOK WHILE HE'S IN. WE GET A PERCENTAGE ON THAT."
JANICE--
YOU GOT A MINUTE?
SURE THING, AL.
READ YOUR SUMMATION ON THE CRITIAN CASE--
NICE JOB BURNING DOWN THE VILLAGE.
WELL, SOMEBODY'S GOTTA PROTECT THESE PHARMACEUTICAL COMPANIES FROM THE STRONG-ARM TACTICS AND CORRUPTION OF THE DISABLED WIDOW'S LOBBY. I'M JUST SORRY WE CAN'T GET THE COUNTERSUIT ANY MOMENTUM.
DON'T WORRY ABOUT IT. I'VE GOT ANOTHER ONE FOR YOU.

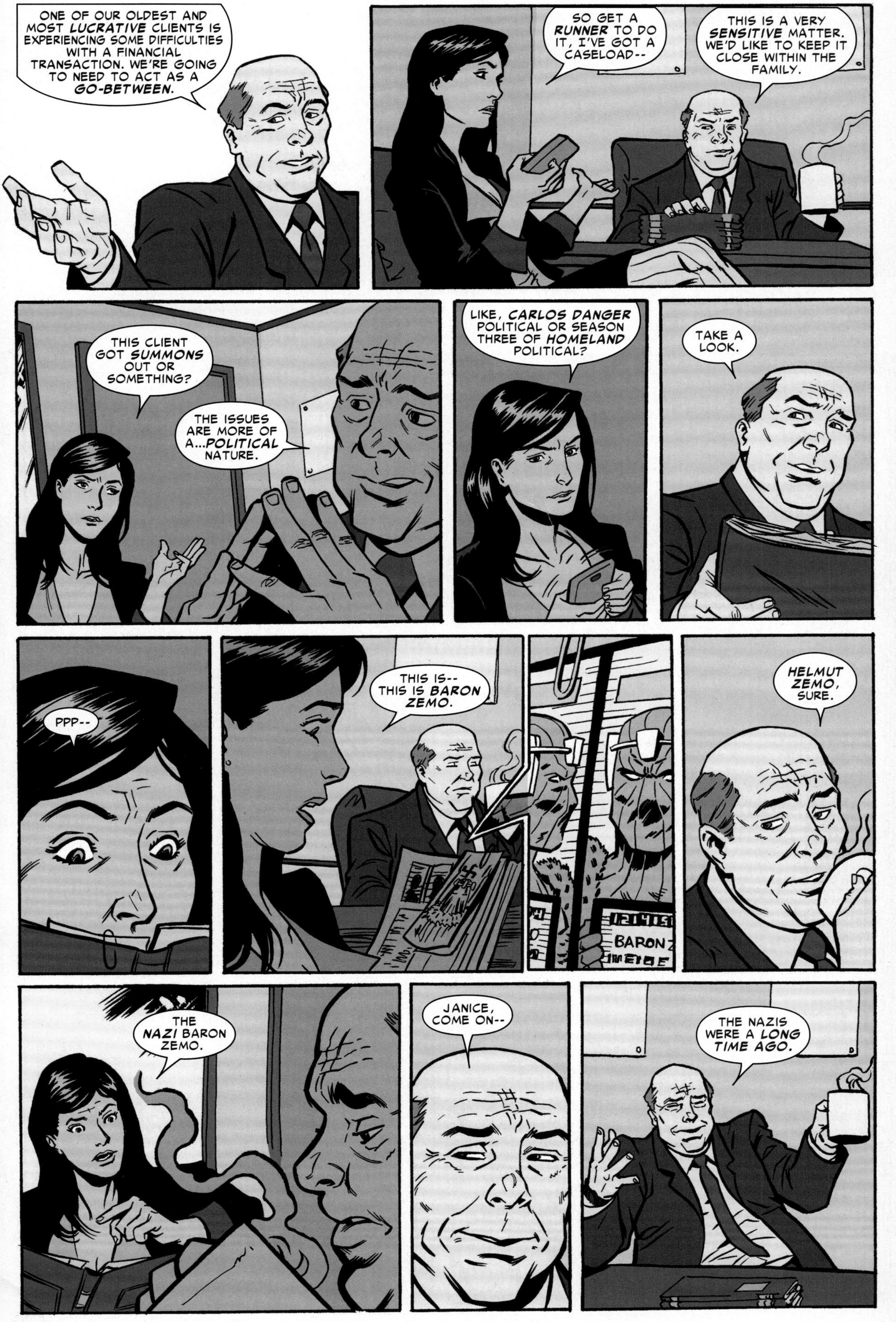
ONE OF OUR OLDEST AND MOST LUCRATIVE CLIENTS IS EXPERIENCING SOME DIFFICULTIES WITH A FINANCIAL TRANSACTION. WE'RE GOING TO NEED TO ACT AS A GO-BETWEEN.
SO GET A RUNNER TO DO IT, I'VE GOT A CASELOAD--
THIS IS A VERY SENSITIVE MATTER. WE'D LIKE TO KEEP IT CLOSE WITHIN THE FAMILY.
THIS CLIENT GOT SUMMONS OUT OR SOMETHING?
THE ISSUES ARE MORE OF A...POLITICAL NATURE.
LIKE, CARLOS DANGER POLITICAL OR SEASON THREE OF HOMELAND POLITICAL?
TAKE A LOOK.
PPP--
THIS IS-- THIS IS BARON ZEMO.
HELMUT ZEMO, SURE.
THE NAZI BARON ZEMO.
JANICE, COME ON--
THE NAZIS WERE A LONG TIME AGO.

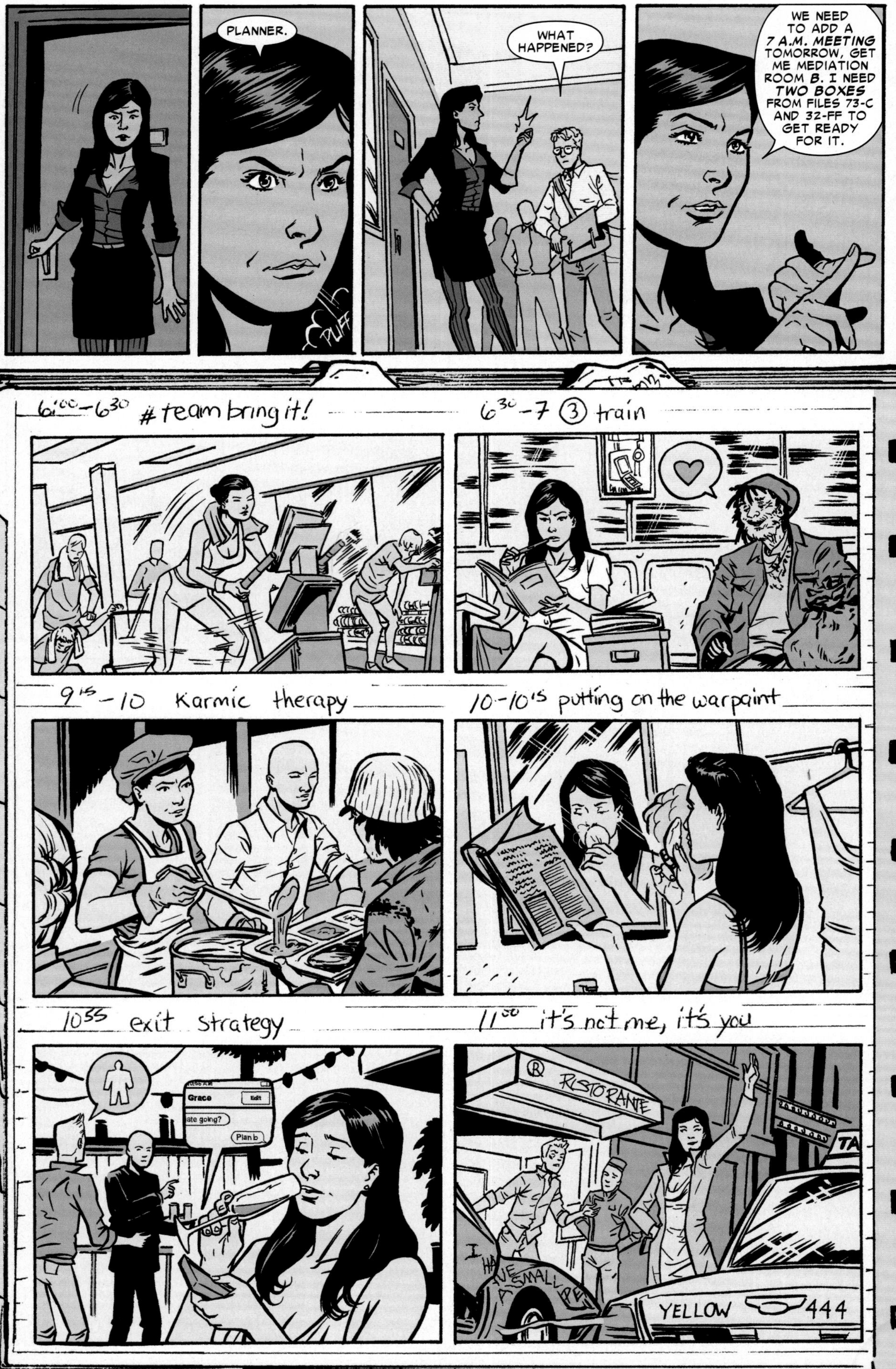
PLANNER.
PUFF
WHAT HAPPENED?
WE NEED TO ADD A 7 A.M. MEETING TOMORROW, GET ME MEDIATION ROOM B. I NEED TWO BOXES FROM FILES 73-C AND 32-FF TO GET READY FOR IT.
6:00-6:30 #team bring it!
6:30-7 ③ train
9:15-10 Karmic therapy
10-10:15 putting on the warpaint
10:55 exit strategy
Grace
Edit
ate going?
Plan b
11:00 it's not me, it's you
RISTORANTE
YELLOW
444

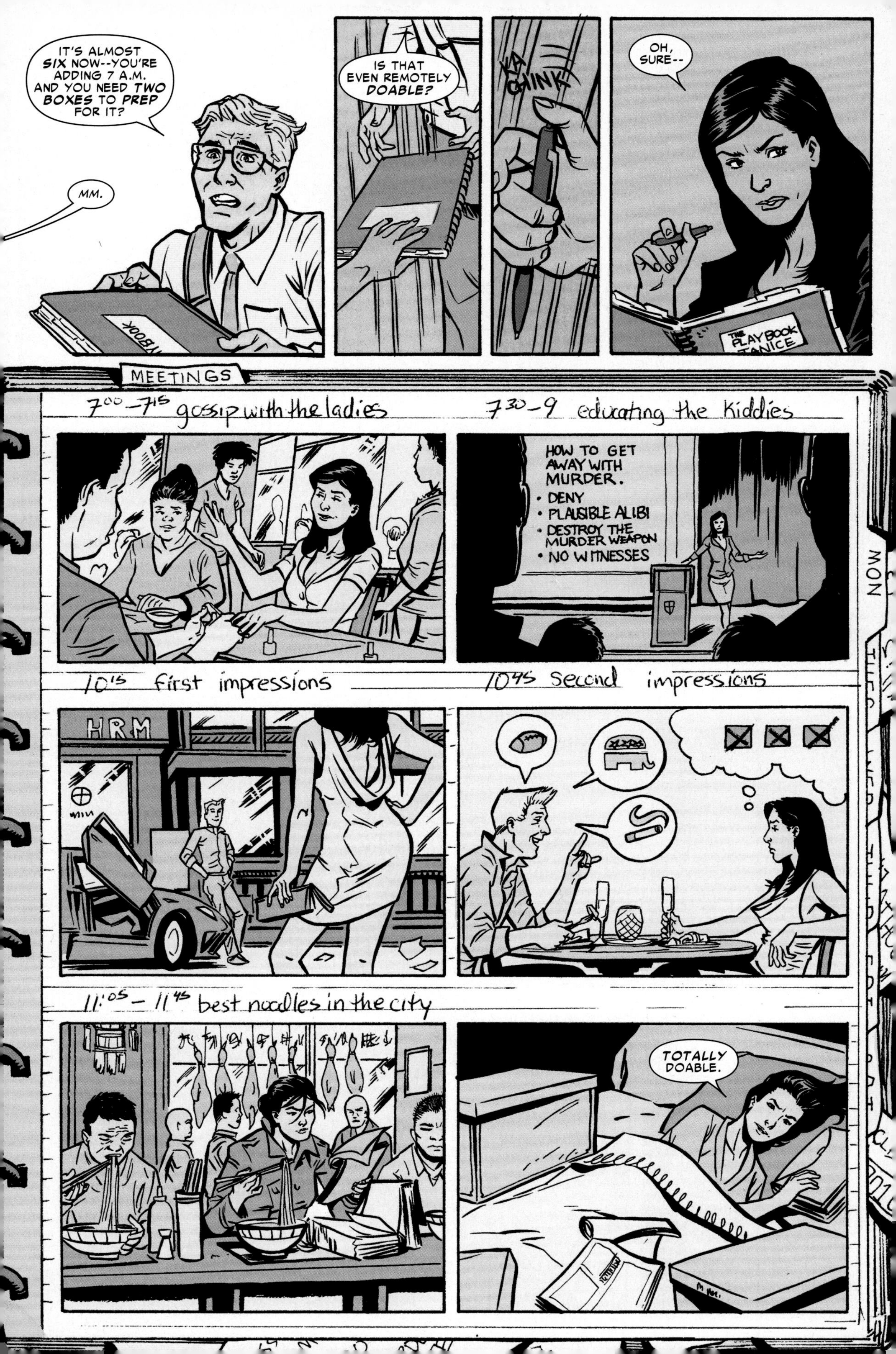
IT'S ALMOST SIX NOW--YOU'RE ADDING 7 A.M. AND YOU NEED TWO BOXES TO PREP FOR IT?
MM.
IS THAT EVEN REMOTELY DOABLE?
CHINK
OH, SURE--
THE PLAYBOOK JANICE
MEETINGS
7^{00}–7^{15} gossip with the ladies
7^{30}–9 educating the kiddies
HOW TO GET AWAY WITH MURDER.
• DENY
• PLAUSIBLE ALIBI
• DESTROY THE MURDER WEAPON
• NO WITNESSES
MON
10^{15} first impressions
10^{45} second impressions
HRM
$11{:}^{05}$ – 11^{45} best noodles in the city
TOTALLY DOABLE.

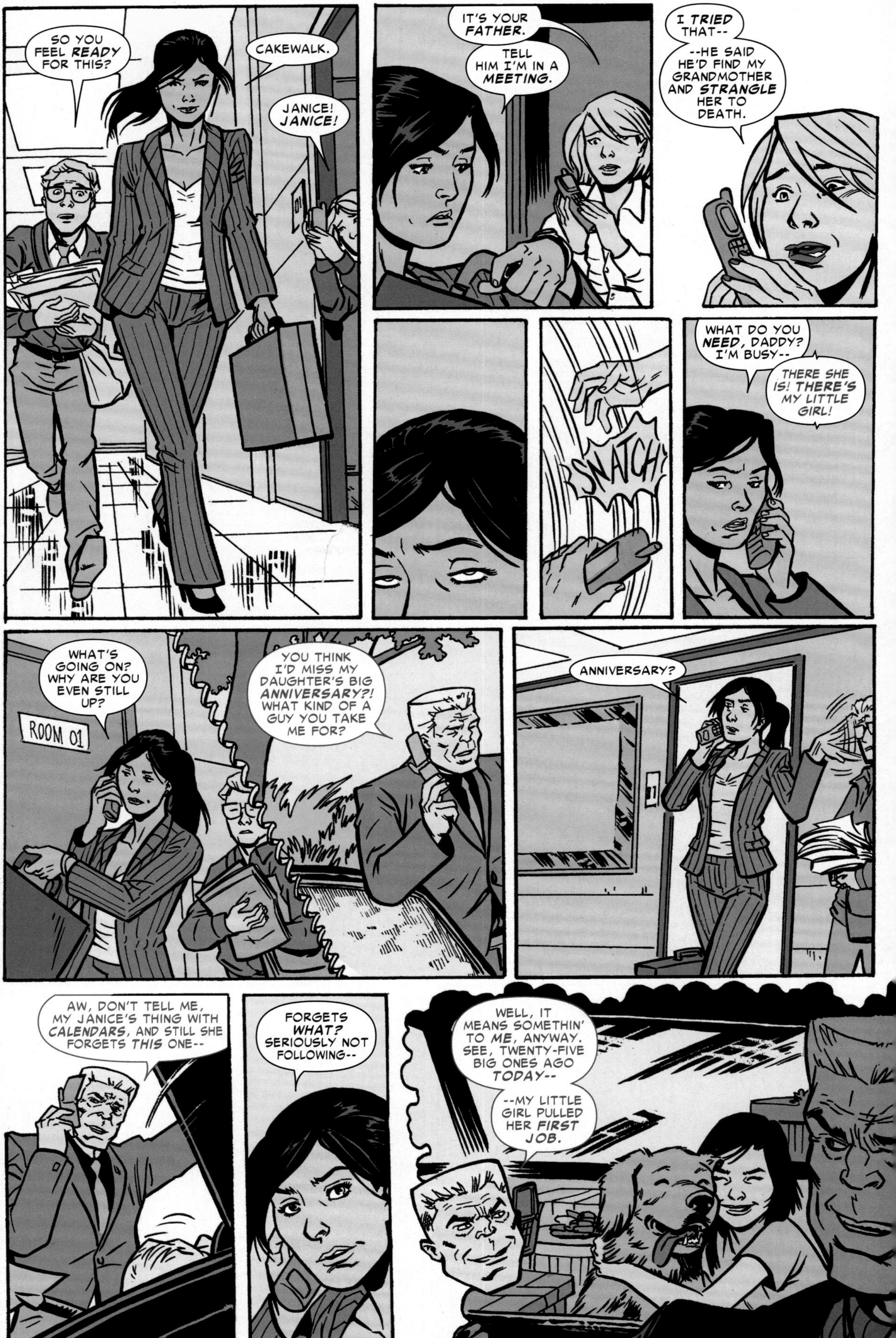
SO YOU FEEL READY FOR THIS?
CAKEWALK.
JANICE! JANICE!
IT'S YOUR FATHER.
TELL HIM I'M IN A MEETING.
I TRIED THAT--
--HE SAID HE'D FIND MY GRANDMOTHER AND STRANGLE HER TO DEATH.
SNATCH!
WHAT DO YOU NEED, DADDY? I'M BUSY--
THERE SHE IS! THERE'S MY LITTLE GIRL!
WHAT'S GOING ON? WHY ARE YOU EVEN STILL UP?
ROOM 01
YOU THINK I'D MISS MY DAUGHTER'S BIG ANNIVERSARY?! WHAT KIND OF A GUY YOU TAKE ME FOR?
ANNIVERSARY?
AW, DON'T TELL ME, MY JANICE'S THING WITH CALENDARS, AND STILL SHE FORGETS THIS ONE--
FORGETS WHAT? SERIOUSLY NOT FOLLOWING--
WELL, IT MEANS SOMETHIN' TO ME, ANYWAY. SEE, TWENTY-FIVE BIG ONES AGO TODAY--
--MY LITTLE GIRL PULLED HER FIRST JOB.

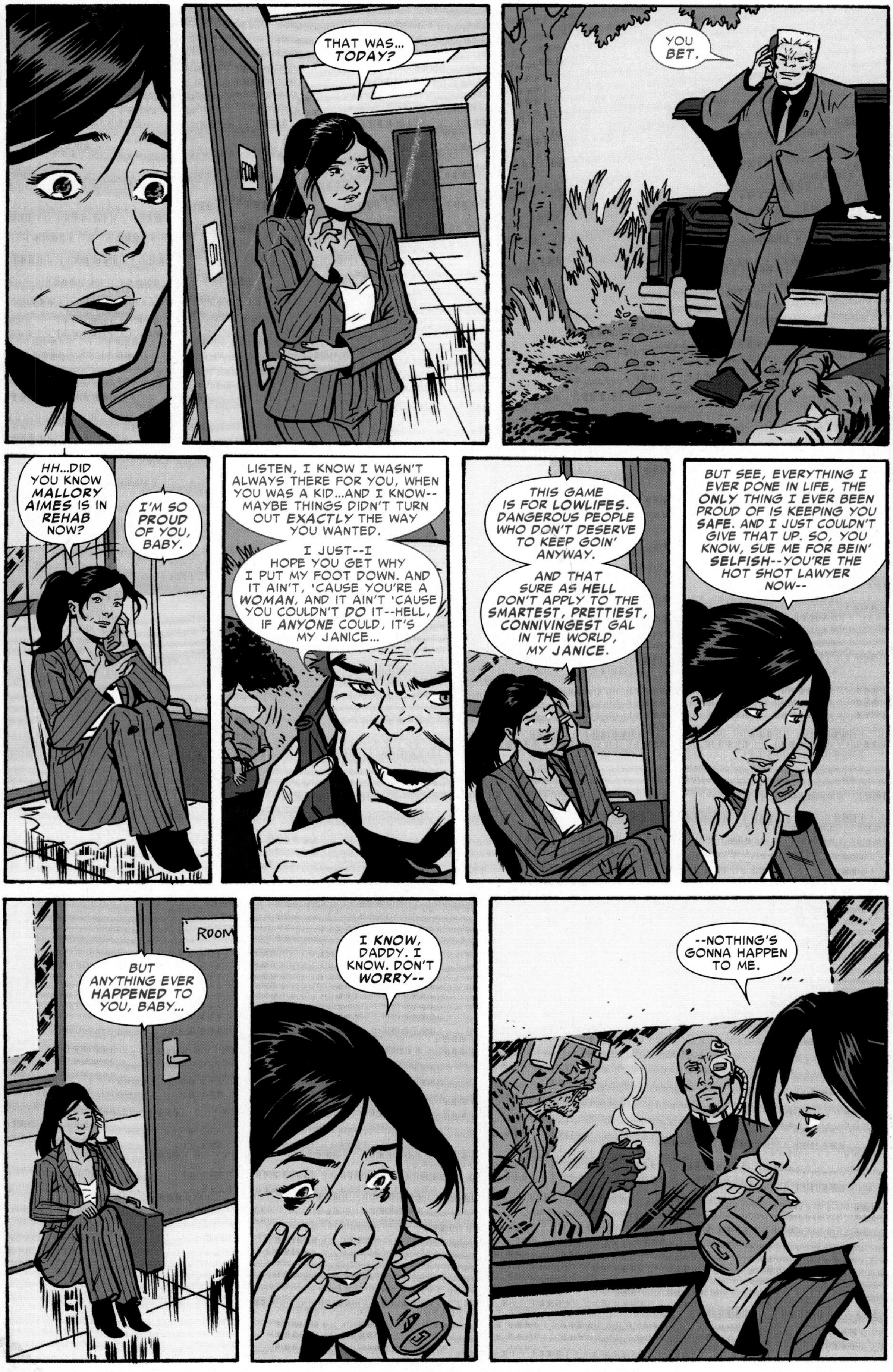
THAT WAS... TODAY?
YOU BET.
HH...DID YOU KNOW MALLORY AIMES IS IN REHAB NOW?
I'M SO PROUD OF YOU, BABY.
LISTEN, I KNOW I WASN'T ALWAYS THERE FOR YOU, WHEN YOU WAS A KID...AND I KNOW--MAYBE THINGS DIDN'T TURN OUT EXACTLY THE WAY YOU WANTED.
I JUST--I HOPE YOU GET WHY I PUT MY FOOT DOWN. AND IT AIN'T, 'CAUSE YOU'RE A WOMAN, AND IT AIN'T 'CAUSE YOU COULDN'T DO IT--HELL, IF ANYONE COULD, IT'S MY JANICE...
THIS GAME IS FOR LOWLIFES. DANGEROUS PEOPLE WHO DON'T DESERVE TO KEEP GOIN' ANYWAY.
AND THAT SURE AS HELL DON'T APPLY TO THE SMARTEST, PRETTIEST, CONNIVINGEST GAL IN THE WORLD, MY JANICE.
BUT SEE, EVERYTHING I EVER DONE IN LIFE, THE ONLY THING I EVER BEEN PROUD OF IS KEEPING YOU SAFE. AND I JUST COULDN'T GIVE THAT UP. SO, YOU KNOW, SUE ME FOR BEIN' SELFISH--YOU'RE THE HOT SHOT LAWYER NOW--
ROOM
BUT ANYTHING EVER HAPPENED TO YOU, BABY...
I KNOW, DADDY. I KNOW. DON'T WORRY--
--NOTHING'S GONNA HAPPEN TO ME.

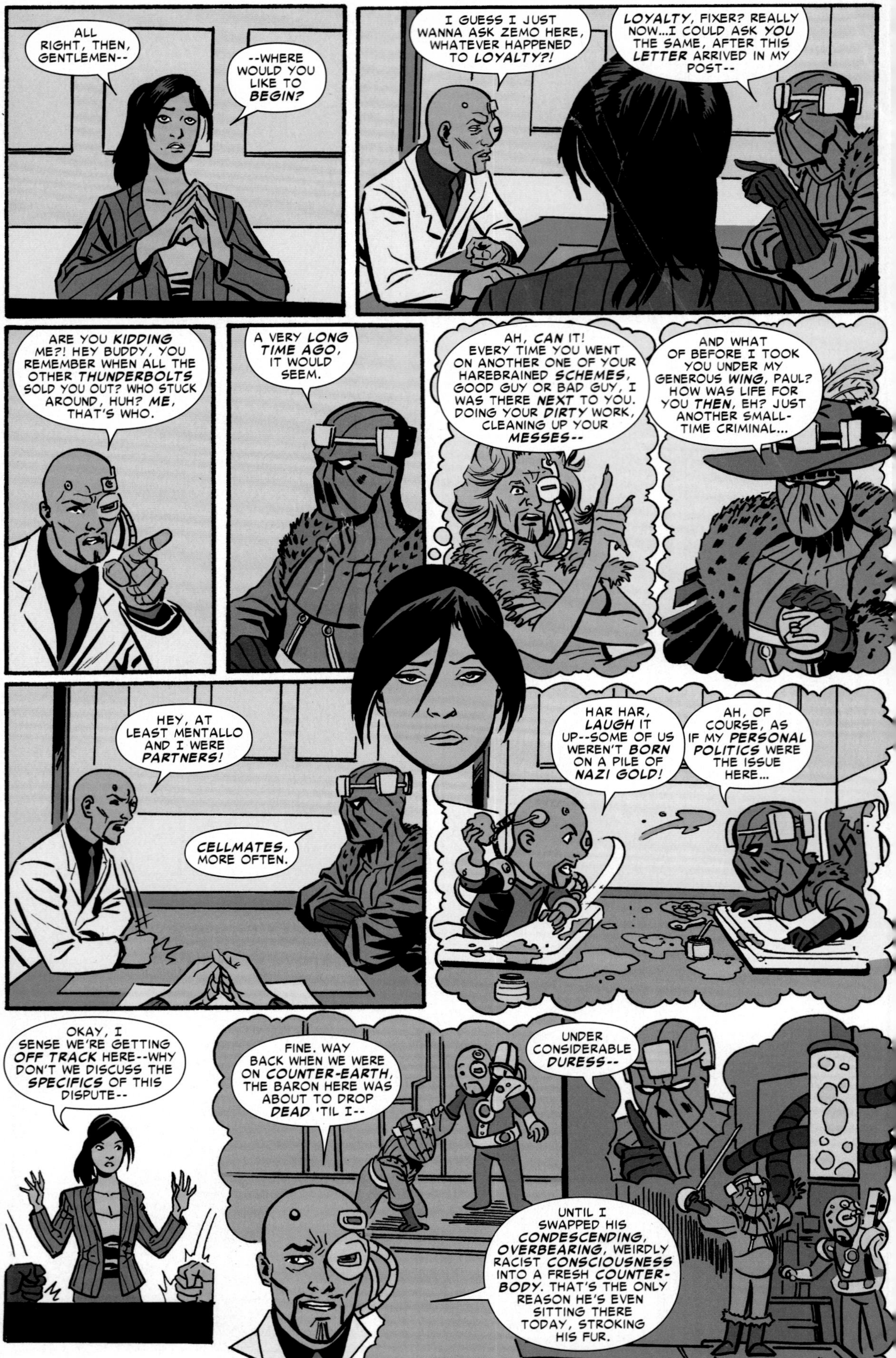
ALL RIGHT, THEN, GENTLEMEN--
--WHERE WOULD YOU LIKE TO BEGIN?
I GUESS I JUST WANNA ASK ZEMO HERE, WHATEVER HAPPENED TO LOYALTY?!
LOYALTY, FIXER? REALLY NOW...I COULD ASK YOU THE SAME, AFTER THIS LETTER ARRIVED IN MY POST--
ARE YOU KIDDING ME?! HEY BUDDY, YOU REMEMBER WHEN ALL THE OTHER THUNDERBOLTS SOLD YOU OUT? WHO STUCK AROUND, HUH? ME, THAT'S WHO.
A VERY LONG TIME AGO, IT WOULD SEEM.
AH, CAN IT! EVERY TIME YOU WENT ON ANOTHER ONE OF YOUR HAREBRAINED SCHEMES, GOOD GUY OR BAD GUY, I WAS THERE NEXT TO YOU. DOING YOUR DIRTY WORK, CLEANING UP YOUR MESSES--
AND WHAT OF BEFORE I TOOK YOU UNDER MY GENEROUS WING, PAUL? HOW WAS LIFE FOR YOU THEN, EH? JUST ANOTHER SMALL-TIME CRIMINAL...
HEY, AT LEAST MENTALLO AND I WERE PARTNERS!
CELLMATES, MORE OFTEN.
HAR HAR, LAUGH IT UP--SOME OF US WEREN'T BORN ON A PILE OF NAZI GOLD!
AH, OF COURSE, AS IF MY PERSONAL POLITICS WERE THE ISSUE HERE...
OKAY, I SENSE WE'RE GETTING OFF TRACK HERE--WHY DON'T WE DISCUSS THE SPECIFICS OF THIS DISPUTE--
FINE. WAY BACK WHEN WE WERE ON COUNTER-EARTH, THE BARON HERE WAS ABOUT TO DROP DEAD 'TIL I--
UNDER CONSIDERABLE DURESS--
UNTIL I SWAPPED HIS CONDESCENDING, OVERBEARING, WEIRDLY RACIST CONSCIOUSNESS INTO A FRESH COUNTER-BODY. THAT'S THE ONLY REASON HE'S EVEN SITTING THERE TODAY, STROKING HIS FUR.

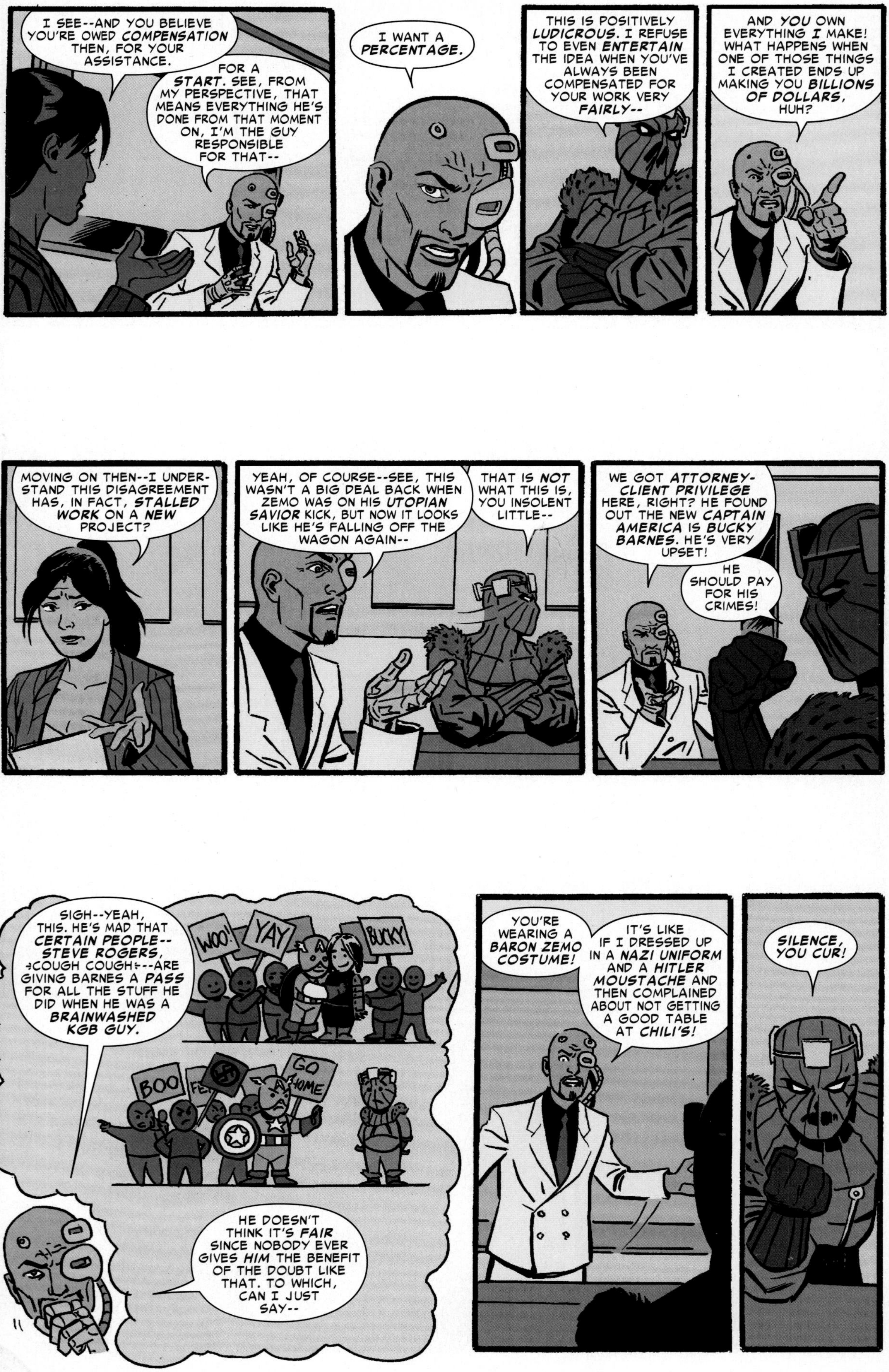

I SEE--AND YOU BELIEVE YOU'RE OWED COMPENSATION THEN, FOR YOUR ASSISTANCE.
FOR A START. SEE, FROM MY PERSPECTIVE, THAT MEANS EVERYTHING HE'S DONE FROM THAT MOMENT ON, I'M THE GUY RESPONSIBLE FOR THAT--
I WANT A PERCENTAGE.
THIS IS POSITIVELY LUDICROUS. I REFUSE TO EVEN ENTERTAIN THE IDEA WHEN YOU'VE ALWAYS BEEN COMPENSATED FOR YOUR WORK VERY FAIRLY--
AND YOU OWN EVERYTHING I MAKE! WHAT HAPPENS WHEN ONE OF THOSE THINGS I CREATED ENDS UP MAKING YOU BILLIONS OF DOLLARS, HUH?
MOVING ON THEN--I UNDERSTAND THIS DISAGREEMENT HAS, IN FACT, STALLED WORK ON A NEW PROJECT?
YEAH, OF COURSE--SEE, THIS WASN'T A BIG DEAL BACK WHEN ZEMO WAS ON HIS UTOPIAN SAVIOR KICK, BUT NOW IT LOOKS LIKE HE'S FALLING OFF THE WAGON AGAIN--
THAT IS NOT WHAT THIS IS, YOU INSOLENT LITTLE--
WE GOT ATTORNEY-CLIENT PRIVILEGE HERE, RIGHT? HE FOUND OUT THE NEW CAPTAIN AMERICA IS BUCKY BARNES. HE'S VERY UPSET!
HE SHOULD PAY FOR HIS CRIMES!
SIGH--YEAH, THIS. HE'S MAD THAT CERTAIN PEOPLE--STEVE ROGERS, *COUGH COUGH*--ARE GIVING BARNES A PASS FOR ALL THE STUFF HE DID WHEN HE WAS A BRAINWASHED KGB GUY.
WOO!
YAY
BUCKY
BOO
GO HOME
HE DOESN'T THINK IT'S FAIR SINCE NOBODY EVER GIVES HIM THE BENEFIT OF THE DOUBT LIKE THAT. TO WHICH, CAN I JUST SAY--
YOU'RE WEARING A BARON ZEMO COSTUME!
IT'S LIKE IF I DRESSED UP IN A NAZI UNIFORM AND A HITLER MOUSTACHE AND THEN COMPLAINED ABOUT NOT GETTING A GOOD TABLE AT CHILI'S!
SILENCE, YOU CUR!

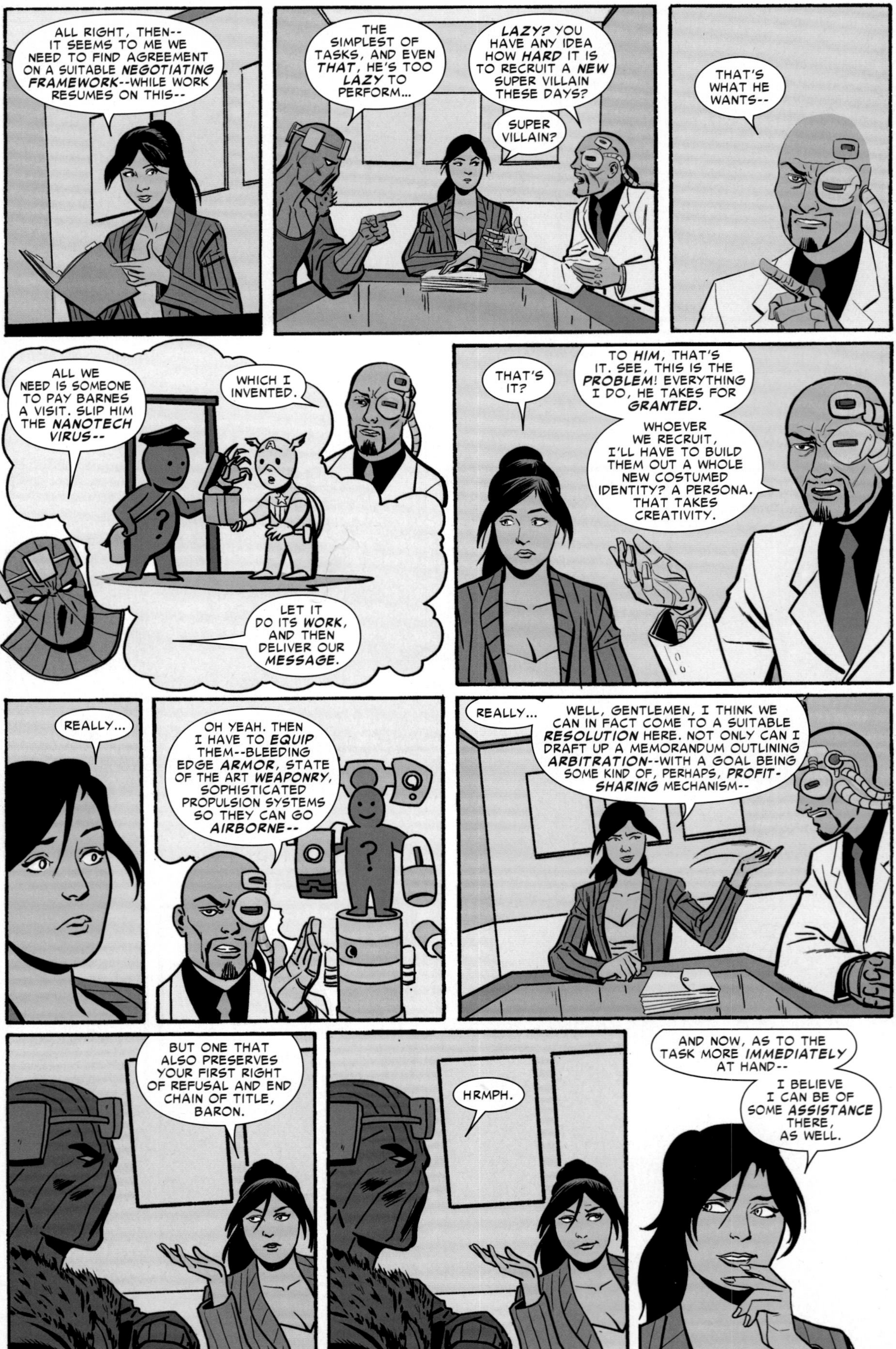

ALL RIGHT, THEN-- IT SEEMS TO ME WE NEED TO FIND AGREEMENT ON A SUITABLE NEGOTIATING FRAMEWORK--WHILE WORK RESUMES ON THIS--
THE SIMPLEST OF TASKS, AND EVEN THAT, HE'S TOO LAZY TO PERFORM...
LAZY? YOU HAVE ANY IDEA HOW HARD IT IS TO RECRUIT A NEW SUPER VILLAIN THESE DAYS?
SUPER VILLAIN?
THAT'S WHAT HE WANTS--
ALL WE NEED IS SOMEONE TO PAY BARNES A VISIT. SLIP HIM THE NANOTECH VIRUS--
WHICH I INVENTED.
LET IT DO ITS WORK, AND THEN DELIVER OUR MESSAGE.
THAT'S IT?
TO HIM, THAT'S IT. SEE, THIS IS THE PROBLEM! EVERYTHING I DO, HE TAKES FOR GRANTED.
WHOEVER WE RECRUIT, I'LL HAVE TO BUILD THEM OUT A WHOLE NEW COSTUMED IDENTITY? A PERSONA. THAT TAKES CREATIVITY.
REALLY...
OH YEAH. THEN I HAVE TO EQUIP THEM--BLEEDING EDGE ARMOR, STATE OF THE ART WEAPONRY, SOPHISTICATED PROPULSION SYSTEMS SO THEY CAN GO AIRBORNE--
REALLY...
WELL, GENTLEMEN, I THINK WE CAN IN FACT COME TO A SUITABLE RESOLUTION HERE. NOT ONLY CAN I DRAFT UP A MEMORANDUM OUTLINING ARBITRATION--WITH A GOAL BEING SOME KIND OF, PERHAPS, PROFIT-SHARING MECHANISM--
BUT ONE THAT ALSO PRESERVES YOUR FIRST RIGHT OF REFUSAL AND END CHAIN OF TITLE, BARON.
HRMPH.
AND NOW, AS TO THE TASK MORE IMMEDIATELY AT HAND--
I BELIEVE I CAN BE OF SOME ASSISTANCE THERE, AS WELL.

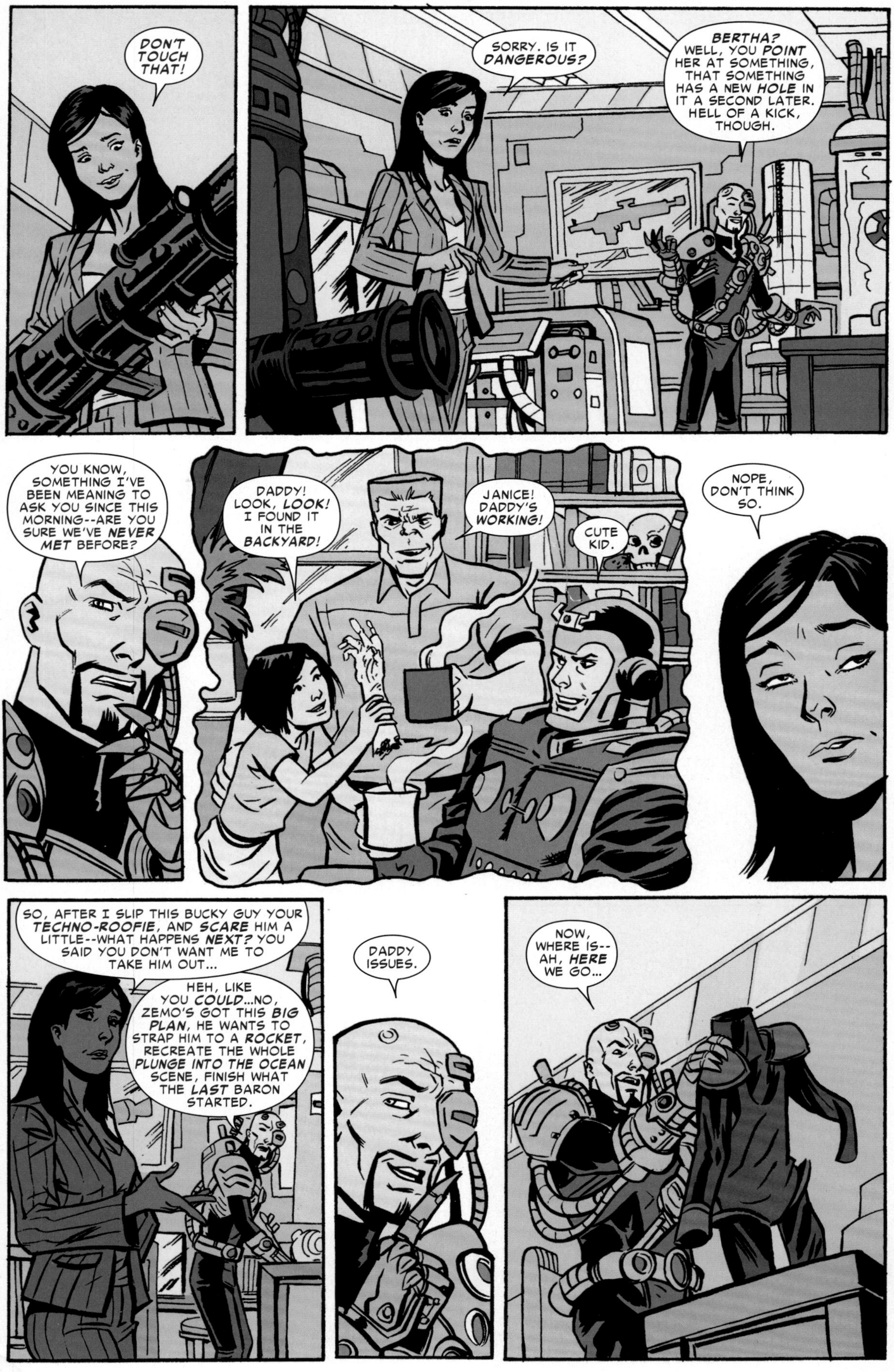
DON'T TOUCH THAT!
SORRY. IS IT DANGEROUS?
BERTHA? WELL, YOU POINT HER AT SOMETHING, THAT SOMETHING HAS A NEW HOLE IN IT A SECOND LATER. HELL OF A KICK, THOUGH.
YOU KNOW, SOMETHING I'VE BEEN MEANING TO ASK YOU SINCE THIS MORNING--ARE YOU SURE WE'VE NEVER MET BEFORE?
DADDY! LOOK, LOOK! I FOUND IT IN THE BACKYARD!
JANICE! DADDY'S WORKING!
CUTE KID.
NOPE, DON'T THINK SO.
SO, AFTER I SLIP THIS BUCKY GUY YOUR TECHNO-ROOFIE, AND SCARE HIM A LITTLE--WHAT HAPPENS NEXT? YOU SAID YOU DON'T WANT ME TO TAKE HIM OUT...
HEH, LIKE YOU COULD...NO, ZEMO'S GOT THIS BIG PLAN, HE WANTS TO STRAP HIM TO A ROCKET, RECREATE THE WHOLE PLUNGE INTO THE OCEAN SCENE, FINISH WHAT THE LAST BARON STARTED.
DADDY ISSUES.
NOW, WHERE IS--AH, HERE WE GO...

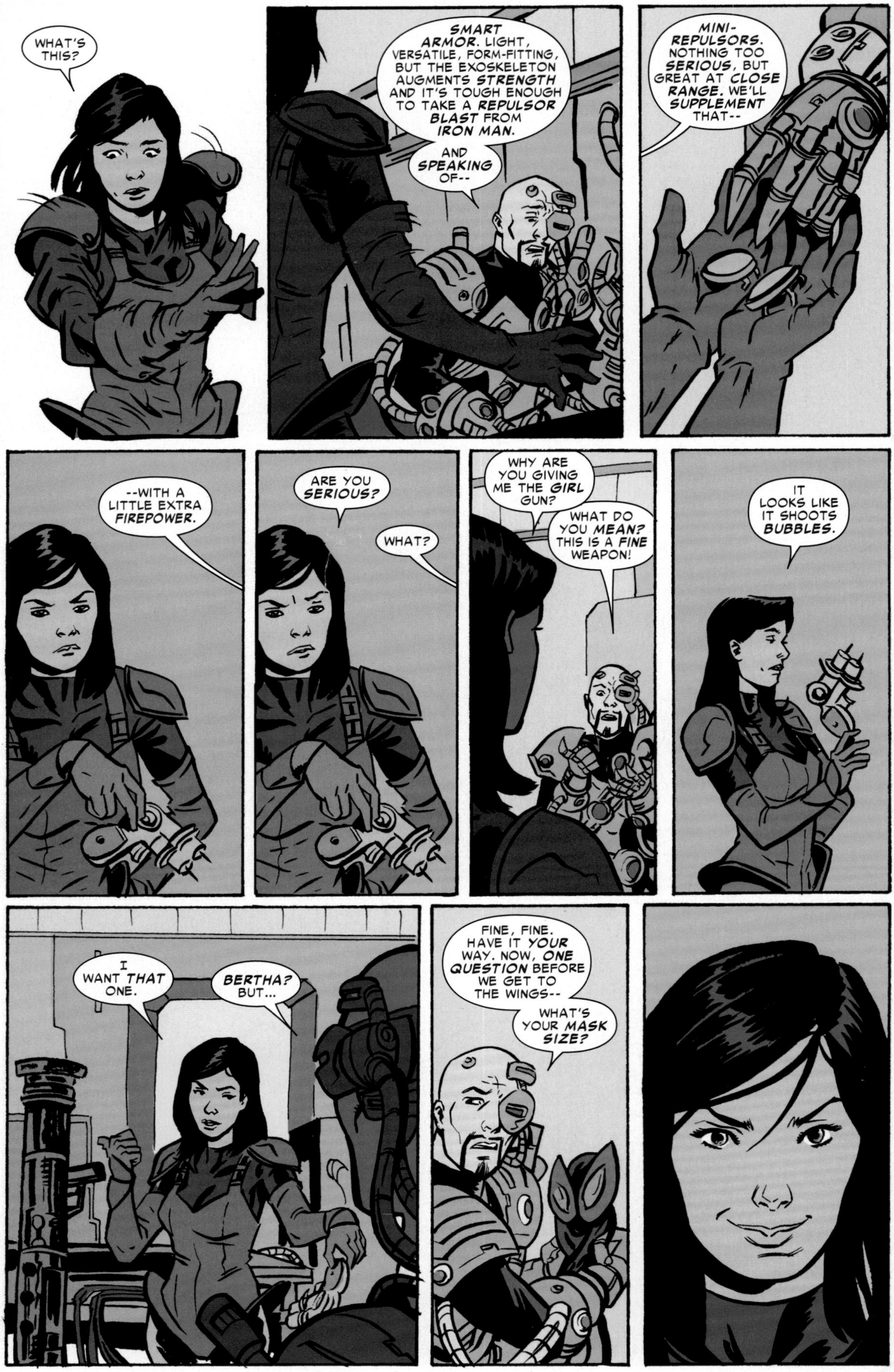
WHAT'S THIS?
SMART ARMOR. LIGHT, VERSATILE, FORM-FITTING, BUT THE EXOSKELETON AUGMENTS STRENGTH AND IT'S TOUGH ENOUGH TO TAKE A REPULSOR BLAST FROM IRON MAN.
AND SPEAKING OF--
MINI-REPULSORS. NOTHING TOO SERIOUS, BUT GREAT AT CLOSE RANGE. WE'LL SUPPLEMENT THAT--
--WITH A LITTLE EXTRA FIREPOWER.
ARE YOU SERIOUS?
WHAT?
WHY ARE YOU GIVING ME THE GIRL GUN?
WHAT DO YOU MEAN? THIS IS A FINE WEAPON!
IT LOOKS LIKE IT SHOOTS BUBBLES.
I WANT THAT ONE.
BERTHA? BUT...
FINE, FINE. HAVE IT YOUR WAY. NOW, ONE QUESTION BEFORE WE GET TO THE WINGS--
WHAT'S YOUR MASK SIZE?

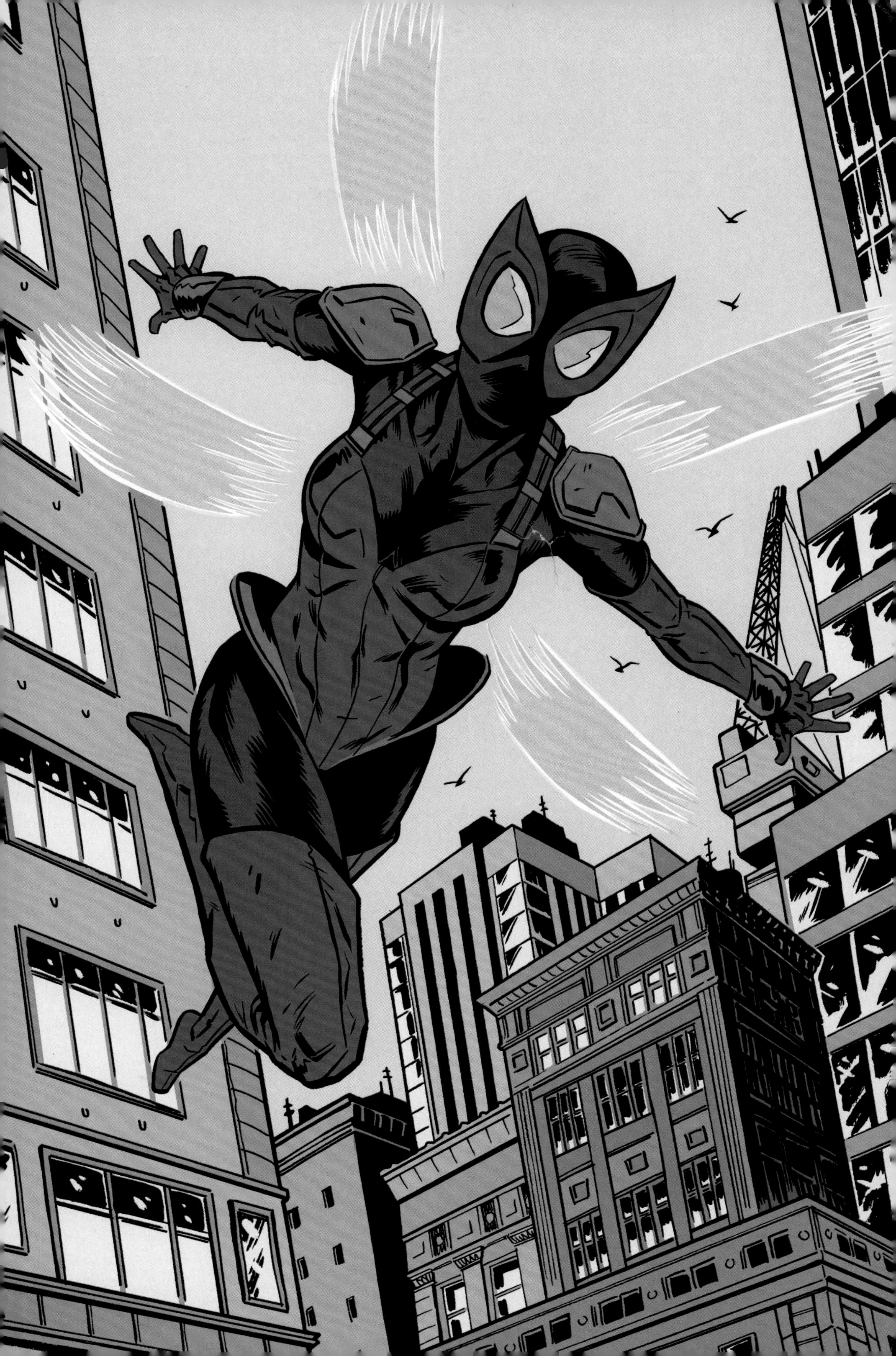

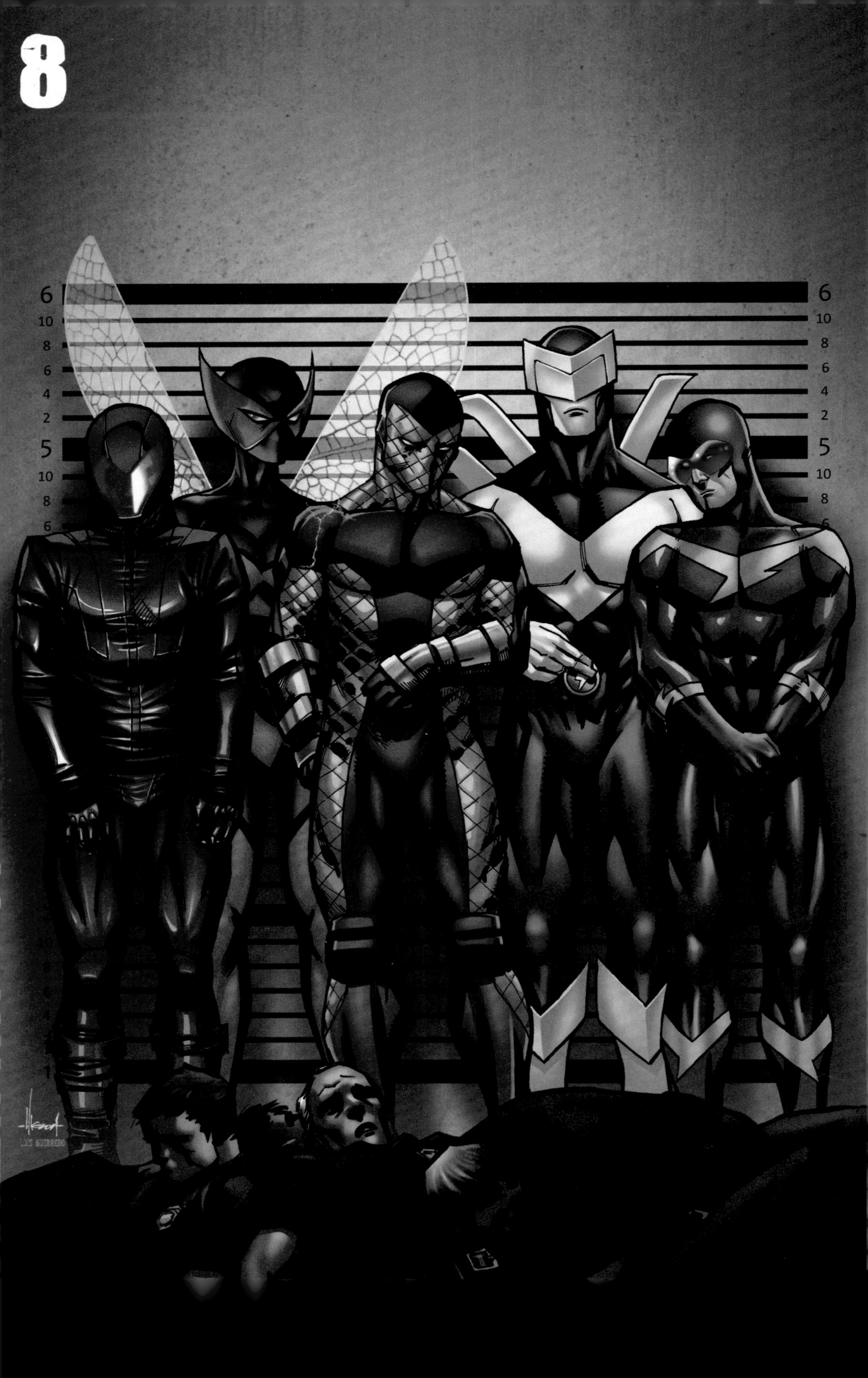
8
6
10
8
6
4
2
5
10
8
6

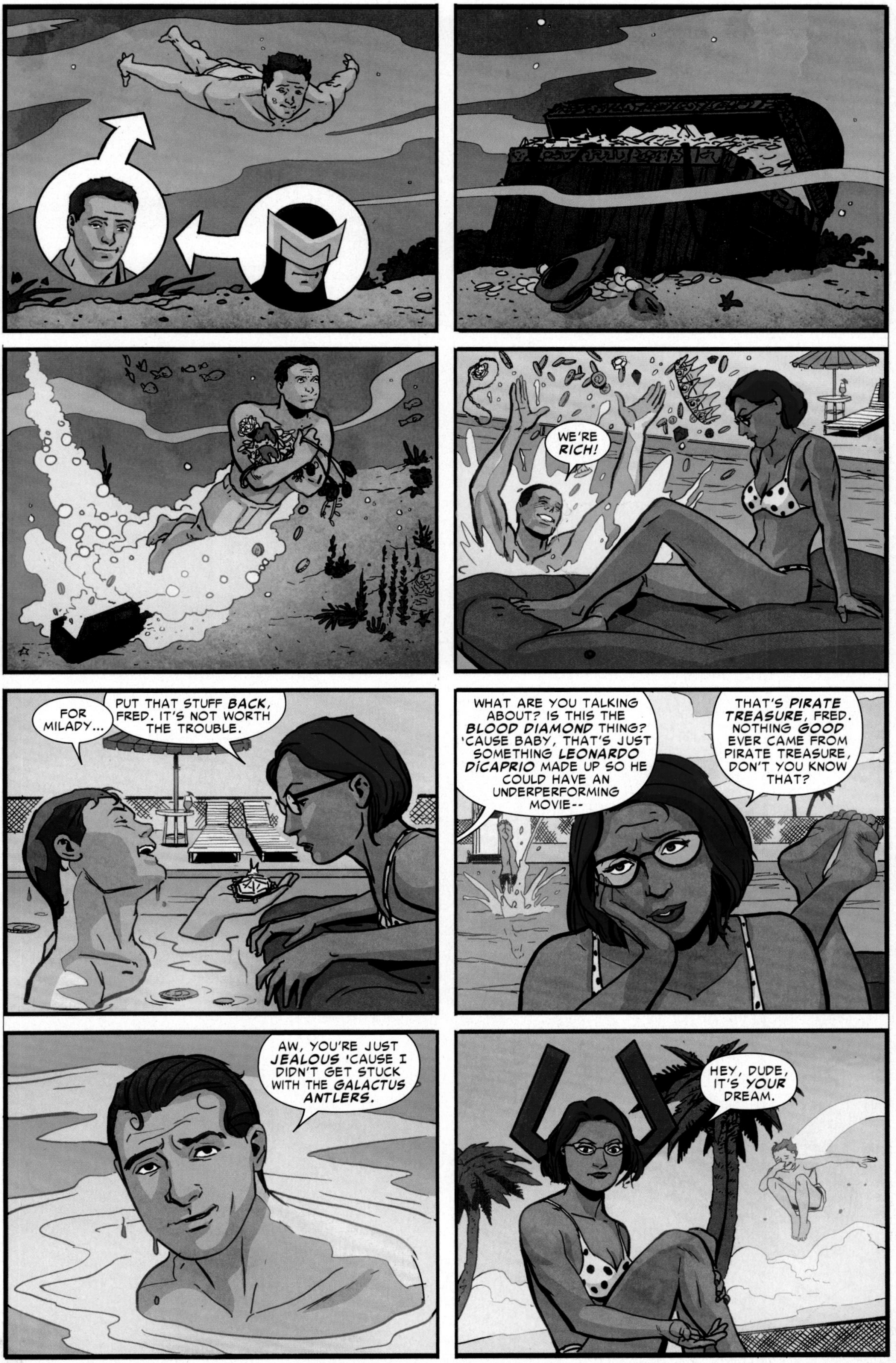
WE'RE RICH!
FOR MILADY...
PUT THAT STUFF BACK, FRED. IT'S NOT WORTH THE TROUBLE.
WHAT ARE YOU TALKING ABOUT? IS THIS THE BLOOD DIAMOND THING? 'CAUSE BABY, THAT'S JUST SOMETHING LEONARDO DiCAPRIO MADE UP SO HE COULD HAVE AN UNDERPERFORMING MOVIE--
THAT'S PIRATE TREASURE, FRED. NOTHING GOOD EVER CAME FROM PIRATE TREASURE, DON'T YOU KNOW THAT?
AW, YOU'RE JUST JEALOUS 'CAUSE I DIDN'T GET STUCK WITH THE GALACTUS ANTLERS.
HEY, DUDE, IT'S YOUR DREAM.

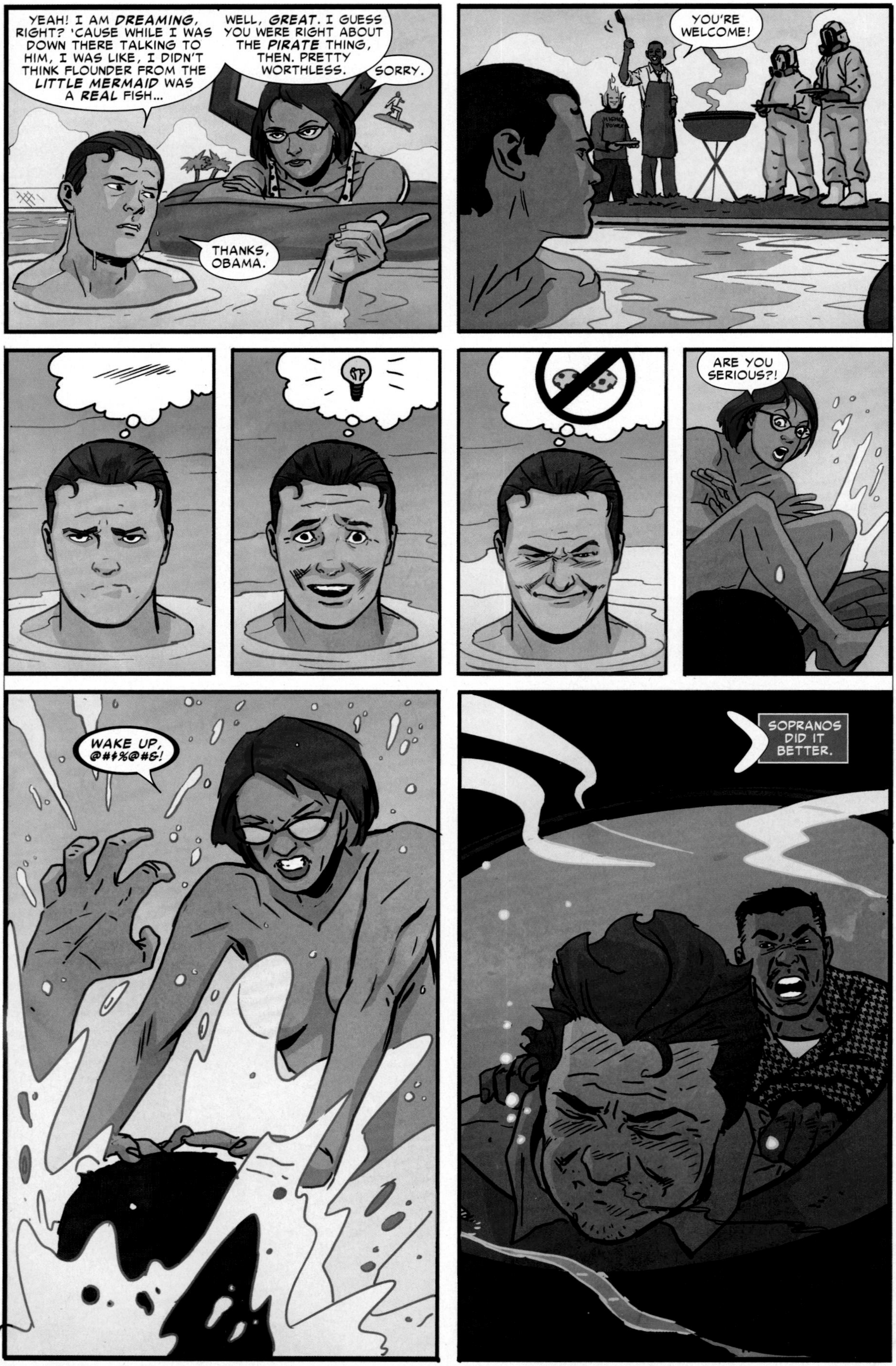

YEAH! I AM DREAMING, RIGHT? 'CAUSE WHILE I WAS DOWN THERE TALKING TO HIM, I WAS LIKE, I DIDN'T THINK FLOUNDER FROM THE LITTLE MERMAID WAS A REAL FISH...
WELL, GREAT. I GUESS YOU WERE RIGHT ABOUT THE PIRATE THING, THEN. PRETTY WORTHLESS.
SORRY.
THANKS, OBAMA.
YOU'RE WELCOME!
ARE YOU SERIOUS?!
WAKE UP, @#$%@#&!
SOPRANOS DID IT BETTER.

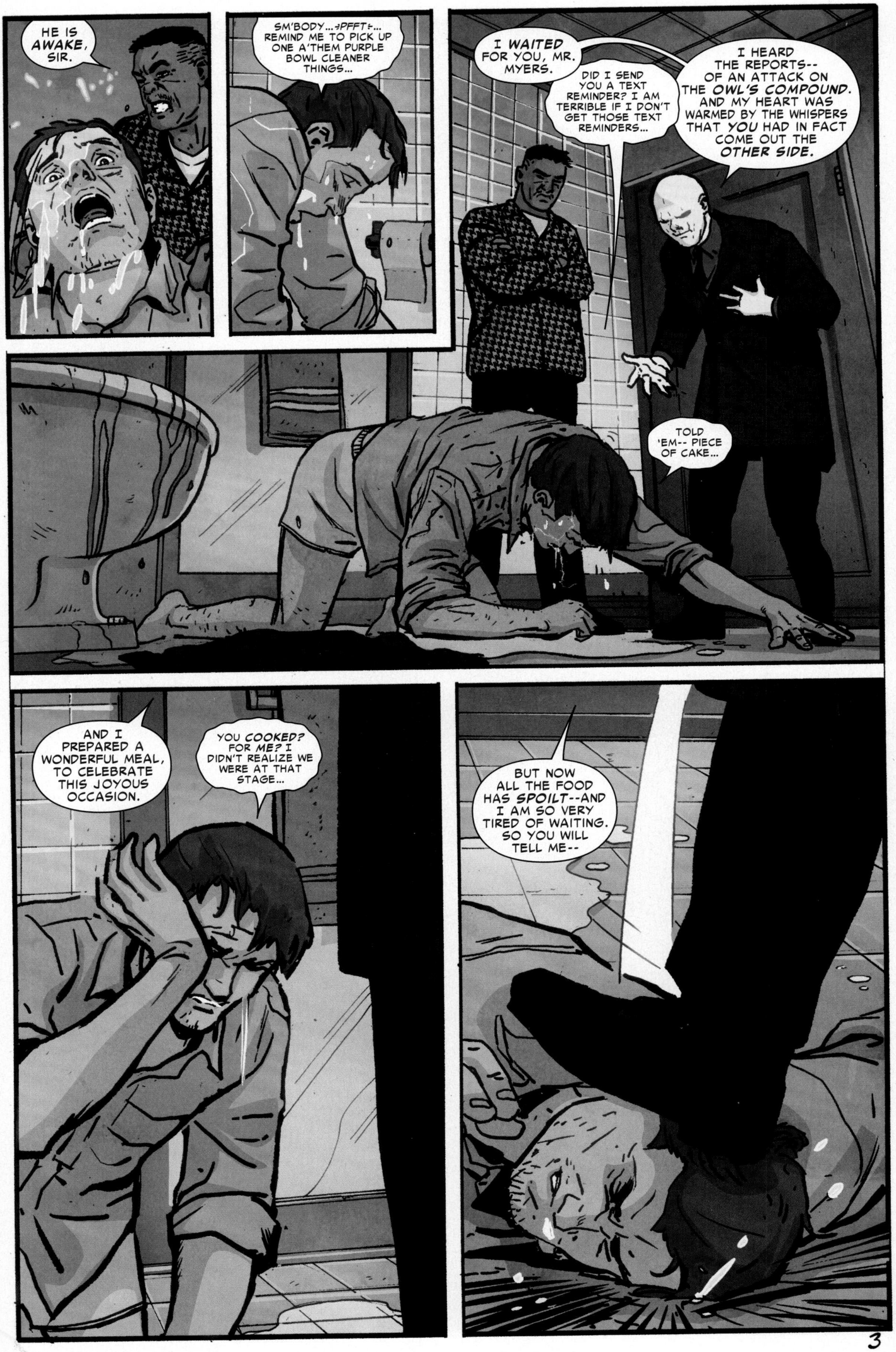

HE IS AWAKE, SIR.
SM'BODY... ≠PFFT≠... REMIND ME TO PICK UP ONE A'THEM PURPLE BOWL CLEANER THINGS...
I WAITED FOR YOU, MR. MYERS.
DID I SEND YOU A TEXT REMINDER? I AM TERRIBLE IF I DON'T GET THOSE TEXT REMINDERS...
I HEARD THE REPORTS-- OF AN ATTACK ON THE OWL'S COMPOUND. AND MY HEART WAS WARMED BY THE WHISPERS THAT YOU HAD IN FACT COME OUT THE OTHER SIDE.
TOLD 'EM-- PIECE OF CAKE...
AND I PREPARED A WONDERFUL MEAL, TO CELEBRATE THIS JOYOUS OCCASION.
YOU COOKED? FOR ME? I DIDN'T REALIZE WE WERE AT THAT STAGE...
BUT NOW ALL THE FOOD HAS SPOILT--AND I AM SO VERY TIRED OF WAITING. SO YOU WILL TELL ME--

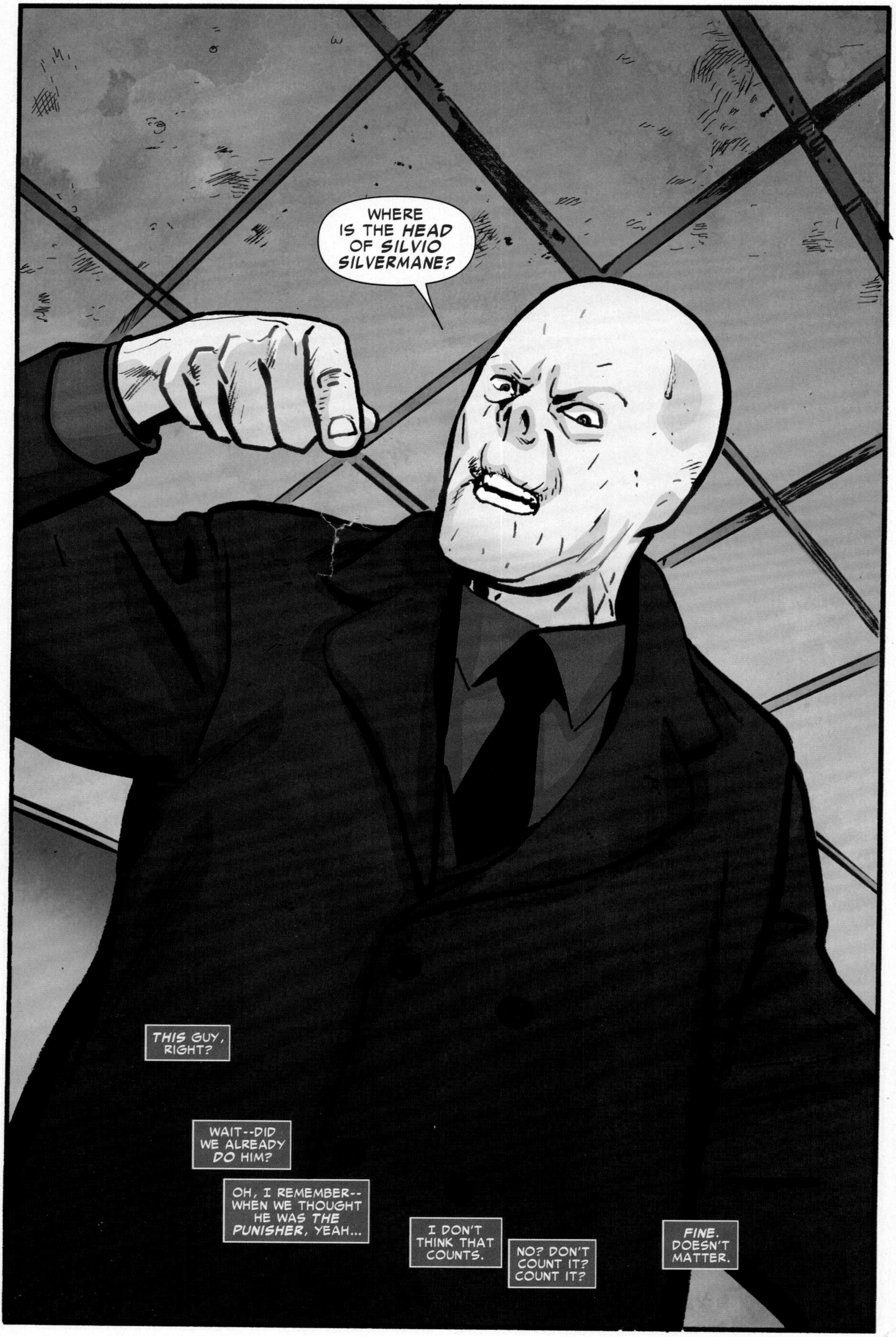
WHERE IS THE HEAD OF SILVIO SILVERMANE?
THIS GUY, RIGHT?
WAIT--DID WE ALREADY DO HIM?
OH, I REMEMBER--WHEN WE THOUGHT HE WAS THE PUNISHER, YEAH...
I DON'T THINK THAT COUNTS.
NO? DON'T COUNT IT? COUNT IT?
FINE. DOESN'T MATTER.

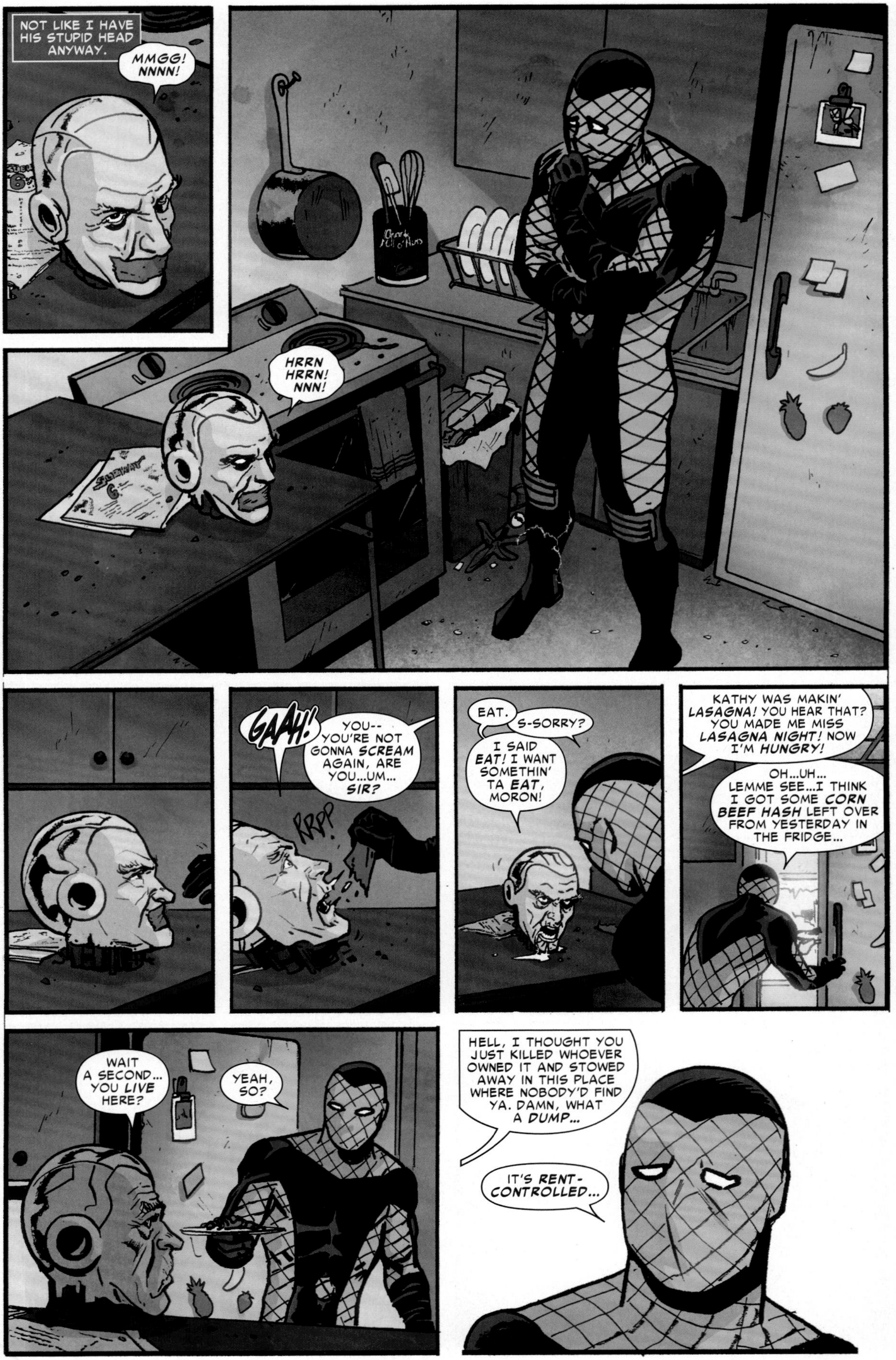
NOT LIKE I HAVE HIS STUPID HEAD ANYWAY.
MMGG! NNNN!
HRRN HRRN! NNN!
GAAH!
YOU-- YOU'RE NOT GONNA SCREAM AGAIN, ARE YOU...UM... SIR?
KRPP
EAT.
S-SORRY?
I SAID EAT! I WANT SOMETHIN' TA EAT, MORON!
KATHY WAS MAKIN' LASAGNA! YOU HEAR THAT? YOU MADE ME MISS LASAGNA NIGHT! NOW I'M HUNGRY!
OH...UH... LEMME SEE...I THINK I GOT SOME CORN BEEF HASH LEFT OVER FROM YESTERDAY IN THE FRIDGE...
WAIT A SECOND... YOU LIVE HERE?
YEAH, SO?
HELL, I THOUGHT YOU JUST KILLED WHOEVER OWNED IT AND STOWED AWAY IN THIS PLACE WHERE NOBODY'D FIND YA. DAMN, WHAT A DUMP...
IT'S RENT-CONTROLLED...

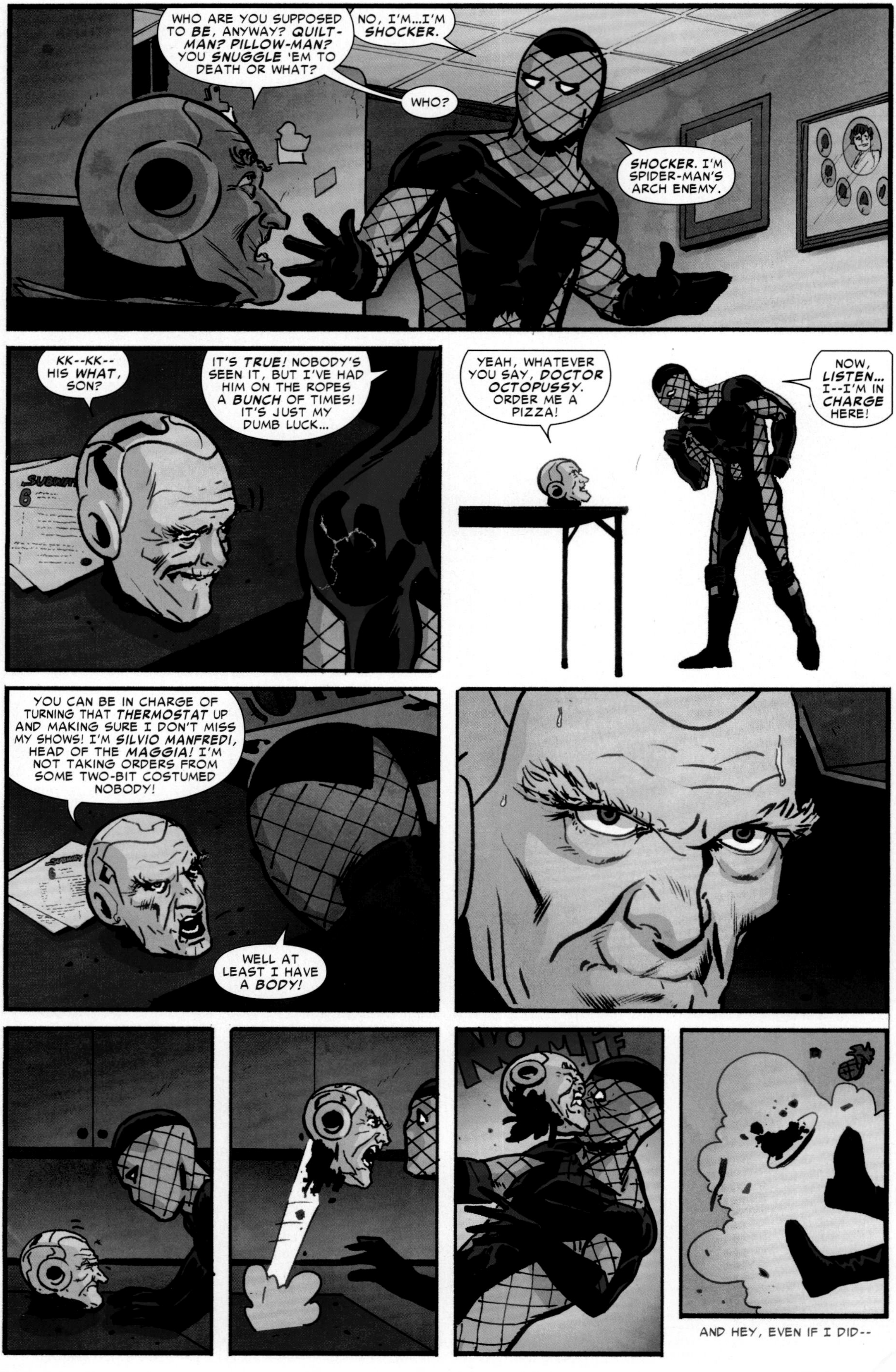
WHO ARE YOU SUPPOSED TO BE, ANYWAY? QUILT-MAN? PILLOW-MAN? YOU SNUGGLE 'EM TO DEATH OR WHAT?
NO, I'M...I'M SHOCKER.
WHO?
SHOCKER. I'M SPIDER-MAN'S ARCH ENEMY.
KK--KK-- HIS WHAT, SON?
IT'S TRUE! NOBODY'S SEEN IT, BUT I'VE HAD HIM ON THE ROPES A BUNCH OF TIMES! IT'S JUST MY DUMB LUCK...
YEAH, WHATEVER YOU SAY, DOCTOR OCTOPUSSY. ORDER ME A PIZZA!
NOW, LISTEN... I--I'M IN CHARGE HERE!
YOU CAN BE IN CHARGE OF TURNING THAT THERMOSTAT UP AND MAKING SURE I DON'T MISS MY SHOWS! I'M SILVIO MANFREDI, HEAD OF THE MAGGIA! I'M NOT TAKING ORDERS FROM SOME TWO-BIT COSTUMED NOBODY!
WELL AT LEAST I HAVE A BODY!
AND HEY, EVEN IF I DID--

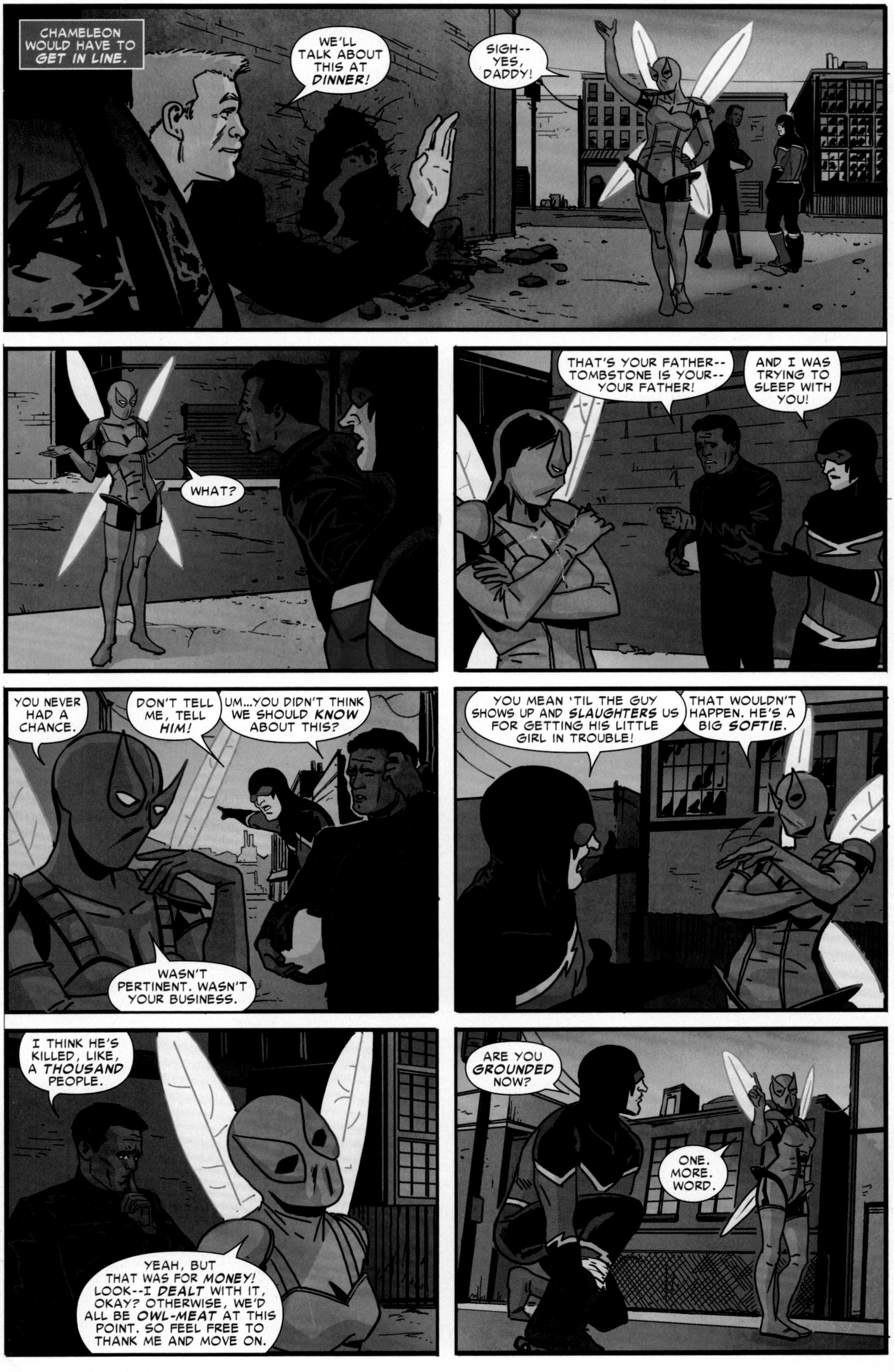
CHAMELEON WOULD HAVE TO GET IN LINE.
WE'LL TALK ABOUT THIS AT DINNER!
SIGH-- YES, DADDY!
WHAT?
THAT'S YOUR FATHER-- TOMBSTONE IS YOUR-- YOUR FATHER!
AND I WAS TRYING TO SLEEP WITH YOU!
YOU NEVER HAD A CHANCE.
DON'T TELL ME, TELL HIM!
UM...YOU DIDN'T THINK WE SHOULD KNOW ABOUT THIS?
WASN'T PERTINENT. WASN'T YOUR BUSINESS.
YOU MEAN 'TIL THE GUY SHOWS UP AND SLAUGHTERS US FOR GETTING HIS LITTLE GIRL IN TROUBLE!
THAT WOULDN'T HAPPEN. HE'S A BIG SOFTIE.
I THINK HE'S KILLED, LIKE, A THOUSAND PEOPLE.
YEAH, BUT THAT WAS FOR MONEY! LOOK--I DEALT WITH IT, OKAY? OTHERWISE, WE'D ALL BE OWL-MEAT AT THIS POINT. SO FEEL FREE TO THANK ME AND MOVE ON.
ARE YOU GROUNDED NOW?
ONE. MORE. WORD.

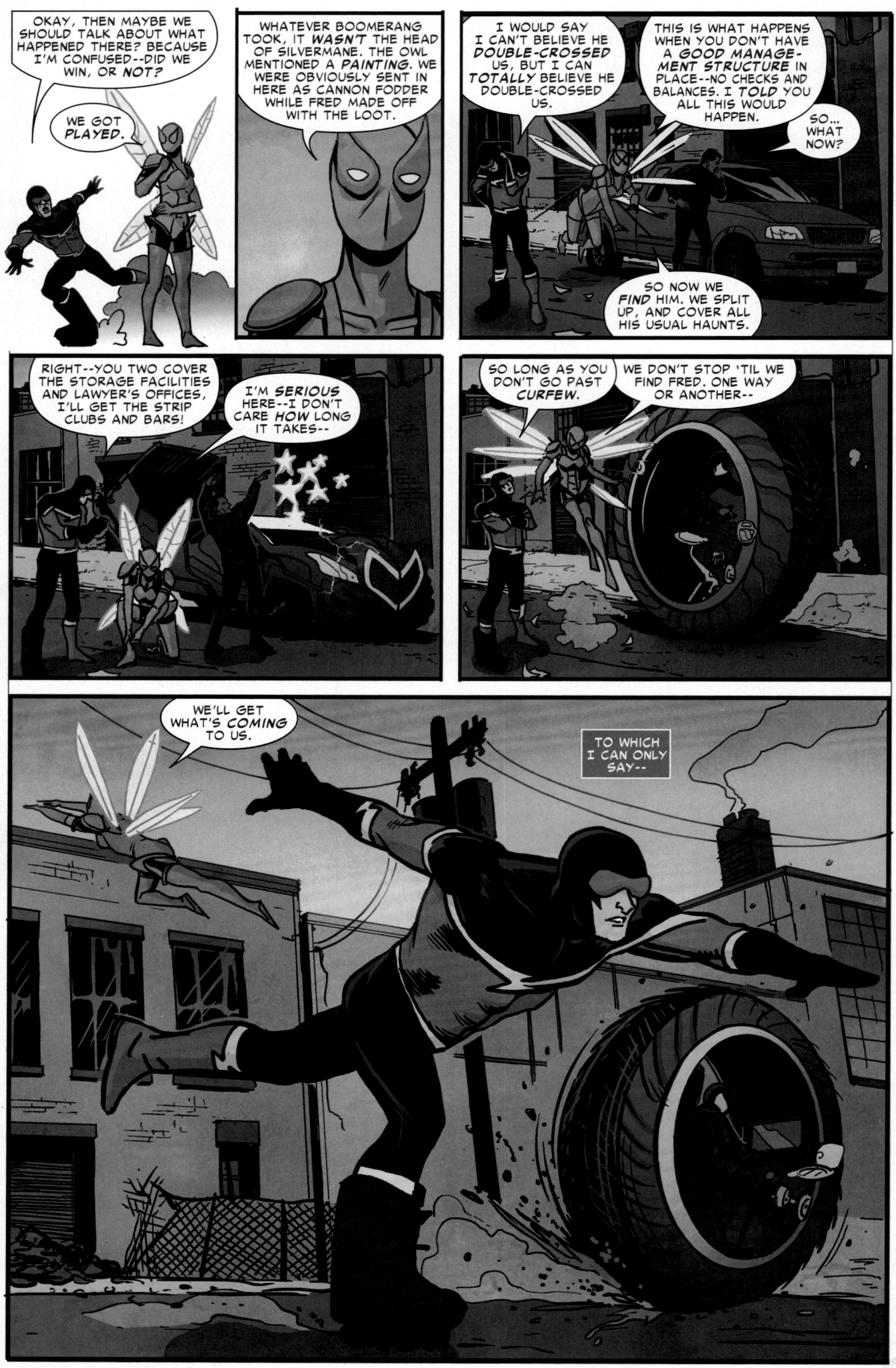

OKAY, THEN MAYBE WE SHOULD TALK ABOUT WHAT HAPPENED THERE? BECAUSE I'M CONFUSED--DID WE WIN, OR NOT?
WE GOT PLAYED.
WHATEVER BOOMERANG TOOK, IT WASN'T THE HEAD OF SILVERMANE. THE OWL MENTIONED A PAINTING. WE WERE OBVIOUSLY SENT IN HERE AS CANNON FODDER WHILE FRED MADE OFF WITH THE LOOT.
I WOULD SAY I CAN'T BELIEVE HE DOUBLE-CROSSED US, BUT I CAN TOTALLY BELIEVE HE DOUBLE-CROSSED US.
THIS IS WHAT HAPPENS WHEN YOU DON'T HAVE A GOOD MANAGEMENT STRUCTURE IN PLACE--NO CHECKS AND BALANCES. I TOLD YOU ALL THIS WOULD HAPPEN.
SO... WHAT NOW?
SO NOW WE FIND HIM. WE SPLIT UP, AND COVER ALL HIS USUAL HAUNTS.
RIGHT--YOU TWO COVER THE STORAGE FACILITIES AND LAWYER'S OFFICES, I'LL GET THE STRIP CLUBS AND BARS!
I'M SERIOUS HERE--I DON'T CARE HOW LONG IT TAKES--
SO LONG AS YOU DON'T GO PAST CURFEW.
WE DON'T STOP 'TIL WE FIND FRED. ONE WAY OR ANOTHER--
WE'LL GET WHAT'S COMING TO US.
TO WHICH I CAN ONLY SAY--

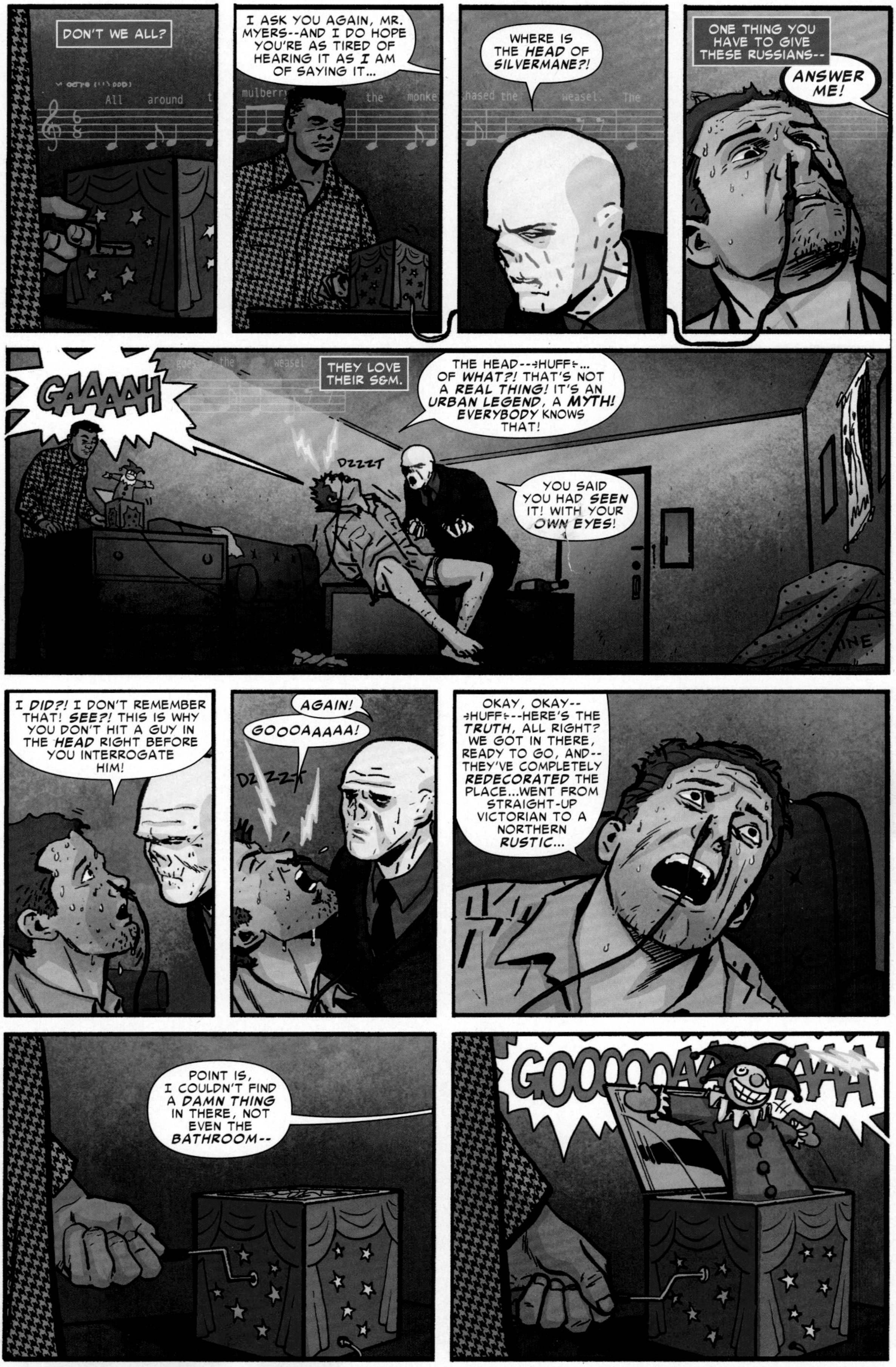
DON'T WE ALL?
All around t
I ASK YOU AGAIN, MR. MYERS--AND I DO HOPE YOU'RE AS TIRED OF HEARING IT AS *I* AM OF SAYING IT...
mulberry
the monke
WHERE IS THE *HEAD* OF *SILVERMANE?!*
weasel. The
ONE THING YOU HAVE TO GIVE THESE RUSSIANS--
ANSWER ME!
GAAAAH
weasel
THEY LOVE THEIR S&M.
THE HEAD--HUFF--... OF *WHAT?!* THAT'S NOT A *REAL THING!* IT'S AN *URBAN LEGEND*, A *MYTH!* *EVERYBODY* KNOWS THAT!
DZZZZT
YOU SAID YOU HAD *SEEN* IT! WITH YOUR *OWN EYES*!
I *DID?!* I DON'T REMEMBER THAT! *SEE?!* THIS IS WHY YOU DON'T HIT A GUY IN THE *HEAD* RIGHT BEFORE YOU INTERROGATE HIM!
AGAIN!
GOOOAAAAA!
DZZZZT
OKAY, OKAY-- HUFF--HERE'S THE *TRUTH*, ALL RIGHT? WE GOT IN THERE, READY TO GO, AND--THEY'VE COMPLETELY *REDECORATED* THE PLACE...WENT FROM STRAIGHT-UP VICTORIAN TO A NORTHERN *RUSTIC*...
POINT IS, I COULDN'T FIND A *DAMN THING* IN THERE, NOT EVEN THE *BATHROOM*--

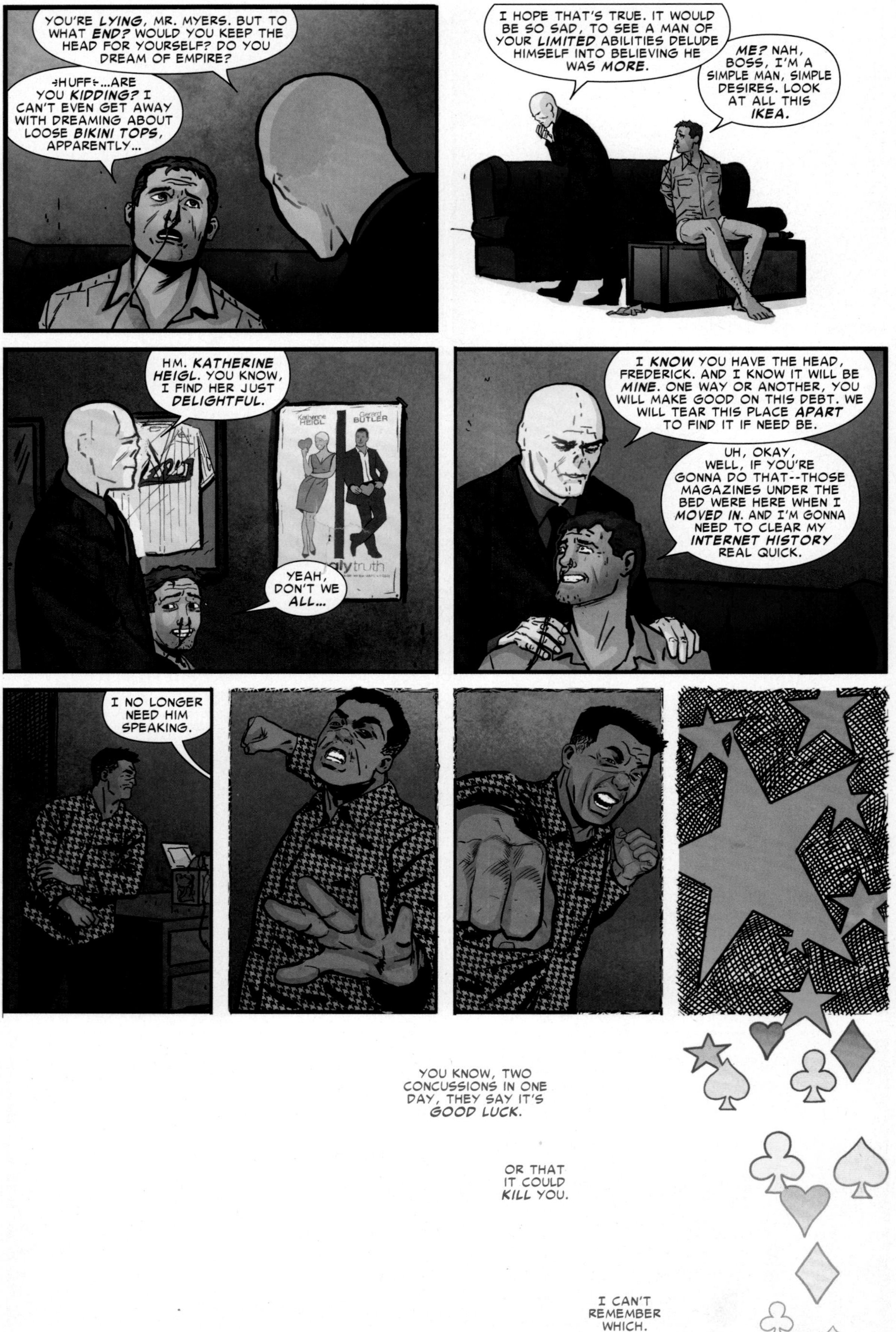
YOU'RE LYING, MR. MYERS. BUT TO WHAT END? WOULD YOU KEEP THE HEAD FOR YOURSELF? DO YOU DREAM OF EMPIRE?
HUFF...ARE YOU KIDDING? I CAN'T EVEN GET AWAY WITH DREAMING ABOUT LOOSE BIKINI TOPS, APPARENTLY...
I HOPE THAT'S TRUE. IT WOULD BE SO SAD, TO SEE A MAN OF YOUR LIMITED ABILITIES DELUDE HIMSELF INTO BELIEVING HE WAS MORE.
ME? NAH, BOSS, I'M A SIMPLE MAN, SIMPLE DESIRES. LOOK AT ALL THIS IKEA.
HM. KATHERINE HEIGL. YOU KNOW, I FIND HER JUST DELIGHTFUL.
Katherine HEIGL
Gerard BUTLER
YEAH, DON'T WE ALL...
I KNOW YOU HAVE THE HEAD, FREDERICK. AND I KNOW IT WILL BE MINE. ONE WAY OR ANOTHER, YOU WILL MAKE GOOD ON THIS DEBT. WE WILL TEAR THIS PLACE APART TO FIND IT IF NEED BE.
UH, OKAY, WELL, IF YOU'RE GONNA DO THAT--THOSE MAGAZINES UNDER THE BED WERE HERE WHEN I MOVED IN. AND I'M GONNA NEED TO CLEAR MY INTERNET HISTORY REAL QUICK.
I NO LONGER NEED HIM SPEAKING.
YOU KNOW, TWO CONCUSSIONS IN ONE DAY, THEY SAY IT'S GOOD LUCK.
OR THAT IT COULD KILL YOU.
I CAN'T REMEMBER WHICH.

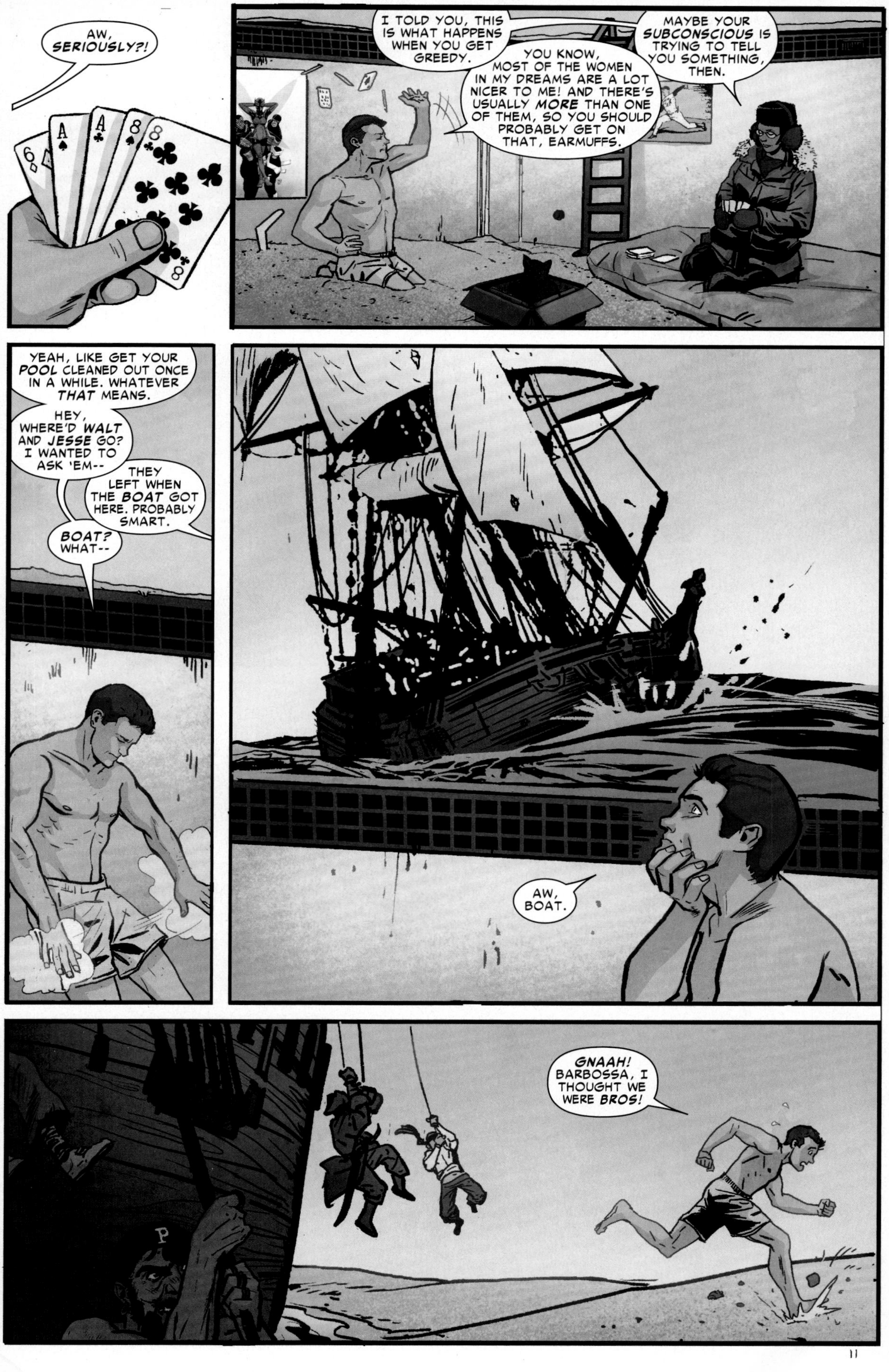
AW, SERIOUSLY?!
I TOLD YOU, THIS IS WHAT HAPPENS WHEN YOU GET GREEDY.
YOU KNOW, MOST OF THE WOMEN IN MY DREAMS ARE A LOT NICER TO ME! AND THERE'S USUALLY MORE THAN ONE OF THEM, SO YOU SHOULD PROBABLY GET ON THAT, EARMUFFS.
MAYBE YOUR SUBCONSCIOUS IS TRYING TO TELL YOU SOMETHING, THEN.
YEAH, LIKE GET YOUR POOL CLEANED OUT ONCE IN A WHILE. WHATEVER THAT MEANS.
HEY, WHERE'D WALT AND JESSE GO? I WANTED TO ASK 'EM--
THEY LEFT WHEN THE BOAT GOT HERE. PROBABLY SMART.
BOAT? WHAT--
AW, BOAT.
GNAAH! BARBOSSA, I THOUGHT WE WERE BROS!

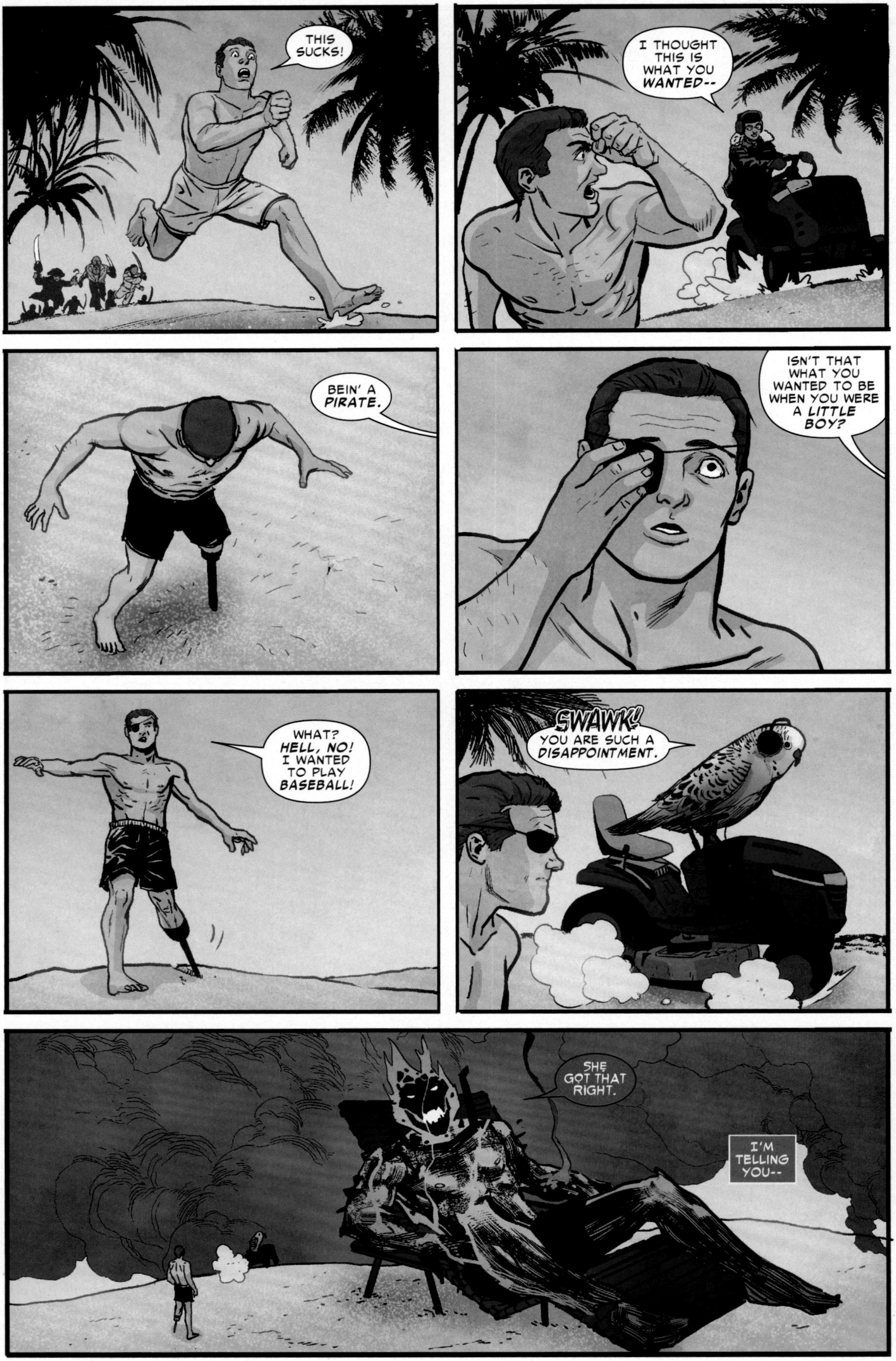

THIS SUCKS!
I THOUGHT THIS IS WHAT YOU WANTED--
BEIN' A PIRATE.
ISN'T THAT WHAT YOU WANTED TO BE WHEN YOU WERE A LITTLE BOY?
WHAT? HELL, NO! I WANTED TO PLAY BASEBALL!
SWAWK!
YOU ARE SUCH A DISAPPOINTMENT.
SHE GOT THAT RIGHT.
I'M TELLING YOU--

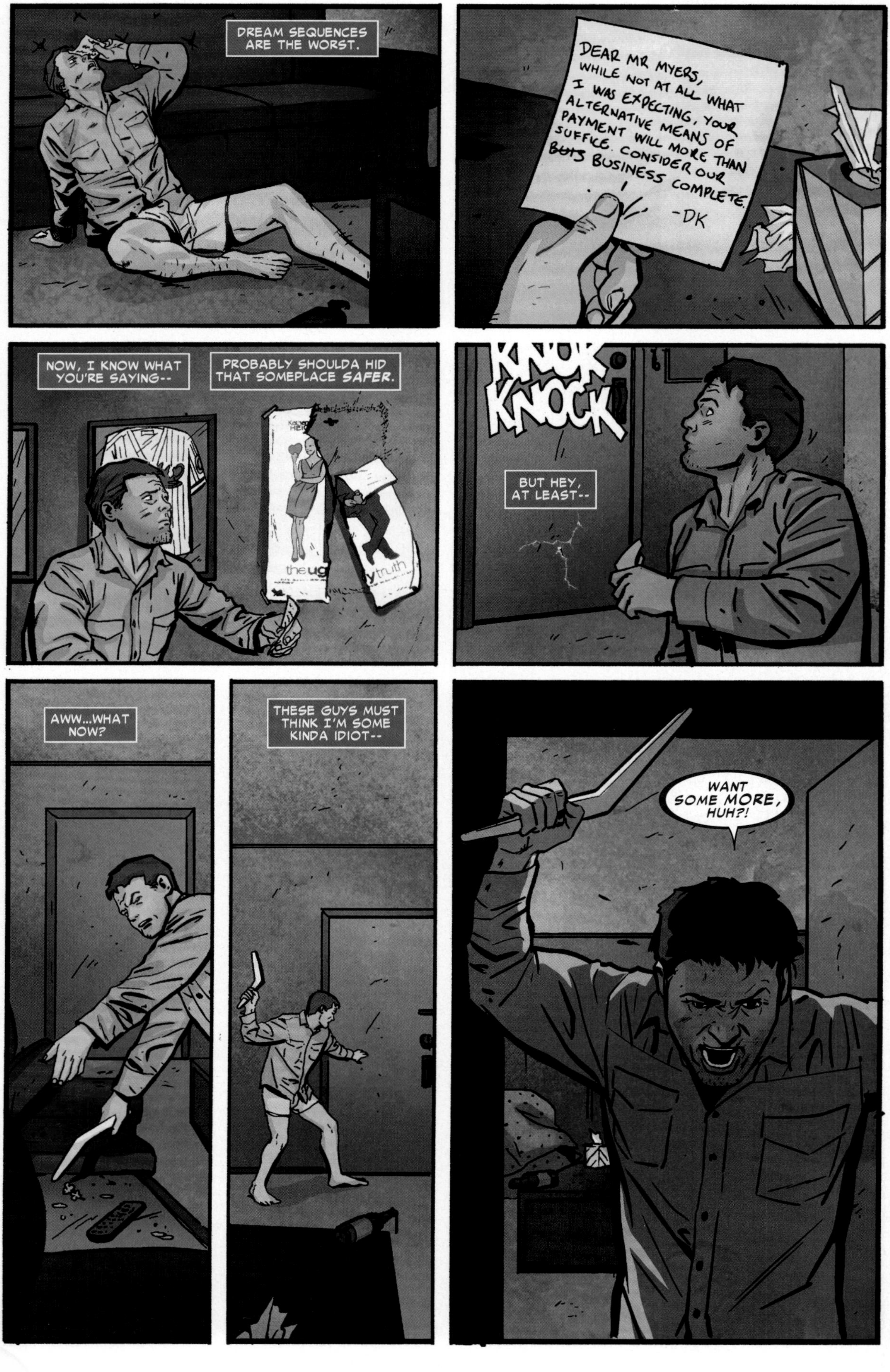
DREAM SEQUENCES ARE THE WORST.
DEAR MR MYERS, WHILE NOT AT ALL WHAT I WAS EXPECTING, YOUR ALTERNATIVE MEANS OF PAYMENT WILL MORE THAN SUFFICE. CONSIDER OUR ~~BUYS~~ BUSINESS COMPLETE.
-DK
NOW, I KNOW WHAT YOU'RE SAYING--
PROBABLY SHOULDA HID THAT SOMEPLACE *SAFER*.
KNOCK
KNOCK
BUT HEY, AT LEAST--
AWW...WHAT NOW?
THESE GUYS MUST THINK I'M SOME KINDA IDIOT--
WANT SOME MORE, HUH?!

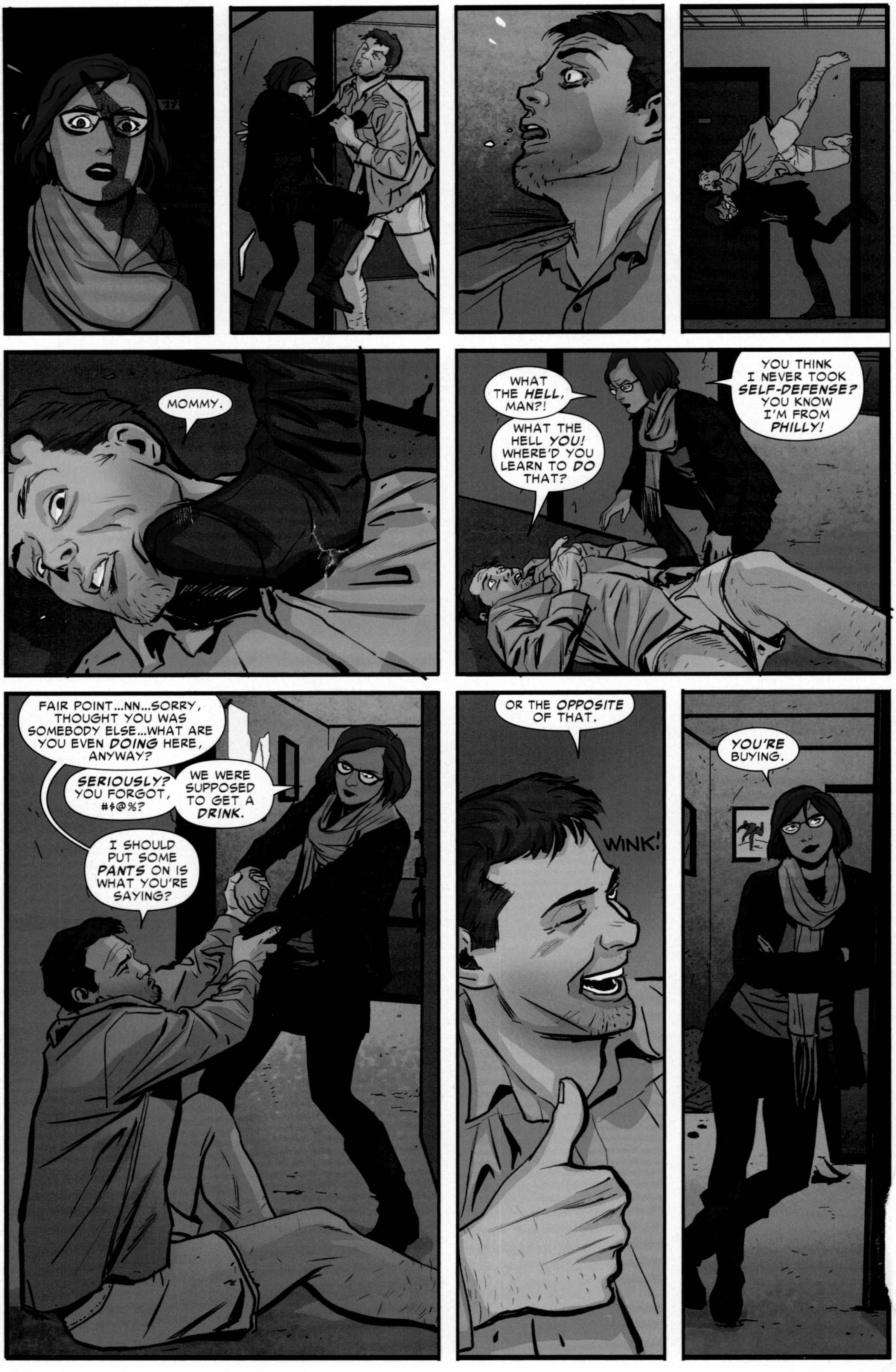
MOMMY.
WHAT THE HELL, MAN?!
WHAT THE HELL YOU! WHERE'D YOU LEARN TO DO THAT?
YOU THINK I NEVER TOOK SELF-DEFENSE? YOU KNOW I'M FROM PHILLY!
FAIR POINT...NN...SORRY, THOUGHT YOU WAS SOMEBODY ELSE...WHAT ARE YOU EVEN DOING HERE, ANYWAY?
SERIOUSLY? YOU FORGOT, #$@%?
WE WERE SUPPOSED TO GET A DRINK.
I SHOULD PUT SOME PANTS ON IS WHAT YOU'RE SAYING?
OR THE OPPOSITE OF THAT.
WINK!
YOU'RE BUYING.

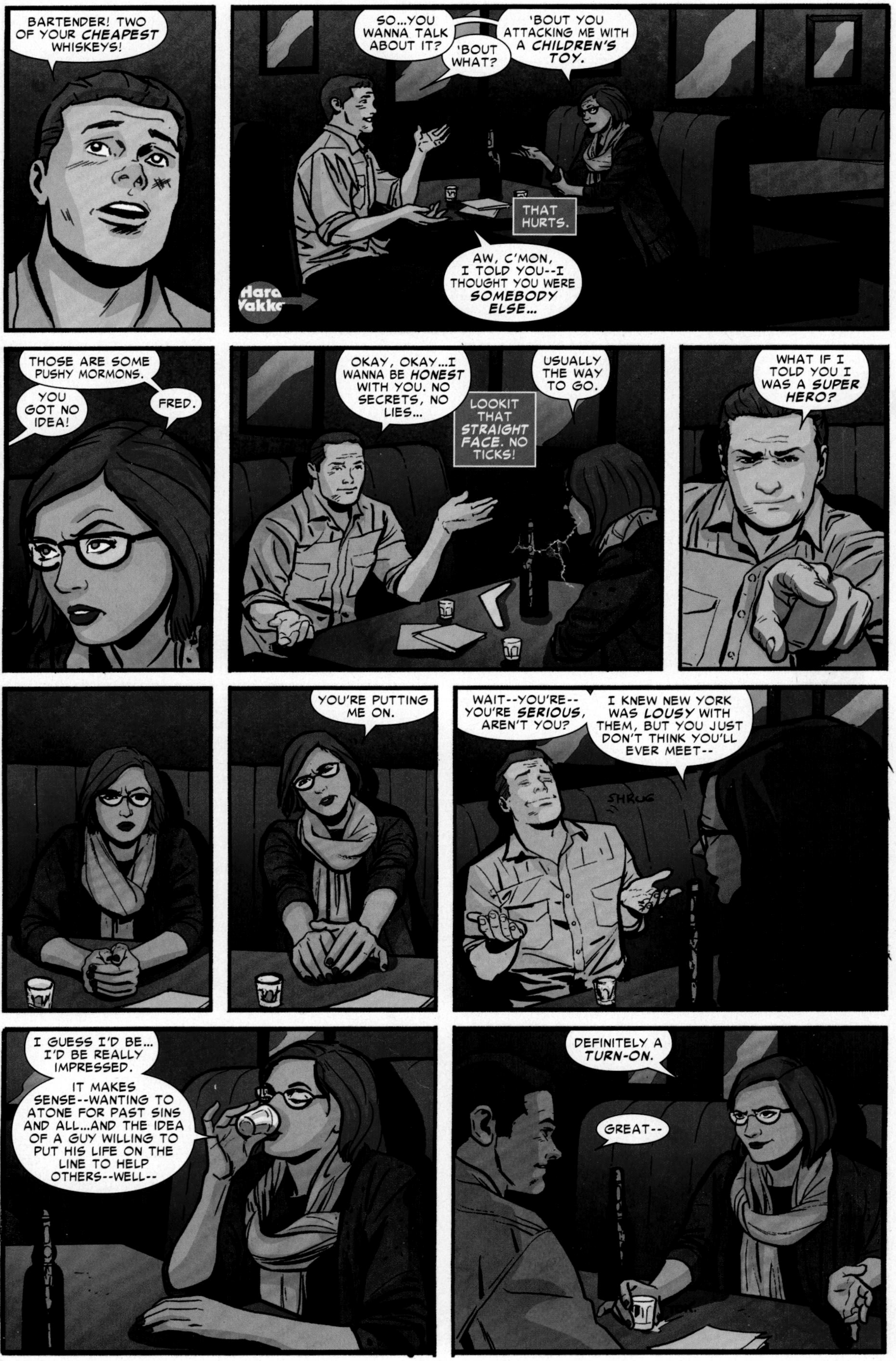
BARTENDER! TWO OF YOUR CHEAPEST WHISKEYS!
SO...YOU WANNA TALK ABOUT IT?
'BOUT WHAT?
'BOUT YOU ATTACKING ME WITH A CHILDREN'S TOY.
THAT HURTS.
AW, C'MON, I TOLD YOU--I THOUGHT YOU WERE SOMEBODY ELSE...
THOSE ARE SOME PUSHY MORMONS.
YOU GOT NO IDEA!
FRED.
OKAY, OKAY...I WANNA BE HONEST WITH YOU. NO SECRETS, NO LIES...
LOOKIT THAT STRAIGHT FACE. NO TICKS!
USUALLY THE WAY TO GO.
WHAT IF I TOLD YOU I WAS A SUPER HERO?
YOU'RE PUTTING ME ON.
WAIT--YOU'RE--YOU'RE SERIOUS, AREN'T YOU?
I KNEW NEW YORK WAS LOUSY WITH THEM, BUT YOU JUST DON'T THINK YOU'LL EVER MEET--
SHRUG
I GUESS I'D BE... I'D BE REALLY IMPRESSED.
IT MAKES SENSE--WANTING TO ATONE FOR PAST SINS AND ALL...AND THE IDEA OF A GUY WILLING TO PUT HIS LIFE ON THE LINE TO HELP OTHERS--WELL--
DEFINITELY A TURN-ON.
GREAT--

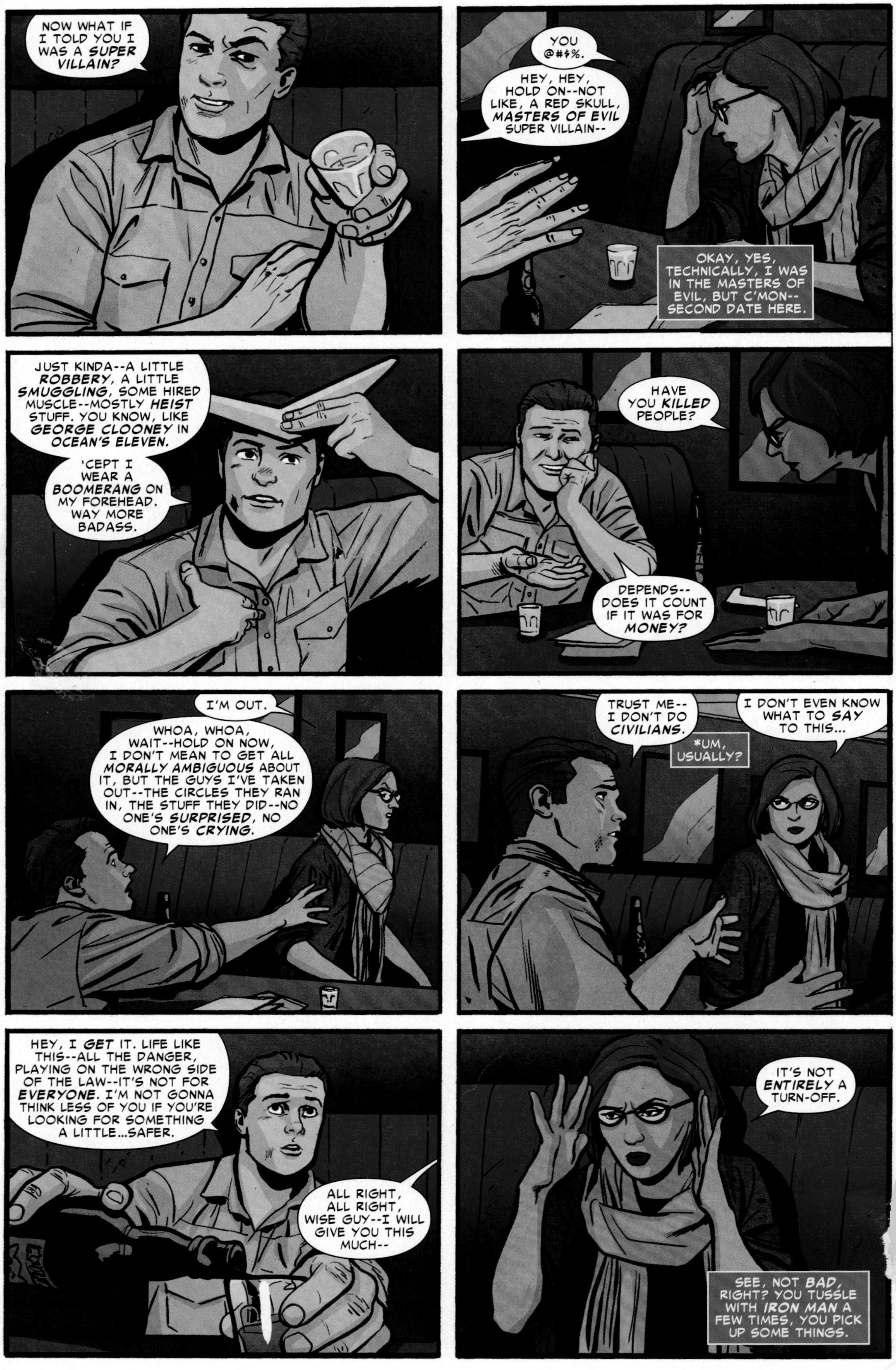
NOW WHAT IF I TOLD YOU I WAS A SUPER VILLAIN?
YOU @#$%.
HEY, HEY, HOLD ON--NOT LIKE, A RED SKULL, MASTERS OF EVIL SUPER VILLAIN--
OKAY, YES, TECHNICALLY, I WAS IN THE MASTERS OF EVIL, BUT C'MON-- SECOND DATE HERE.
JUST KINDA--A LITTLE ROBBERY, A LITTLE SMUGGLING, SOME HIRED MUSCLE--MOSTLY HEIST STUFF. YOU KNOW, LIKE GEORGE CLOONEY IN OCEAN'S ELEVEN.
'CEPT I WEAR A BOOMERANG ON MY FOREHEAD. WAY MORE BADASS.
HAVE YOU KILLED PEOPLE?
DEPENDS-- DOES IT COUNT IF IT WAS FOR MONEY?
I'M OUT.
WHOA, WHOA, WAIT--HOLD ON NOW, I DON'T MEAN TO GET ALL MORALLY AMBIGUOUS ABOUT IT, BUT THE GUYS I'VE TAKEN OUT--THE CIRCLES THEY RAN IN, THE STUFF THEY DID--NO ONE'S SURPRISED, NO ONE'S CRYING.
TRUST ME-- I DON'T DO CIVILIANS.
*UM, USUALLY?
I DON'T EVEN KNOW WHAT TO SAY TO THIS...
HEY, I GET IT. LIFE LIKE THIS--ALL THE DANGER, PLAYING ON THE WRONG SIDE OF THE LAW--IT'S NOT FOR EVERYONE. I'M NOT GONNA THINK LESS OF YOU IF YOU'RE LOOKING FOR SOMETHING A LITTLE...SAFER.
ALL RIGHT, ALL RIGHT, WISE GUY--I WILL GIVE YOU THIS MUCH--
IT'S NOT ENTIRELY A TURN-OFF.
SEE, NOT BAD, RIGHT? YOU TUSSLE WITH IRON MAN A FEW TIMES, YOU PICK UP SOME THINGS.

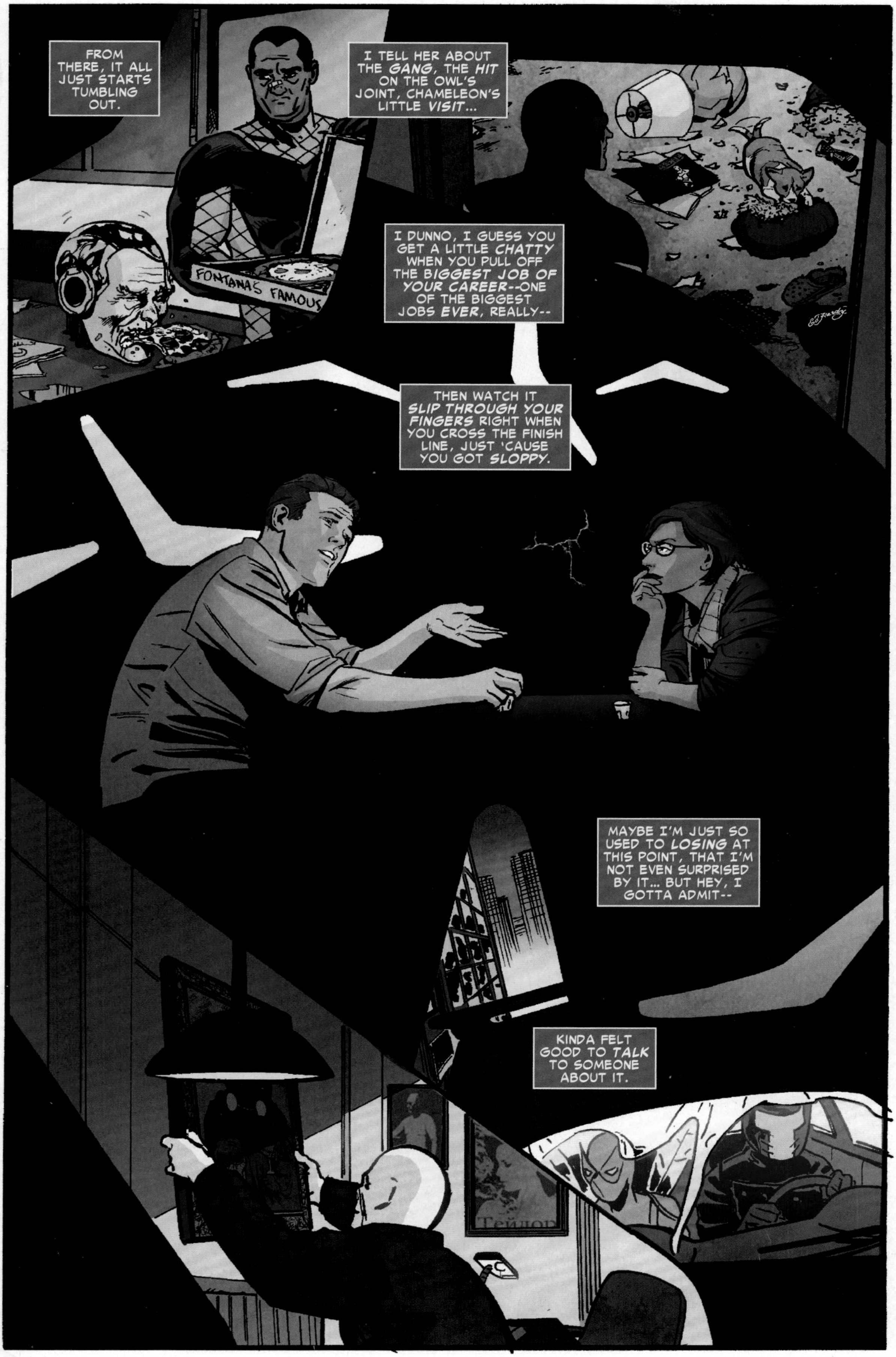
FROM THERE, IT ALL JUST STARTS TUMBLING OUT.
I TELL HER ABOUT THE GANG, THE HIT ON THE OWL'S JOINT, CHAMELEON'S LITTLE VISIT...
FONTANA'S FAMOUS
I DUNNO, I GUESS YOU GET A LITTLE CHATTY WHEN YOU PULL OFF THE BIGGEST JOB OF YOUR CAREER--ONE OF THE BIGGEST JOBS EVER, REALLY--
THEN WATCH IT SLIP THROUGH YOUR FINGERS RIGHT WHEN YOU CROSS THE FINISH LINE, JUST 'CAUSE YOU GOT SLOPPY.
MAYBE I'M JUST SO USED TO LOSING AT THIS POINT, THAT I'M NOT EVEN SURPRISED BY IT... BUT HEY, I GOTTA ADMIT--
KINDA FELT GOOD TO TALK TO SOMEONE ABOUT IT.

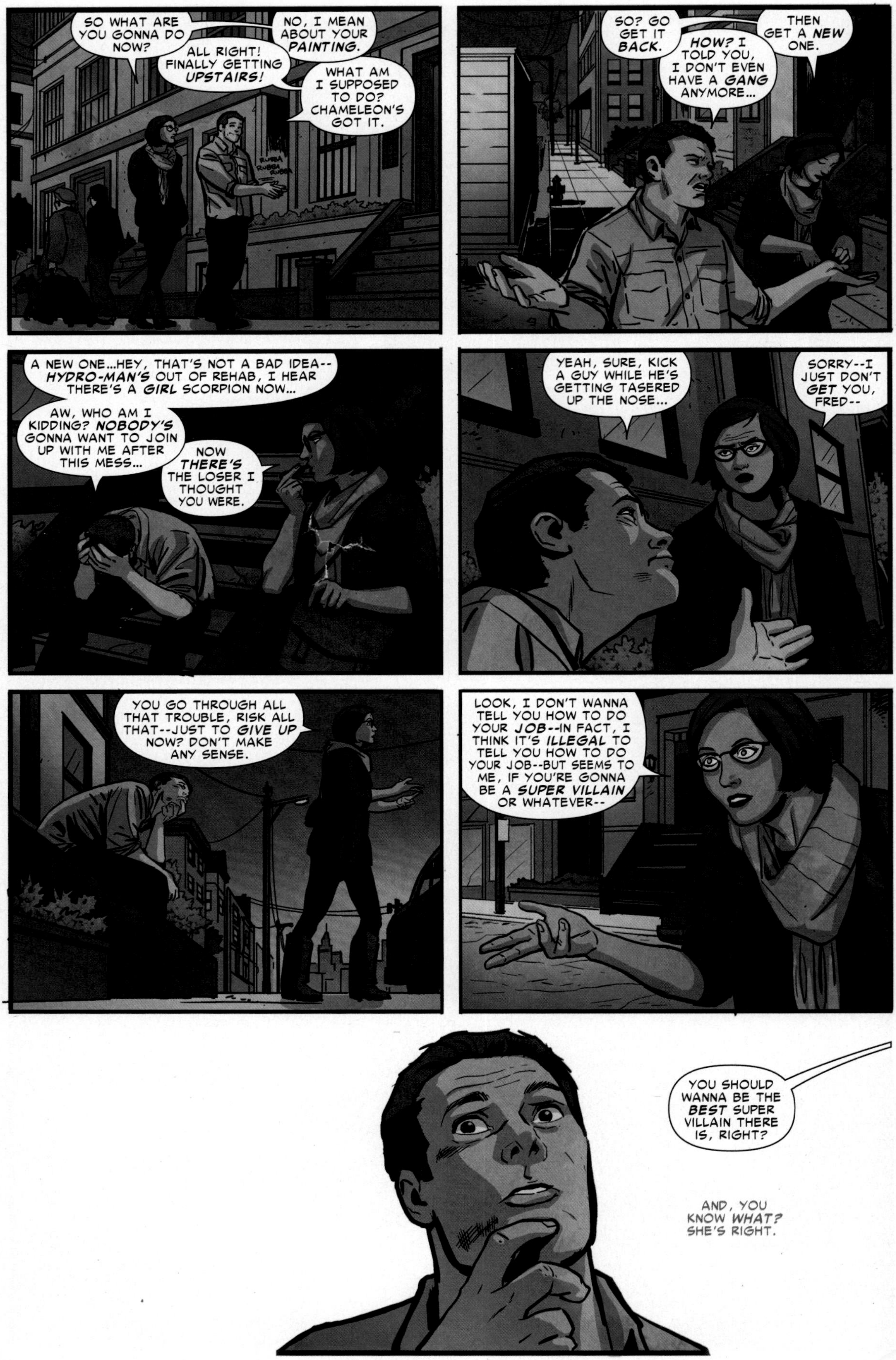
SO WHAT ARE YOU GONNA DO NOW?
ALL RIGHT! FINALLY GETTING UPSTAIRS!
NO, I MEAN ABOUT YOUR PAINTING.
WHAT AM I SUPPOSED TO DO? CHAMELEON'S GOT IT.
SO? GO GET IT BACK.
HOW? I TOLD YOU, I DON'T EVEN HAVE A GANG ANYMORE...
THEN GET A NEW ONE.
A NEW ONE...HEY, THAT'S NOT A BAD IDEA-- HYDRO-MAN'S OUT OF REHAB, I HEAR THERE'S A GIRL SCORPION NOW...
AW, WHO AM I KIDDING? NOBODY'S GONNA WANT TO JOIN UP WITH ME AFTER THIS MESS...
NOW THERE'S THE LOSER I THOUGHT YOU WERE.
YEAH, SURE, KICK A GUY WHILE HE'S GETTING TASERED UP THE NOSE...
SORRY--I JUST DON'T GET YOU, FRED--
YOU GO THROUGH ALL THAT TROUBLE, RISK ALL THAT--JUST TO GIVE UP NOW? DON'T MAKE ANY SENSE.
LOOK, I DON'T WANNA TELL YOU HOW TO DO YOUR JOB--IN FACT, I THINK IT'S ILLEGAL TO TELL YOU HOW TO DO YOUR JOB--BUT SEEMS TO ME, IF YOU'RE GONNA BE A SUPER VILLAIN OR WHATEVER--
YOU SHOULD WANNA BE THE BEST SUPER VILLAIN THERE IS, RIGHT?
AND, YOU KNOW WHAT? SHE'S RIGHT.

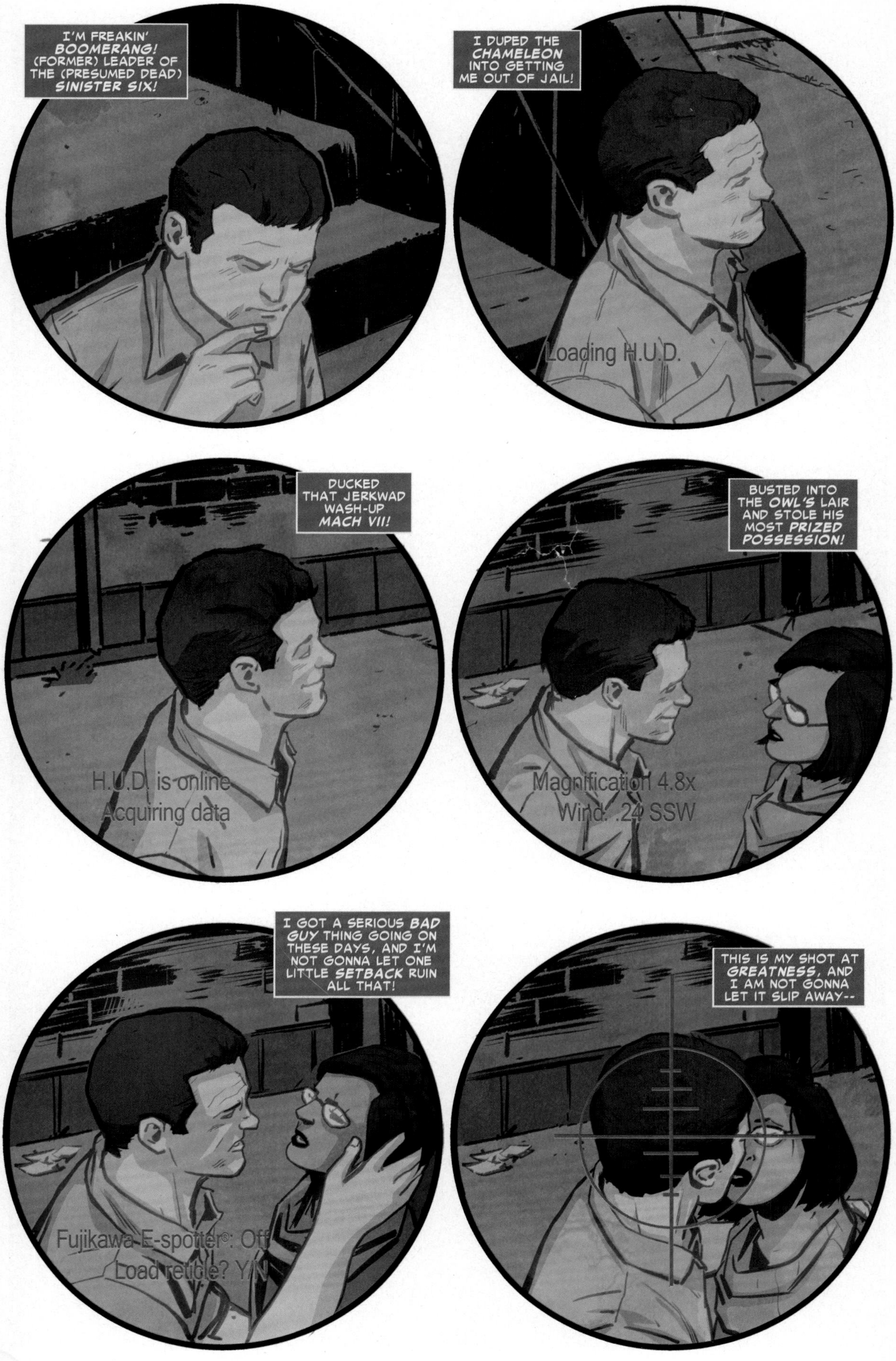
I'M FREAKIN' BOOMERANG! (FORMER) LEADER OF THE (PRESUMED DEAD) SINISTER SIX!
I DUPED THE CHAMELEON INTO GETTING ME OUT OF JAIL!
Loading H.U.D.
DUCKED THAT JERKWAD WASH-UP MACH VII!
H.U.D. is online
Acquiring data
BUSTED INTO THE OWL'S LAIR AND STOLE HIS MOST PRIZED POSSESSION!
Magnification 4.8x
Wind: .24 SSW
I GOT A SERIOUS BAD GUY THING GOING ON THESE DAYS, AND I'M NOT GONNA LET ONE LITTLE SETBACK RUIN ALL THAT!
Fujikawa E-spotter®: Off
Load reticle? Y/N
THIS IS MY SHOT AT GREATNESS, AND I AM NOT GONNA LET IT SLIP AWAY--

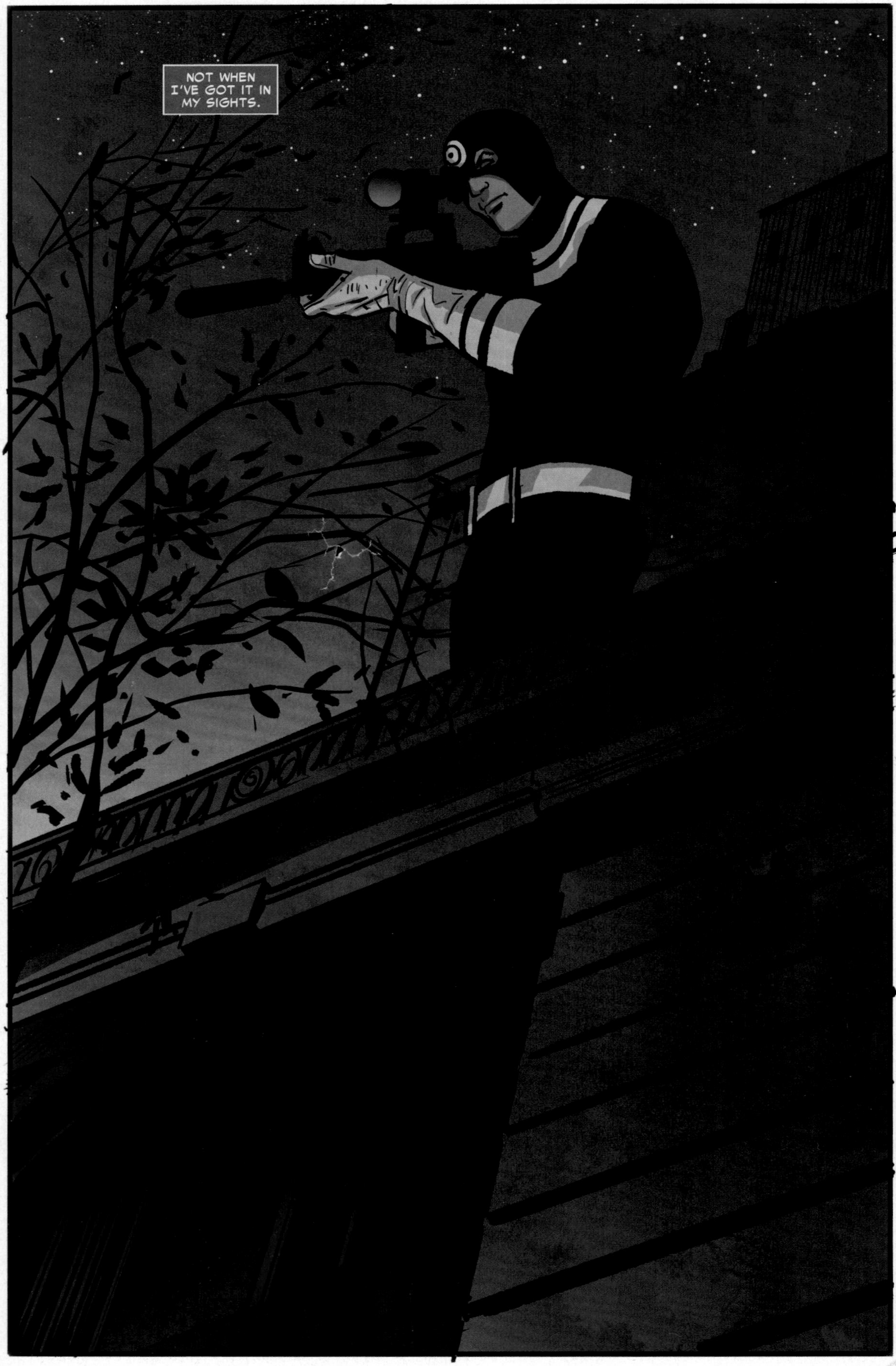
NOT WHEN I'VE GOT IT IN MY SIGHTS.

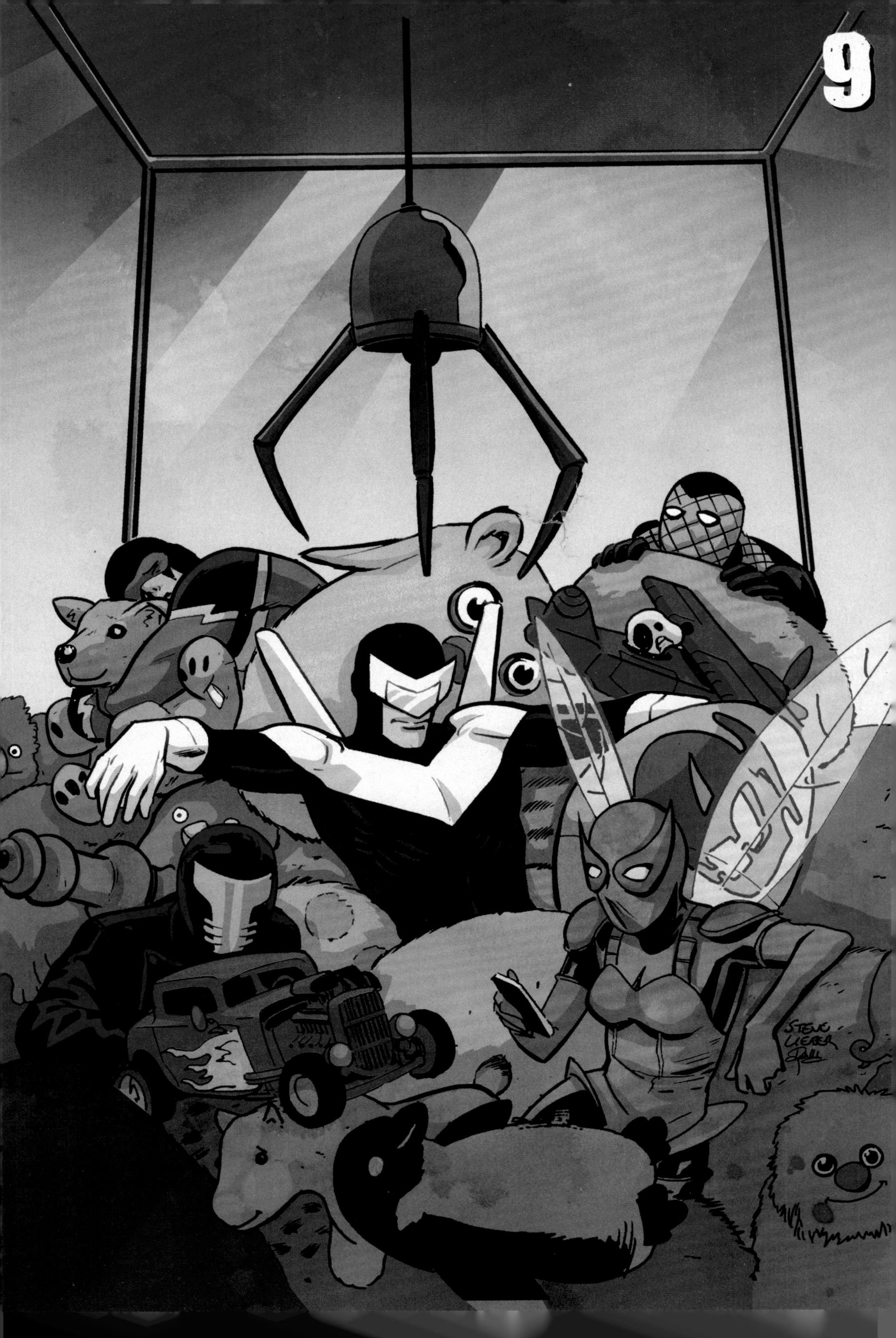
9

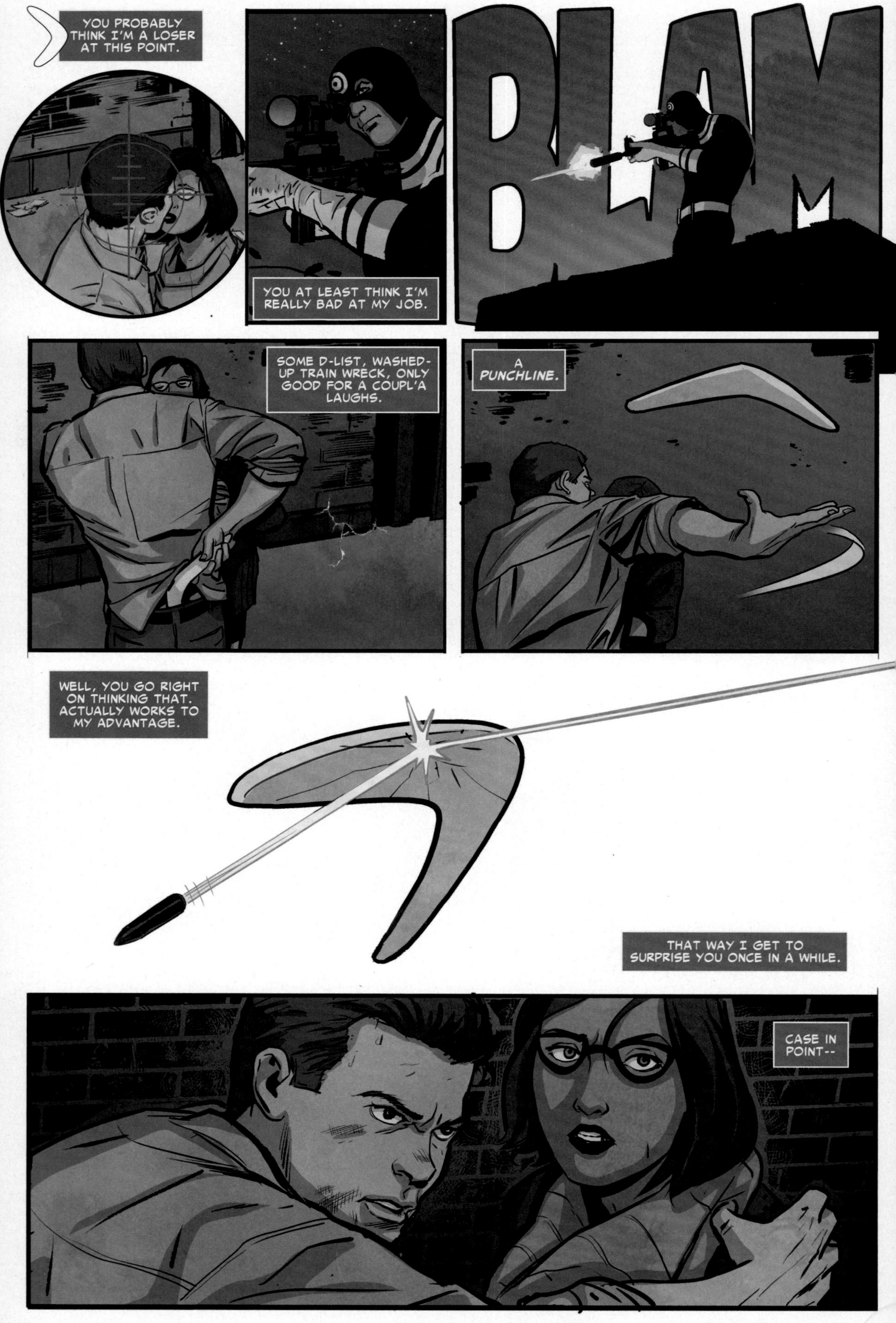
YOU PROBABLY THINK I'M A LOSER AT THIS POINT.
YOU AT LEAST THINK I'M REALLY BAD AT MY JOB.
BLAM
SOME D-LIST, WASHED-UP TRAIN WRECK, ONLY GOOD FOR A COUPL'A LAUGHS.
A *PUNCHLINE.*
WELL, YOU GO RIGHT ON THINKING THAT. ACTUALLY WORKS TO MY ADVANTAGE.
THAT WAY I GET TO SURPRISE YOU ONCE IN A WHILE.
CASE IN POINT--

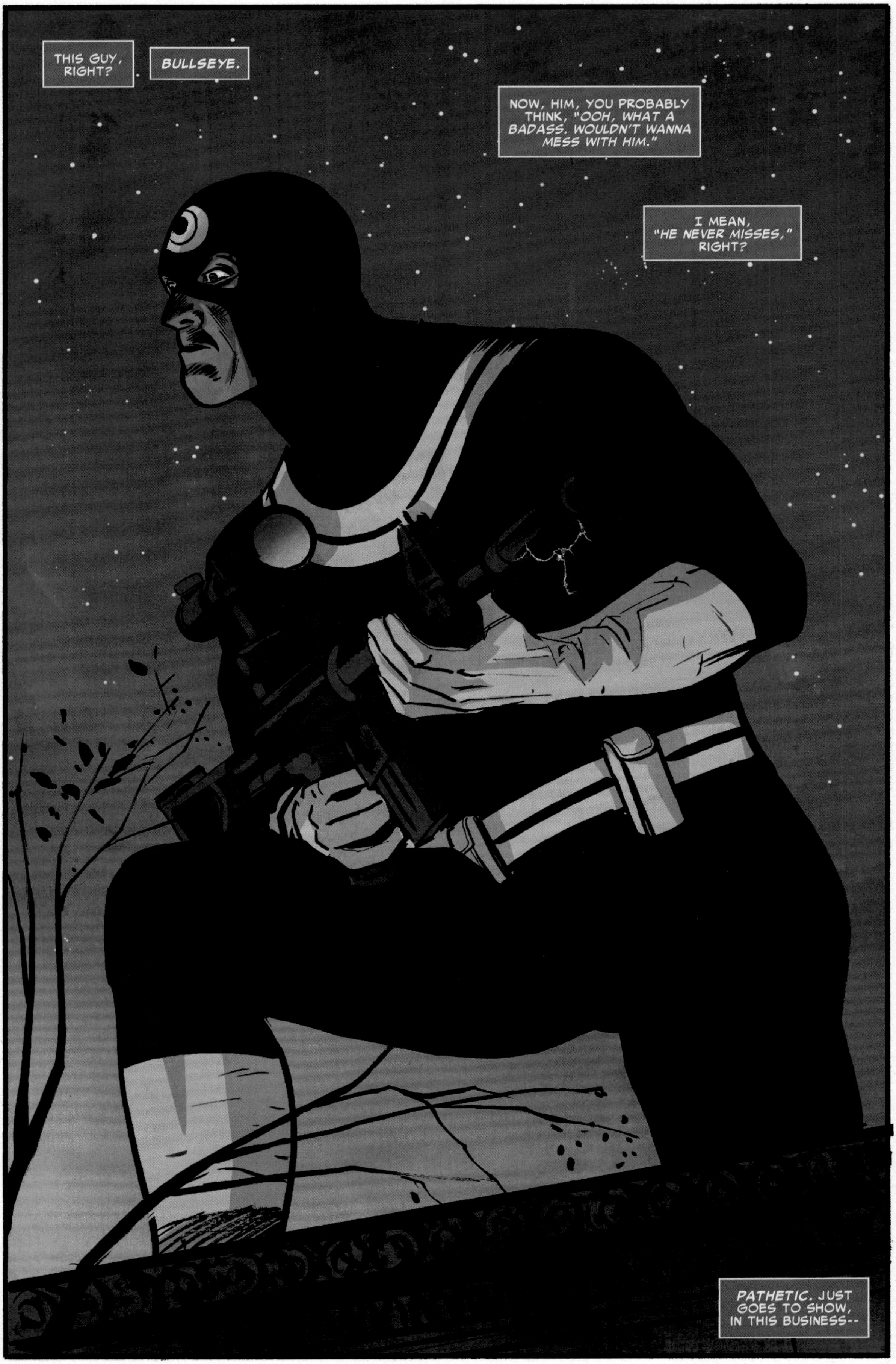
THIS GUY, RIGHT?
BULLSEYE.
NOW, HIM, YOU PROBABLY THINK, "OOH, WHAT A BADASS. WOULDN'T WANNA MESS WITH HIM."
I MEAN, "HE NEVER MISSES," RIGHT?
PATHETIC. JUST GOES TO SHOW, IN THIS BUSINESS--

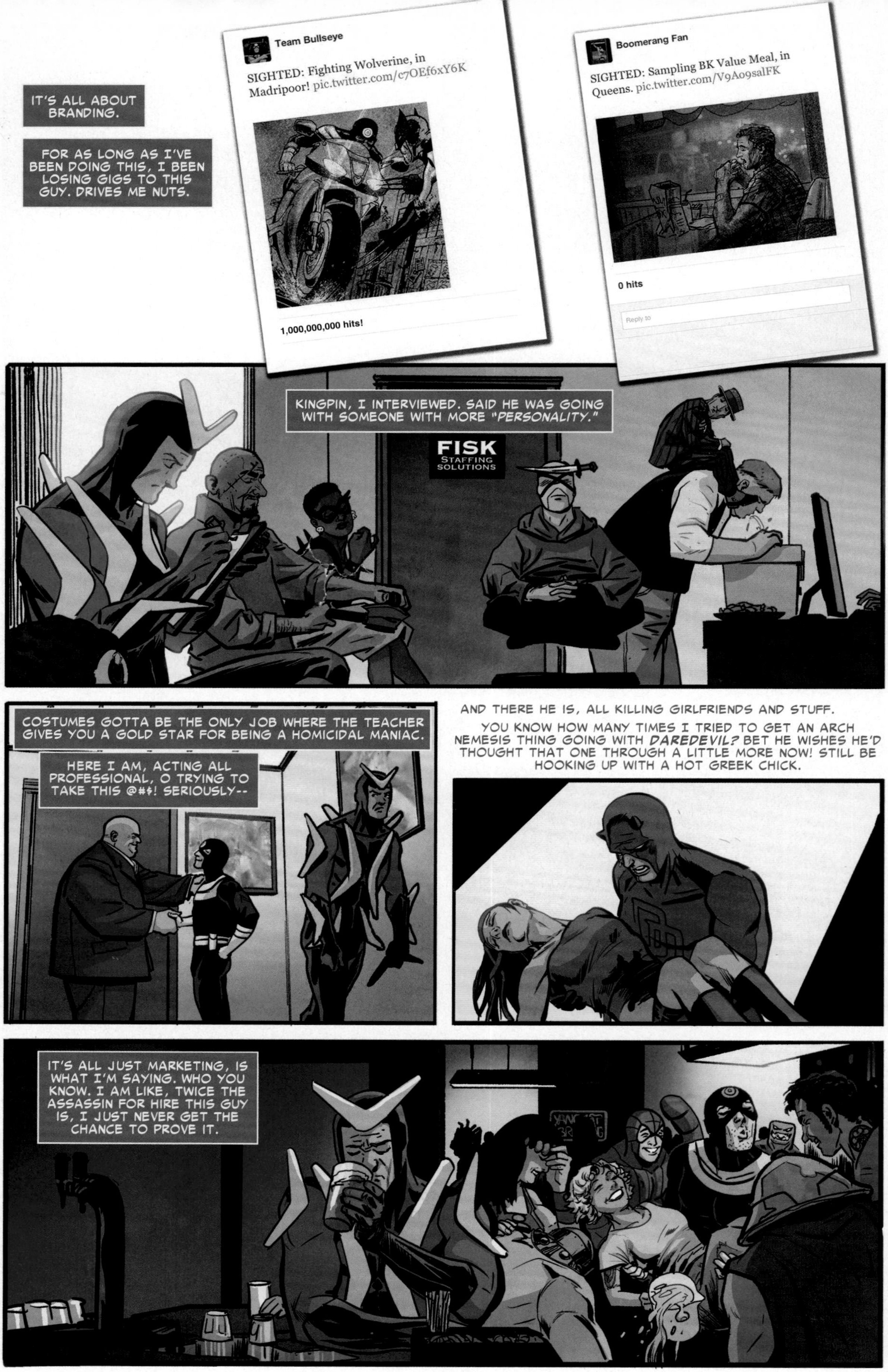
IT'S ALL ABOUT BRANDING.
FOR AS LONG AS I'VE BEEN DOING THIS, I BEEN LOSING GIGS TO THIS GUY. DRIVES ME NUTS.
Team Bullseye
SIGHTED: Fighting Wolverine, in Madripoor! pic.twitter.com/c7OEf6xY6K
1,000,000,000 hits!
Boomerang Fan
SIGHTED: Sampling BK Value Meal, in Queens. pic.twitter.com/V9Ao9salFK
0 hits
Reply to
KINGPIN, I INTERVIEWED. SAID HE WAS GOING WITH SOMEONE WITH MORE "PERSONALITY."
FISK STAFFING SOLUTIONS
COSTUMES GOTTA BE THE ONLY JOB WHERE THE TEACHER GIVES YOU A GOLD STAR FOR BEING A HOMICIDAL MANIAC.
HERE I AM, ACTING ALL PROFESSIONAL, O TRYING TO TAKE THIS @#$! SERIOUSLY--
AND THERE HE IS, ALL KILLING GIRLFRIENDS AND STUFF.
YOU KNOW HOW MANY TIMES I TRIED TO GET AN ARCH NEMESIS THING GOING WITH DAREDEVIL? BET HE WISHES HE'D THOUGHT THAT ONE THROUGH A LITTLE MORE NOW! STILL BE HOOKING UP WITH A HOT GREEK CHICK.
IT'S ALL JUST MARKETING, IS WHAT I'M SAYING. WHO YOU KNOW. I AM LIKE, TWICE THE ASSASSIN FOR HIRE THIS GUY IS, I JUST NEVER GET THE CHANCE TO PROVE IT.

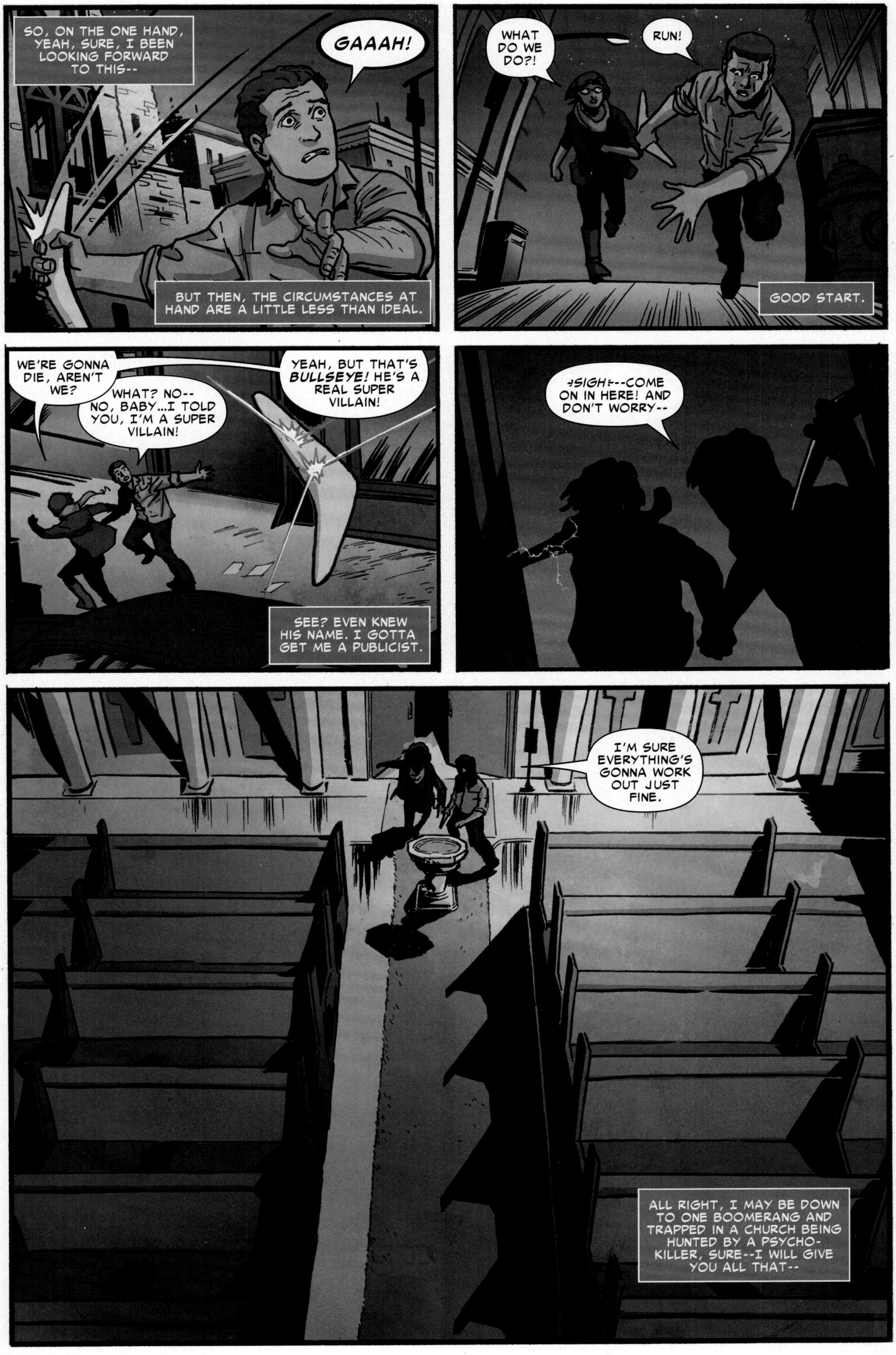
SO, ON THE ONE HAND, YEAH, SURE, I BEEN LOOKING FORWARD TO THIS--
GAAAH!
BUT THEN, THE CIRCUMSTANCES AT HAND ARE A LITTLE LESS THAN IDEAL.
WHAT DO WE DO?!
RUN!
GOOD START.
WE'RE GONNA DIE, AREN'T WE?
WHAT? NO-- NO, BABY...I TOLD YOU, I'M A SUPER VILLAIN!
YEAH, BUT THAT'S BULLSEYE! HE'S A REAL SUPER VILLAIN!
SEE? EVEN KNEW HIS NAME. I GOTTA GET ME A PUBLICIST.
-SIGH---COME ON IN HERE! AND DON'T WORRY--
I'M SURE EVERYTHING'S GONNA WORK OUT JUST FINE.
ALL RIGHT, I MAY BE DOWN TO ONE BOOMERANG AND TRAPPED IN A CHURCH BEING HUNTED BY A PSYCHO-KILLER, SURE--I WILL GIVE YOU ALL THAT--

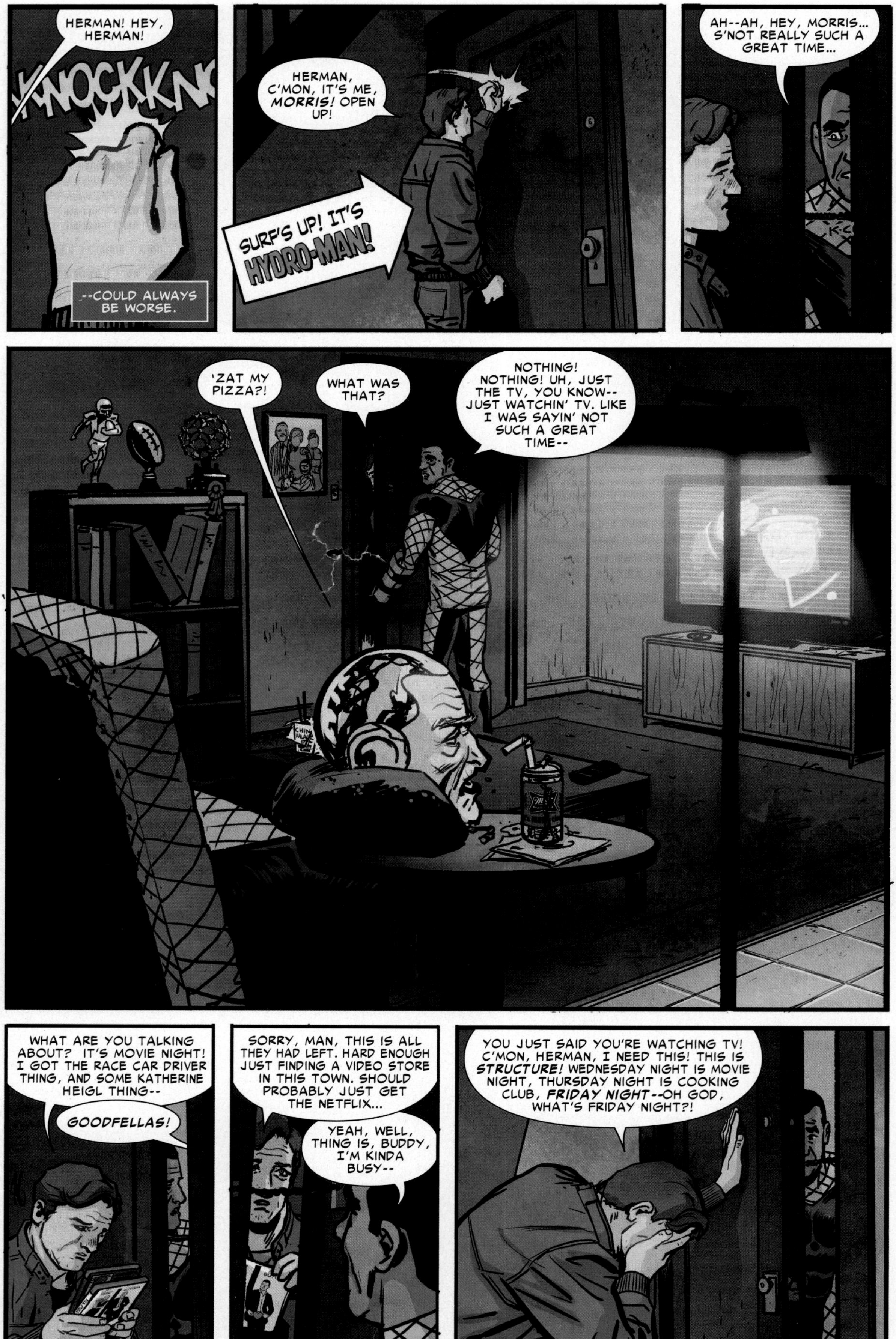
HERMAN! HEY, HERMAN!
KNOCKKNO
--COULD ALWAYS BE WORSE.
HERMAN, C'MON, IT'S ME, MORRIS! OPEN UP!
SURF'S UP! IT'S HYDRO-MAN!
AH--AH, HEY, MORRIS... S'NOT REALLY SUCH A GREAT TIME...
'ZAT MY PIZZA?!
WHAT WAS THAT?
NOTHING! NOTHING! UH, JUST THE TV, YOU KNOW-- JUST WATCHIN' TV. LIKE I WAS SAYIN' NOT SUCH A GREAT TIME--
WHAT ARE YOU TALKING ABOUT? IT'S MOVIE NIGHT! I GOT THE RACE CAR DRIVER THING, AND SOME KATHERINE HEIGL THING--
GOODFELLAS!
SORRY, MAN, THIS IS ALL THEY HAD LEFT. HARD ENOUGH JUST FINDING A VIDEO STORE IN THIS TOWN. SHOULD PROBABLY JUST GET THE NETFLIX...
YEAH, WELL, THING IS, BUDDY, I'M KINDA BUSY--
YOU JUST SAID YOU'RE WATCHING TV! C'MON, HERMAN, I NEED THIS! THIS IS STRUCTURE! WEDNESDAY NIGHT IS MOVIE NIGHT, THURSDAY NIGHT IS COOKING CLUB, FRIDAY NIGHT--OH GOD, WHAT'S FRIDAY NIGHT?!

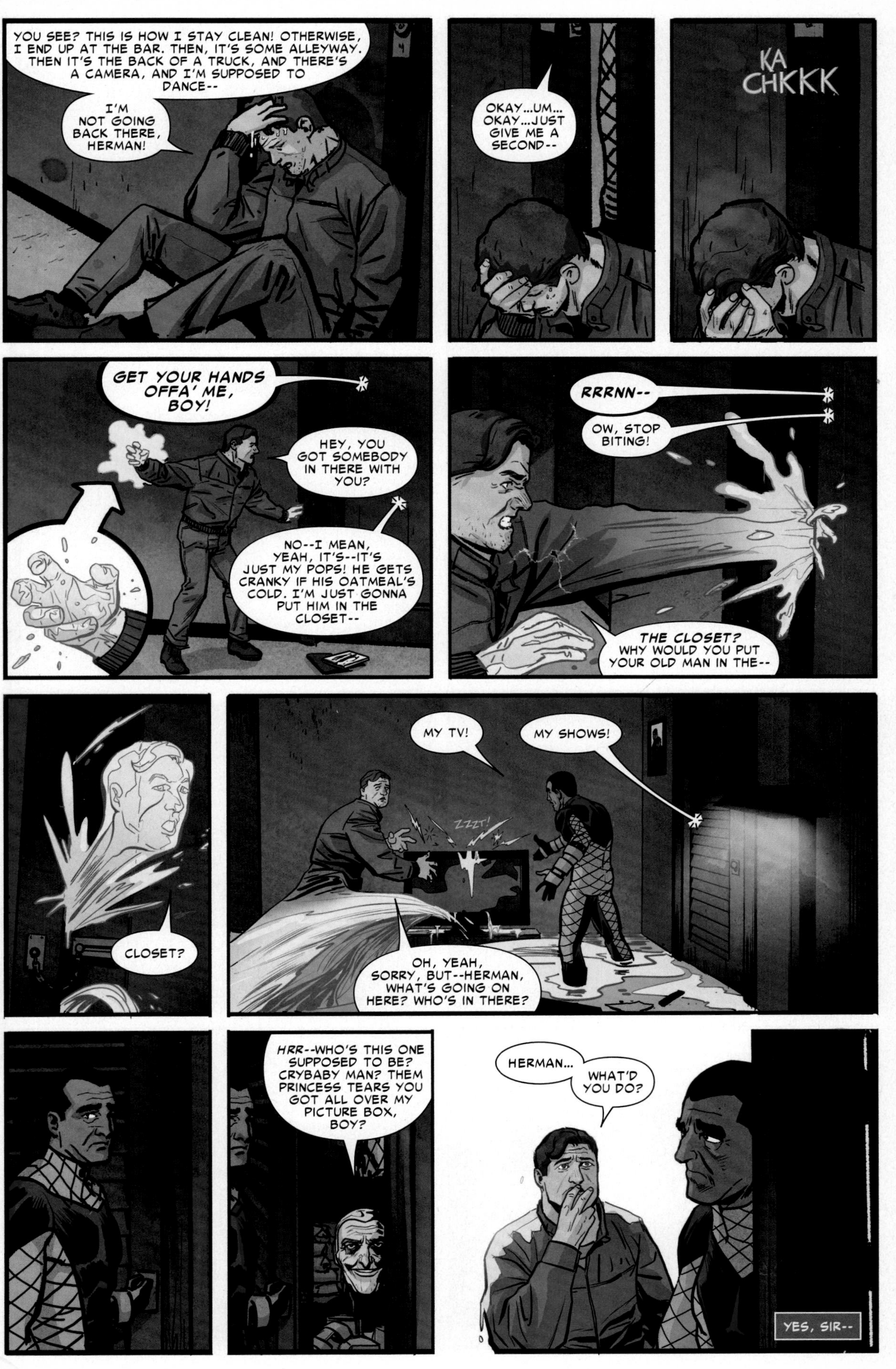
YOU SEE? THIS IS HOW I STAY CLEAN! OTHERWISE, I END UP AT THE BAR. THEN, IT'S SOME ALLEYWAY. THEN IT'S THE BACK OF A TRUCK, AND THERE'S A CAMERA, AND I'M SUPPOSED TO DANCE--
I'M NOT GOING BACK THERE, HERMAN!
OKAY...UM... OKAY...JUST GIVE ME A SECOND--
KA CHKKK
GET YOUR HANDS OFFA' ME, BOY!
HEY, YOU GOT SOMEBODY IN THERE WITH YOU?
NO--I MEAN, YEAH, IT'S--IT'S JUST MY POPS! HE GETS CRANKY IF HIS OATMEAL'S COLD. I'M JUST GONNA PUT HIM IN THE CLOSET--
RRRNN--
OW, STOP BITING!
THE CLOSET? WHY WOULD YOU PUT YOUR OLD MAN IN THE--
CLOSET?
MY TV!
MY SHOWS!
ZZZT!
OH, YEAH, SORRY, BUT--HERMAN, WHAT'S GOING ON HERE? WHO'S IN THERE?
HRR--WHO'S THIS ONE SUPPOSED TO BE? CRYBABY MAN? THEM PRINCESS TEARS YOU GOT ALL OVER MY PICTURE BOX, BOY?
HERMAN...
WHAT'D YOU DO?
YES, SIR--

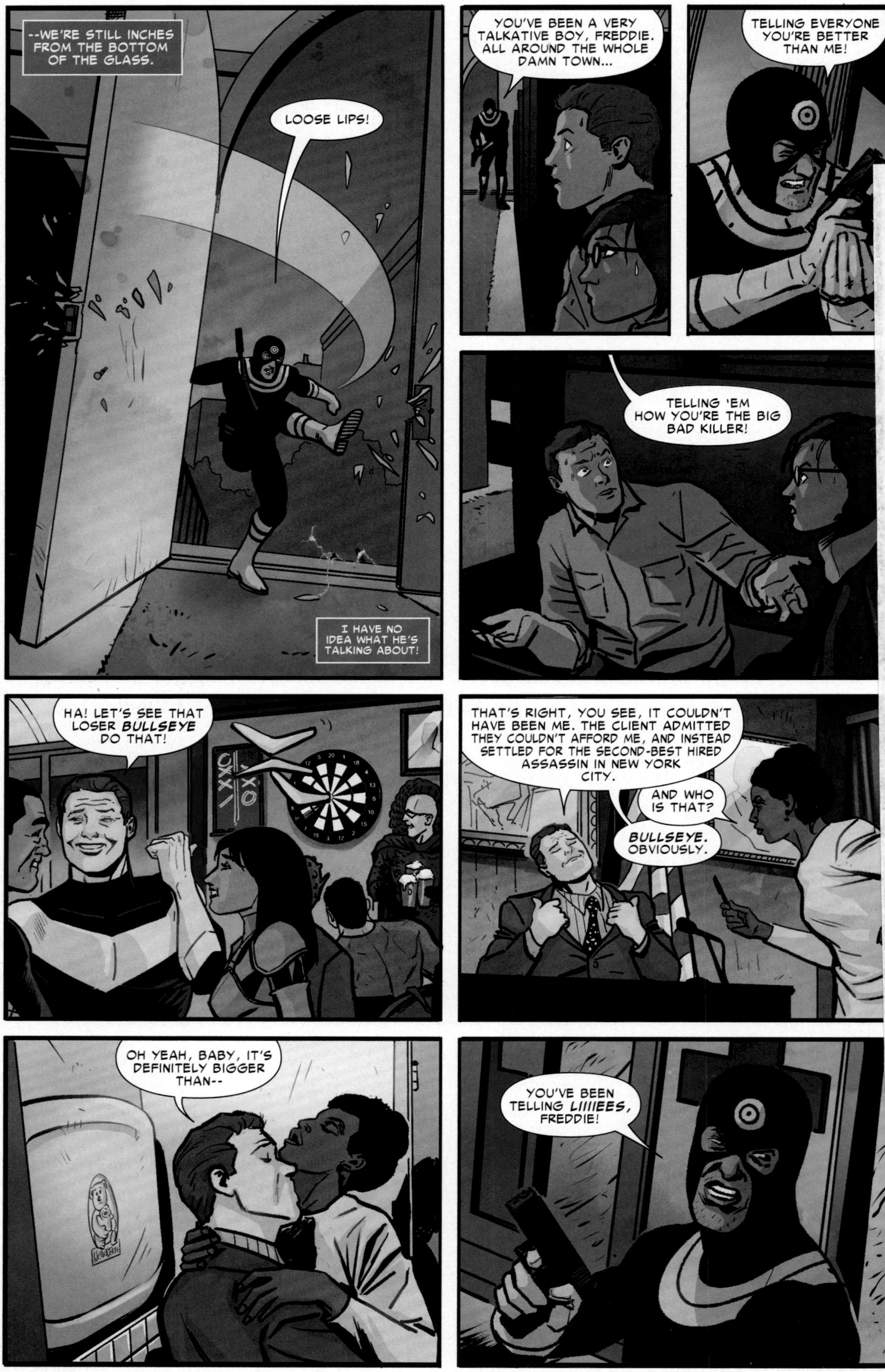
--WE'RE STILL INCHES FROM THE BOTTOM OF THE GLASS.
LOOSE LIPS!
I HAVE NO IDEA WHAT HE'S TALKING ABOUT!
YOU'VE BEEN A VERY TALKATIVE BOY, FREDDIE. ALL AROUND THE WHOLE DAMN TOWN...
TELLING EVERYONE YOU'RE BETTER THAN ME!
TELLING 'EM HOW YOU'RE THE BIG BAD KILLER!
HA! LET'S SEE THAT LOSER BULLSEYE DO THAT!
THAT'S RIGHT, YOU SEE, IT COULDN'T HAVE BEEN ME. THE CLIENT ADMITTED THEY COULDN'T AFFORD ME, AND INSTEAD SETTLED FOR THE SECOND-BEST HIRED ASSASSIN IN NEW YORK CITY.
AND WHO IS THAT?
BULLSEYE. OBVIOUSLY.
OH YEAH, BABY, IT'S DEFINITELY BIGGER THAN--
YOU'VE BEEN TELLING LIIIIEES, FREDDIE!

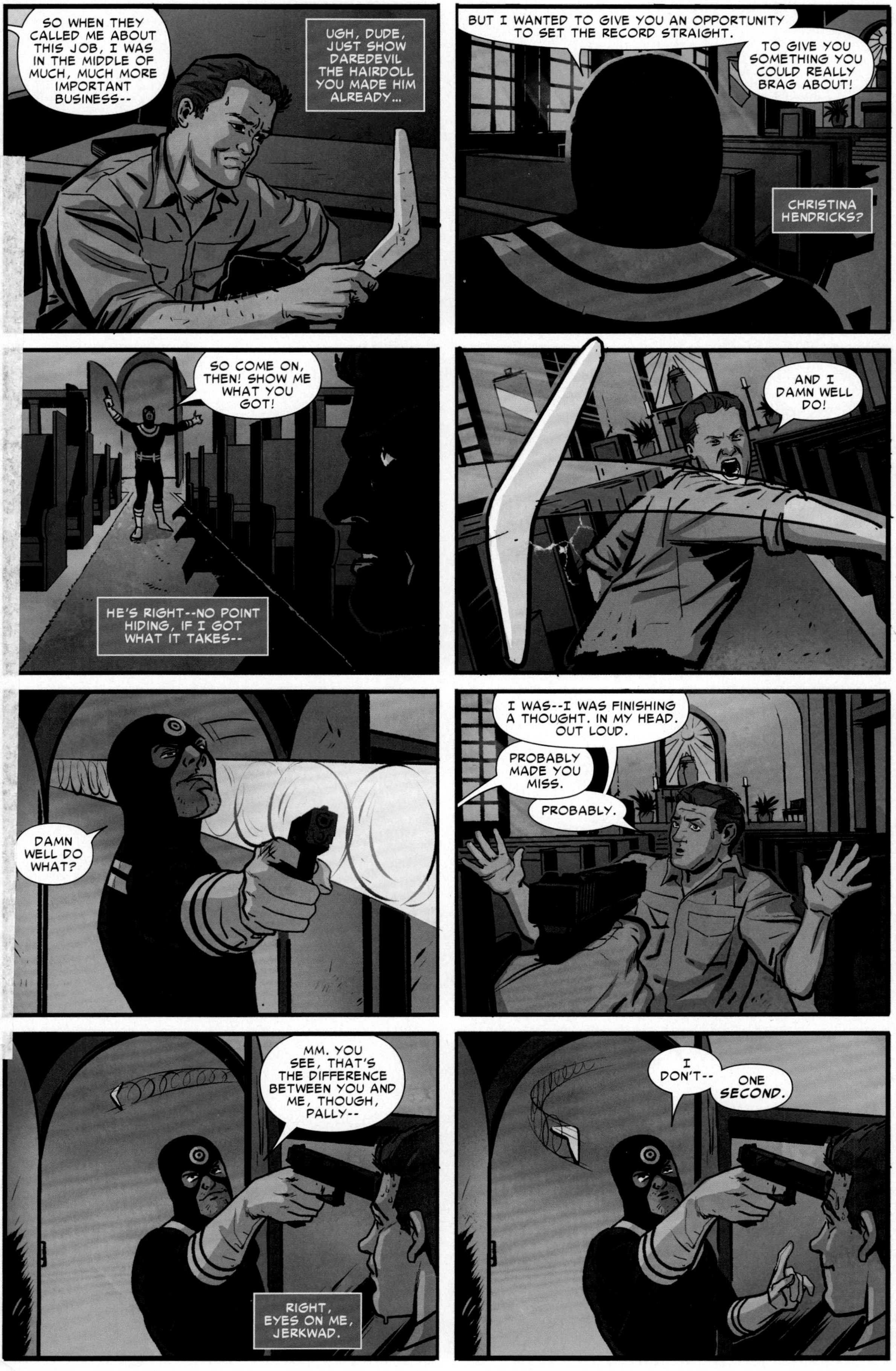
SO WHEN THEY CALLED ME ABOUT THIS JOB, I WAS IN THE MIDDLE OF MUCH, MUCH MORE IMPORTANT BUSINESS--
UGH, DUDE, JUST SHOW DAREDEVIL THE HAIRDOLL YOU MADE HIM ALREADY...
BUT I WANTED TO GIVE YOU AN OPPORTUNITY TO SET THE RECORD STRAIGHT.
TO GIVE YOU SOMETHING YOU COULD REALLY BRAG ABOUT!
CHRISTINA HENDRICKS?
SO COME ON, THEN! SHOW ME WHAT YOU GOT!
HE'S RIGHT--NO POINT HIDING, IF I GOT WHAT IT TAKES--
AND I DAMN WELL DO!
DAMN WELL DO WHAT?
I WAS--I WAS FINISHING A THOUGHT. IN MY HEAD. OUT LOUD.
PROBABLY MADE YOU MISS.
PROBABLY.
MM. YOU SEE, THAT'S THE DIFFERENCE BETWEEN YOU AND ME, THOUGH, PALLY--
RIGHT, EYES ON ME, JERKWAD.
I DON'T--
ONE SECOND.

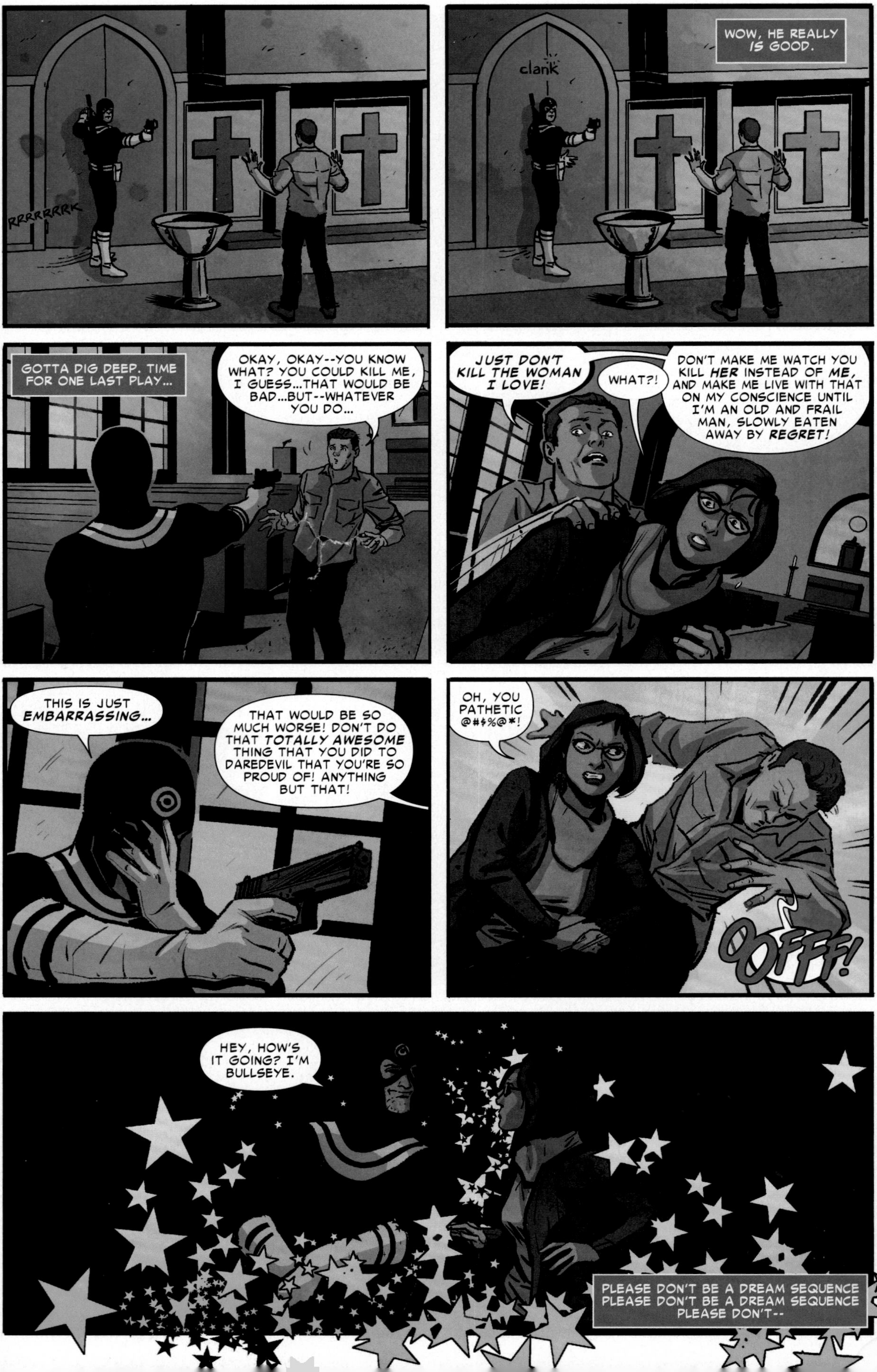
RRRRRRRK
clank
WOW, HE REALLY IS GOOD.
GOTTA DIG DEEP. TIME FOR ONE LAST PLAY...
OKAY, OKAY--YOU KNOW WHAT? YOU COULD KILL ME, I GUESS...THAT WOULD BE BAD...BUT--WHATEVER YOU DO...
JUST DON'T KILL THE WOMAN I LOVE!
WHAT?!
DON'T MAKE ME WATCH YOU KILL HER INSTEAD OF ME, AND MAKE ME LIVE WITH THAT ON MY CONSCIENCE UNTIL I'M AN OLD AND FRAIL MAN, SLOWLY EATEN AWAY BY REGRET!
THIS IS JUST EMBARRASSING...
THAT WOULD BE SO MUCH WORSE! DON'T DO THAT TOTALLY AWESOME THING THAT YOU DID TO DAREDEVIL THAT YOU'RE SO PROUD OF! ANYTHING BUT THAT!
OH, YOU PATHETIC @#$%@*!
OOFFF!
HEY, HOW'S IT GOING? I'M BULLSEYE.
PLEASE DON'T BE A DREAM SEQUENCE PLEASE DON'T BE A DREAM SEQUENCE PLEASE DON'T--

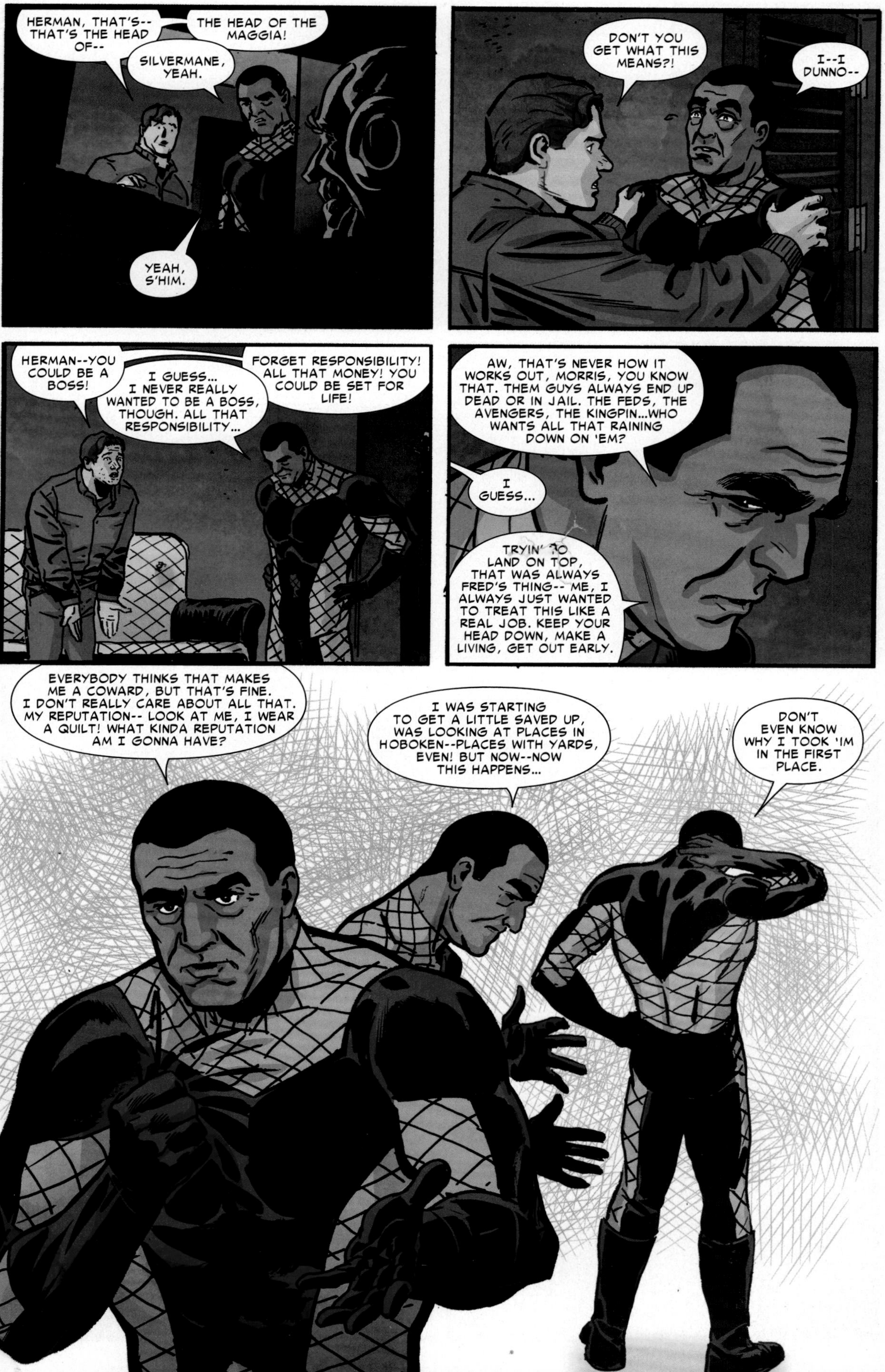
HERMAN, THAT'S-- THAT'S THE HEAD OF--
THE HEAD OF THE MAGGIA!
SILVERMANE, YEAH.
YEAH, S'HIM.
DON'T YOU GET WHAT THIS MEANS?!
I--I DUNNO--
HERMAN--YOU COULD BE A BOSS!
I GUESS... I NEVER REALLY WANTED TO BE A BOSS, THOUGH. ALL THAT RESPONSIBILITY...
FORGET RESPONSIBILITY! ALL THAT MONEY! YOU COULD BE SET FOR LIFE!
AW, THAT'S NEVER HOW IT WORKS OUT, MORRIS, YOU KNOW THAT. THEM GUYS ALWAYS END UP DEAD OR IN JAIL. THE FEDS, THE AVENGERS, THE KINGPIN...WHO WANTS ALL THAT RAINING DOWN ON 'EM?
I GUESS...
TRYIN' TO LAND ON TOP, THAT WAS ALWAYS FRED'S THING-- ME, I ALWAYS JUST WANTED TO TREAT THIS LIKE A REAL JOB. KEEP YOUR HEAD DOWN, MAKE A LIVING, GET OUT EARLY.
EVERYBODY THINKS THAT MAKES ME A COWARD, BUT THAT'S FINE. I DON'T REALLY CARE ABOUT ALL THAT. MY REPUTATION-- LOOK AT ME, I WEAR A QUILT! WHAT KINDA REPUTATION AM I GONNA HAVE?
I WAS STARTING TO GET A LITTLE SAVED UP, WAS LOOKING AT PLACES IN HOBOKEN--PLACES WITH YARDS, EVEN! BUT NOW--NOW THIS HAPPENS...
DON'T EVEN KNOW WHY I TOOK 'IM IN THE FIRST PLACE.

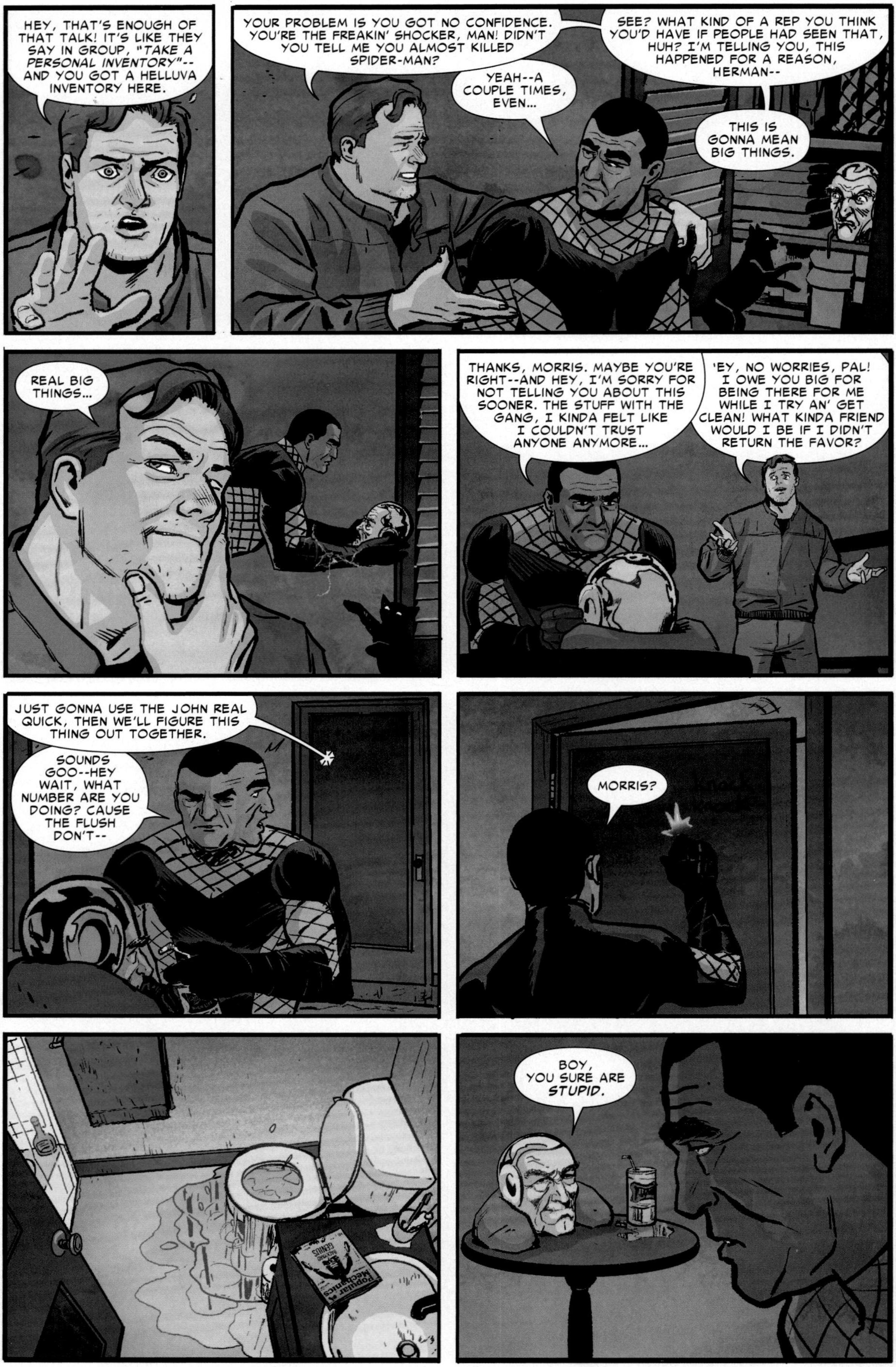

HEY, THAT'S ENOUGH OF THAT TALK! IT'S LIKE THEY SAY IN GROUP, *"TAKE A PERSONAL INVENTORY"*--AND YOU GOT A HELLUVA INVENTORY HERE.
YOUR PROBLEM IS YOU GOT NO CONFIDENCE. YOU'RE THE FREAKIN' SHOCKER, MAN! DIDN'T YOU TELL ME YOU ALMOST KILLED SPIDER-MAN?
YEAH--A COUPLE TIMES, EVEN...
SEE? WHAT KIND OF A REP YOU THINK YOU'D HAVE IF PEOPLE HAD SEEN THAT, HUH? I'M TELLING YOU, THIS HAPPENED FOR A REASON, HERMAN--
THIS IS GONNA MEAN BIG THINGS.
REAL BIG THINGS...
THANKS, MORRIS. MAYBE YOU'RE RIGHT--AND HEY, I'M SORRY FOR NOT TELLING YOU ABOUT THIS SOONER. THE STUFF WITH THE GANG, I KINDA FELT LIKE I COULDN'T TRUST ANYONE ANYMORE...
'EY, NO WORRIES, PAL! I OWE YOU BIG FOR BEING THERE FOR ME WHILE I TRY AN' GET CLEAN! WHAT KINDA FRIEND WOULD I BE IF I DIDN'T RETURN THE FAVOR?
JUST GONNA USE THE JOHN REAL QUICK, THEN WE'LL FIGURE THIS THING OUT TOGETHER.
SOUNDS GOO--HEY WAIT, WHAT NUMBER ARE YOU DOING? CAUSE THE FLUSH DON'T--
MORRIS?
Popular Mechanics
BOY, YOU SURE ARE *STUPID*.

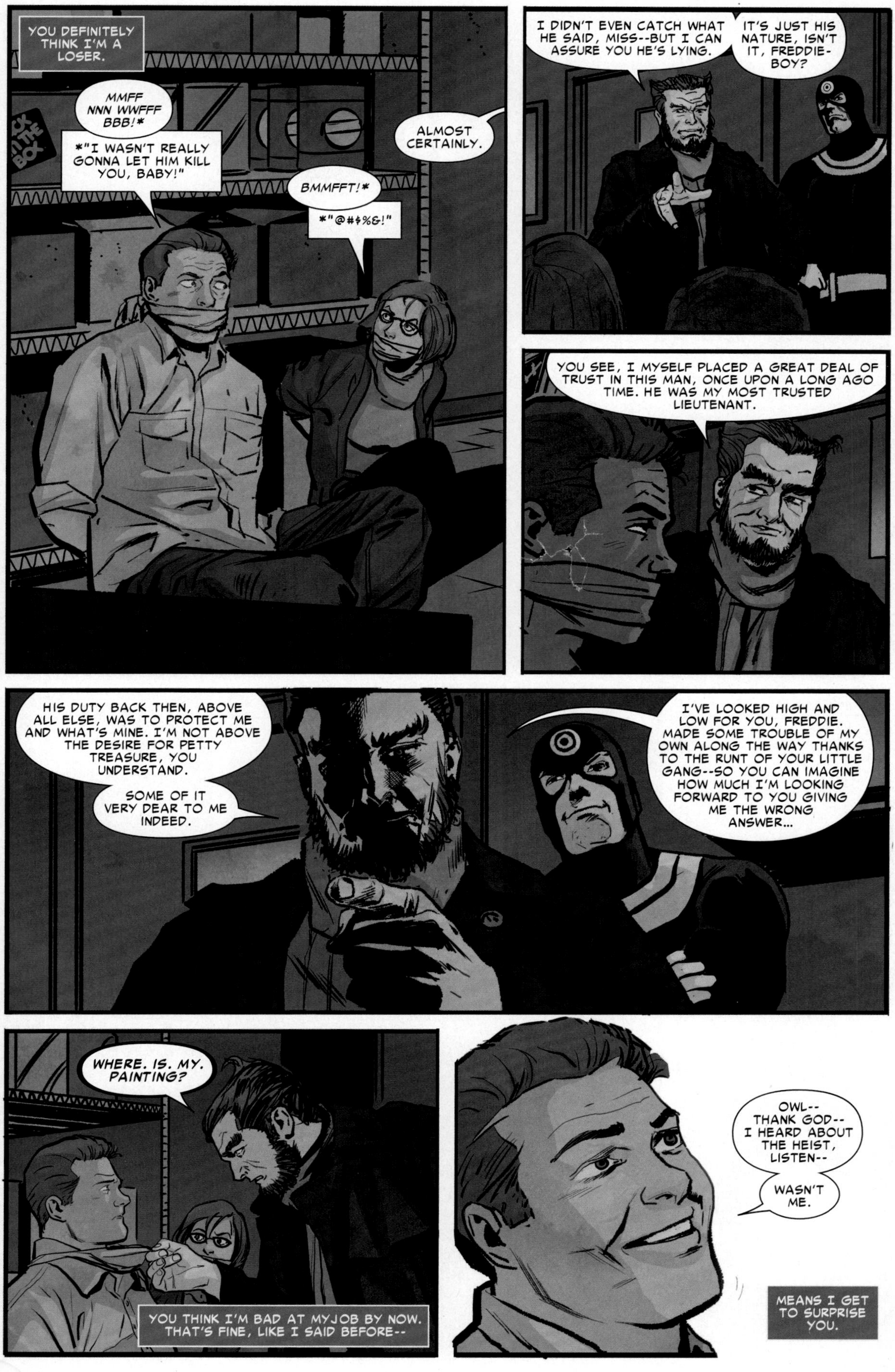
YOU DEFINITELY THINK I'M A LOSER.
MMFF NNN WWFFF BBB!*
*"I WASN'T REALLY GONNA LET HIM KILL YOU, BABY!"
ALMOST CERTAINLY.
BMMFFT!*
*"@#$%&!"
I DIDN'T EVEN CATCH WHAT HE SAID, MISS--BUT I CAN ASSURE YOU HE'S LYING.
IT'S JUST HIS NATURE, ISN'T IT, FREDDIE-BOY?
YOU SEE, I MYSELF PLACED A GREAT DEAL OF TRUST IN THIS MAN, ONCE UPON A LONG AGO TIME. HE WAS MY MOST TRUSTED LIEUTENANT.
HIS DUTY BACK THEN, ABOVE ALL ELSE, WAS TO PROTECT ME AND WHAT'S MINE. I'M NOT ABOVE THE DESIRE FOR PETTY TREASURE, YOU UNDERSTAND.
SOME OF IT VERY DEAR TO ME INDEED.
I'VE LOOKED HIGH AND LOW FOR YOU, FREDDIE. MADE SOME TROUBLE OF MY OWN ALONG THE WAY THANKS TO THE RUNT OF YOUR LITTLE GANG--SO YOU CAN IMAGINE HOW MUCH I'M LOOKING FORWARD TO YOU GIVING ME THE WRONG ANSWER...
WHERE. IS. MY. PAINTING?
YOU THINK I'M BAD AT MYJOB BY NOW. THAT'S FINE, LIKE I SAID BEFORE--
OWL-- THANK GOD-- I HEARD ABOUT THE HEIST, LISTEN--
WASN'T ME.
MEANS I GET TO SURPRISE YOU.

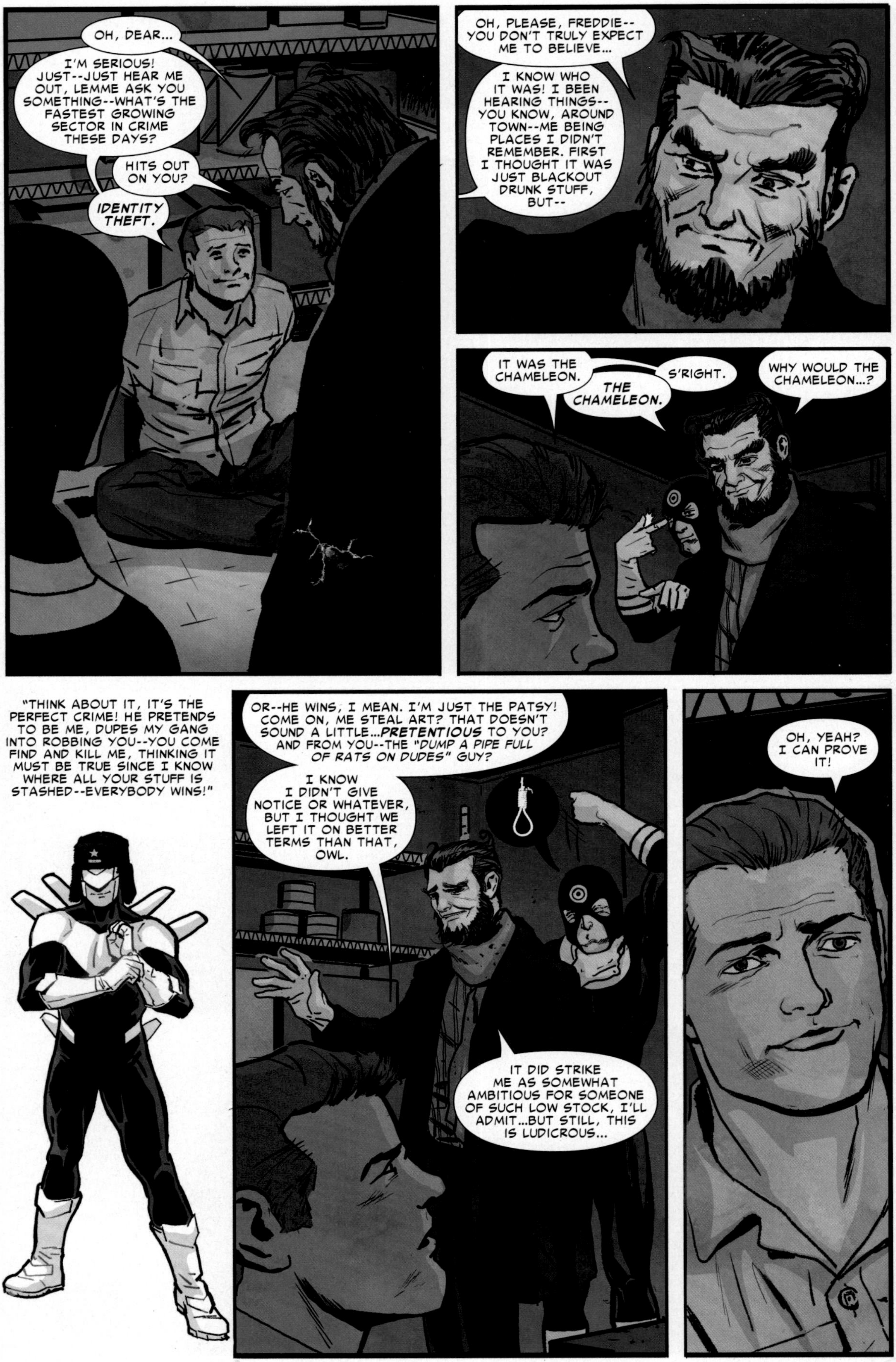
OH, DEAR...
I'M SERIOUS! JUST--JUST HEAR ME OUT, LEMME ASK YOU SOMETHING--WHAT'S THE FASTEST GROWING SECTOR IN CRIME THESE DAYS?
HITS OUT ON YOU?
IDENTITY THEFT.
OH, PLEASE, FREDDIE-- YOU DON'T TRULY EXPECT ME TO BELIEVE...
I KNOW WHO IT WAS! I BEEN HEARING THINGS-- YOU KNOW, AROUND TOWN--ME BEING PLACES I DIDN'T REMEMBER. FIRST I THOUGHT IT WAS JUST BLACKOUT DRUNK STUFF, BUT--
IT WAS THE CHAMELEON.
THE CHAMELEON.
S'RIGHT.
WHY WOULD THE CHAMELEON...?
"THINK ABOUT IT, IT'S THE PERFECT CRIME! HE PRETENDS TO BE ME, DUPES MY GANG INTO ROBBING YOU--YOU COME FIND AND KILL ME, THINKING IT MUST BE TRUE SINCE I KNOW WHERE ALL YOUR STUFF IS STASHED--EVERYBODY WINS!"
OR--HE WINS, I MEAN. I'M JUST THE PATSY! COME ON, ME STEAL ART? THAT DOESN'T SOUND A LITTLE...PRETENTIOUS TO YOU? AND FROM YOU--THE "DUMP A PIPE FULL OF RATS ON DUDES" GUY?
I KNOW I DIDN'T GIVE NOTICE OR WHATEVER, BUT I THOUGHT WE LEFT IT ON BETTER TERMS THAN THAT, OWL.
IT DID STRIKE ME AS SOMEWHAT AMBITIOUS FOR SOMEONE OF SUCH LOW STOCK, I'LL ADMIT...BUT STILL, THIS IS LUDICROUS...
OH, YEAH? I CAN PROVE IT!

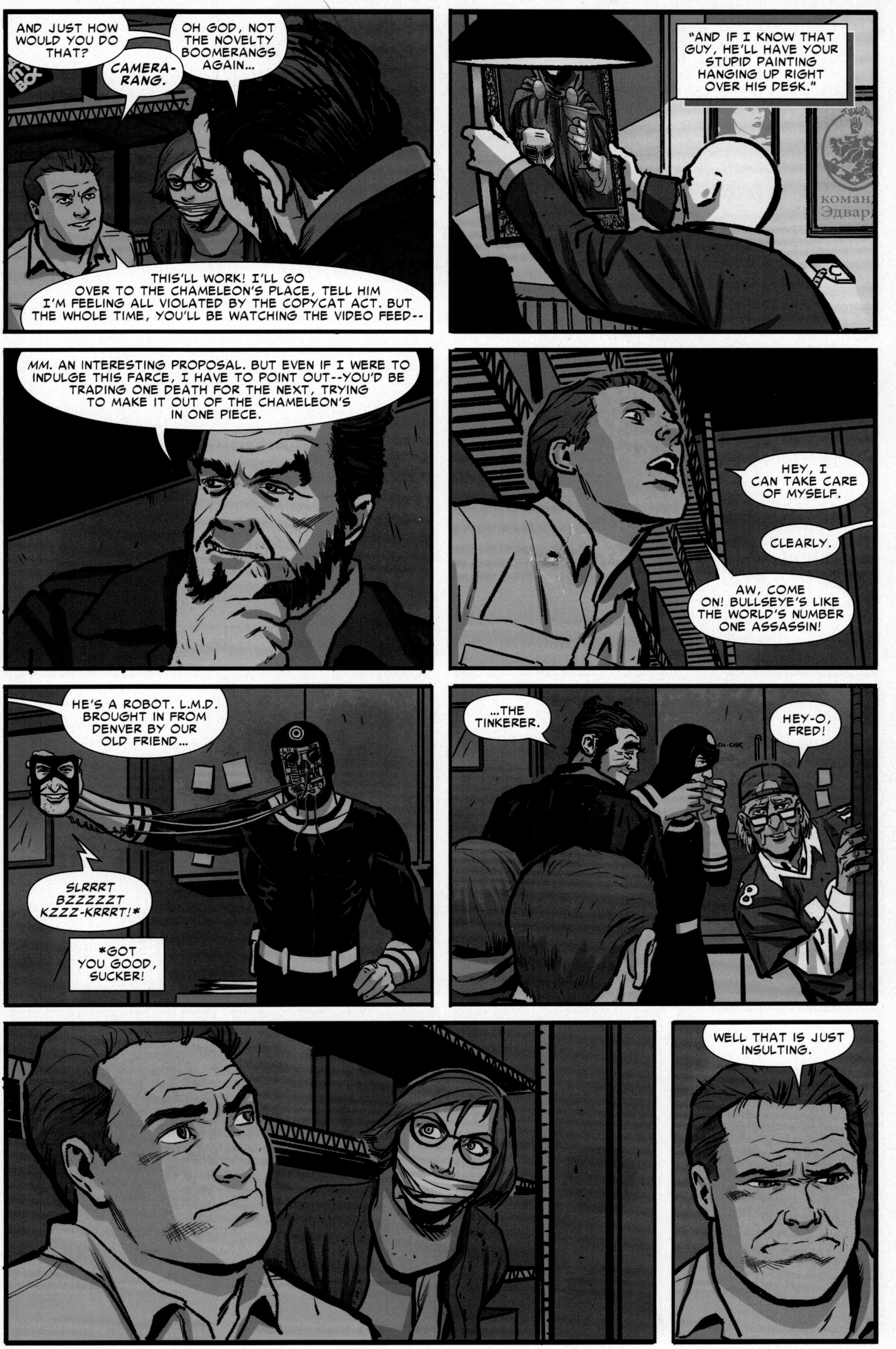
AND JUST HOW WOULD YOU DO THAT?
OH GOD, NOT THE NOVELTY BOOMERANGS AGAIN...
CAMERA-RANG.
THIS'LL WORK! I'LL GO OVER TO THE CHAMELEON'S PLACE, TELL HIM I'M FEELING ALL VIOLATED BY THE COPYCAT ACT. BUT THE WHOLE TIME, YOU'LL BE WATCHING THE VIDEO FEED--
"AND IF I KNOW THAT GUY, HE'LL HAVE YOUR STUPID PAINTING HANGING UP RIGHT OVER HIS DESK."
MM. AN INTERESTING PROPOSAL. BUT EVEN IF I WERE TO INDULGE THIS FARCE, I HAVE TO POINT OUT--YOU'D BE TRADING ONE DEATH FOR THE NEXT, TRYING TO MAKE IT OUT OF THE CHAMELEON'S IN ONE PIECE.
HEY, I CAN TAKE CARE OF MYSELF.
CLEARLY.
AW, COME ON! BULLSEYE'S LIKE THE WORLD'S NUMBER ONE ASSASSIN!
HE'S A ROBOT. L.M.D. BROUGHT IN FROM DENVER BY OUR OLD FRIEND...
SLRRRT BZZZZZT KZZZ-KRRRT!*
*GOT YOU GOOD, SUCKER!
...THE TINKERER.
CH-CHK
HEY-O, FRED!
WELL THAT IS JUST INSULTING.

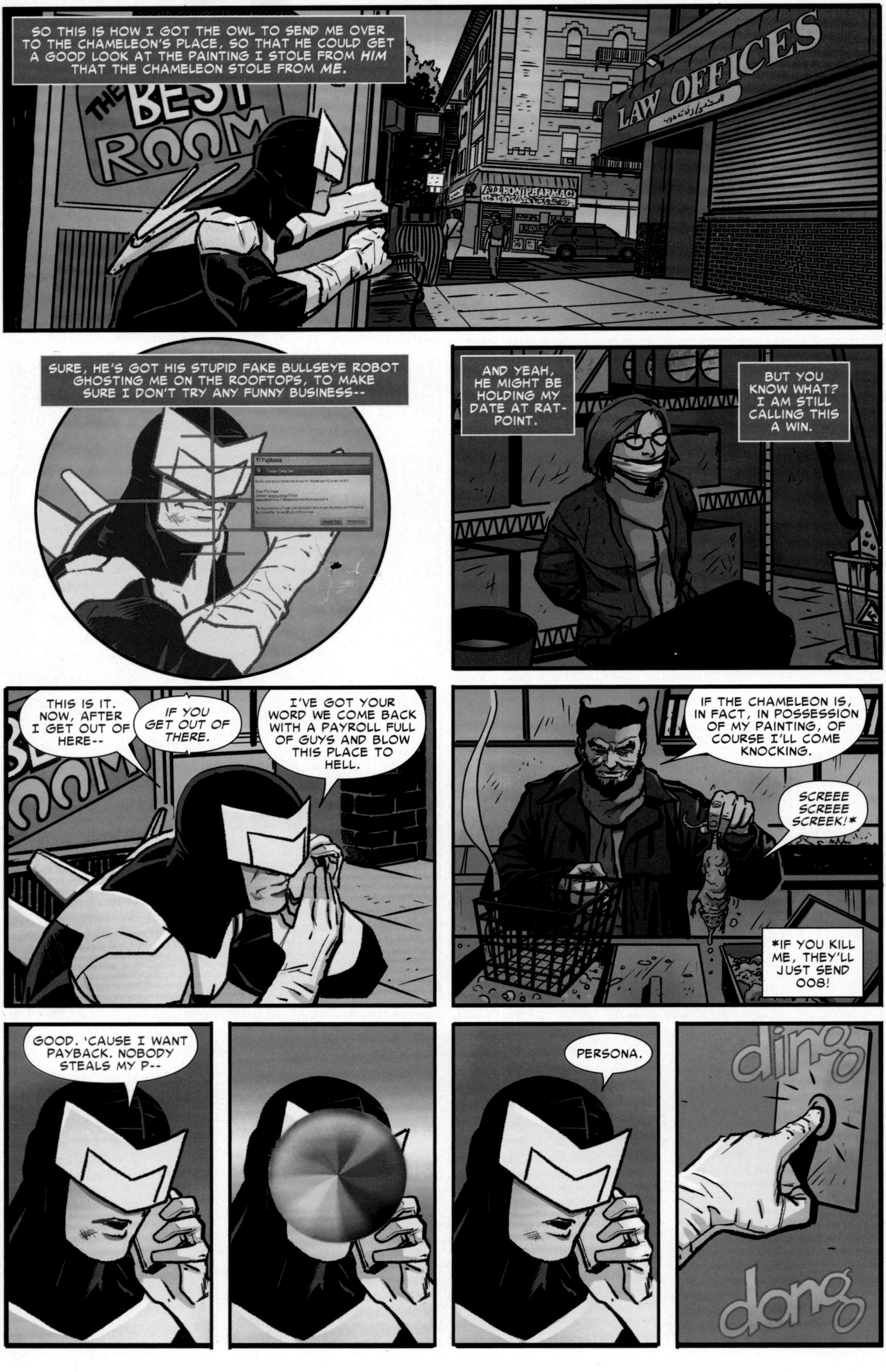
SO THIS IS HOW I GOT THE OWL TO SEND ME OVER TO THE CHAMELEON'S PLACE, SO THAT HE COULD GET A GOOD LOOK AT THE PAINTING I STOLE FROM *HIM* THAT THE CHAMELEON STOLE FROM *ME*.
THE BEST ROOM
LAW OFFICES
SURE, HE'S GOT HIS STUPID FAKE BULLSEYE ROBOT GHOSTING ME ON THE ROOFTOPS, TO MAKE SURE I DON'T TRY ANY FUNNY BUSINESS--
AND YEAH, HE MIGHT BE HOLDING MY DATE AT RAT-POINT.
BUT YOU KNOW WHAT? I AM STILL CALLING THIS A WIN.
THIS IS IT. NOW, AFTER I GET OUT OF HERE--
IF YOU GET OUT OF THERE.
I'VE GOT YOUR WORD WE COME BACK WITH A PAYROLL FULL OF GUYS AND BLOW THIS PLACE TO HELL.
IF THE CHAMELEON IS, IN FACT, IN POSSESSION OF MY PAINTING, OF COURSE I'LL COME KNOCKING.
SCREEE SCREEE SCREEK!*
*IF YOU KILL ME, THEY'LL JUST SEND 008!
GOOD. 'CAUSE I WANT PAYBACK. NOBODY STEALS MY P--
PERSONA.
ding
dong

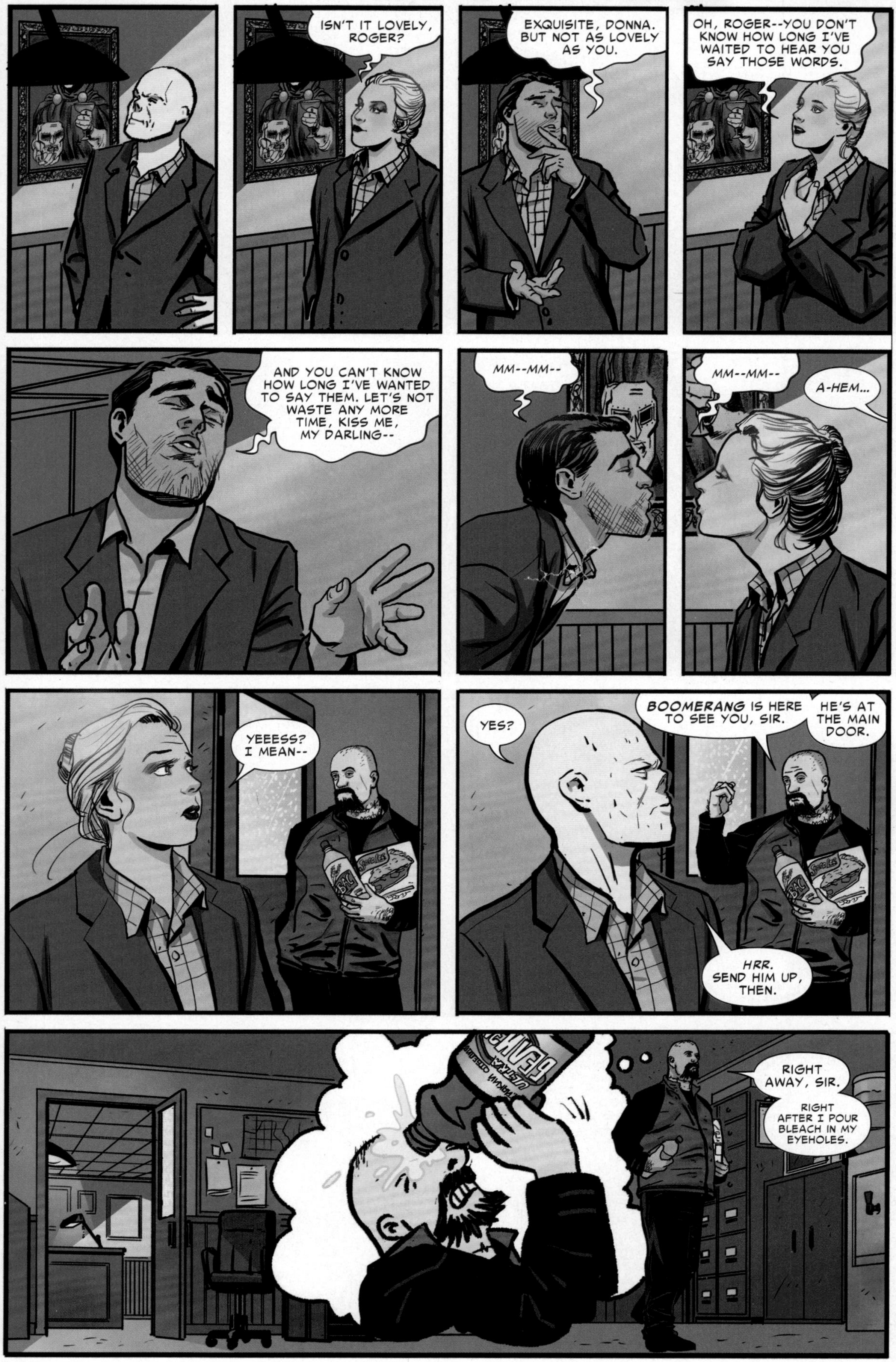
ISN'T IT LOVELY, ROGER?
EXQUISITE, DONNA. BUT NOT AS LOVELY AS YOU.
OH, ROGER--YOU DON'T KNOW HOW LONG I'VE WAITED TO HEAR YOU SAY THOSE WORDS.
AND YOU CAN'T KNOW HOW LONG I'VE WANTED TO SAY THEM. LET'S NOT WASTE ANY MORE TIME, KISS ME, MY DARLING--
MM--MM--
MM--MM--
A-HEM...
YEEESS? I MEAN--
YES?
BOOMERANG IS HERE TO SEE YOU, SIR.
HE'S AT THE MAIN DOOR.
HRR. SEND HIM UP, THEN.
RIGHT AWAY, SIR.
RIGHT AFTER I POUR BLEACH IN MY EYEHOLES.

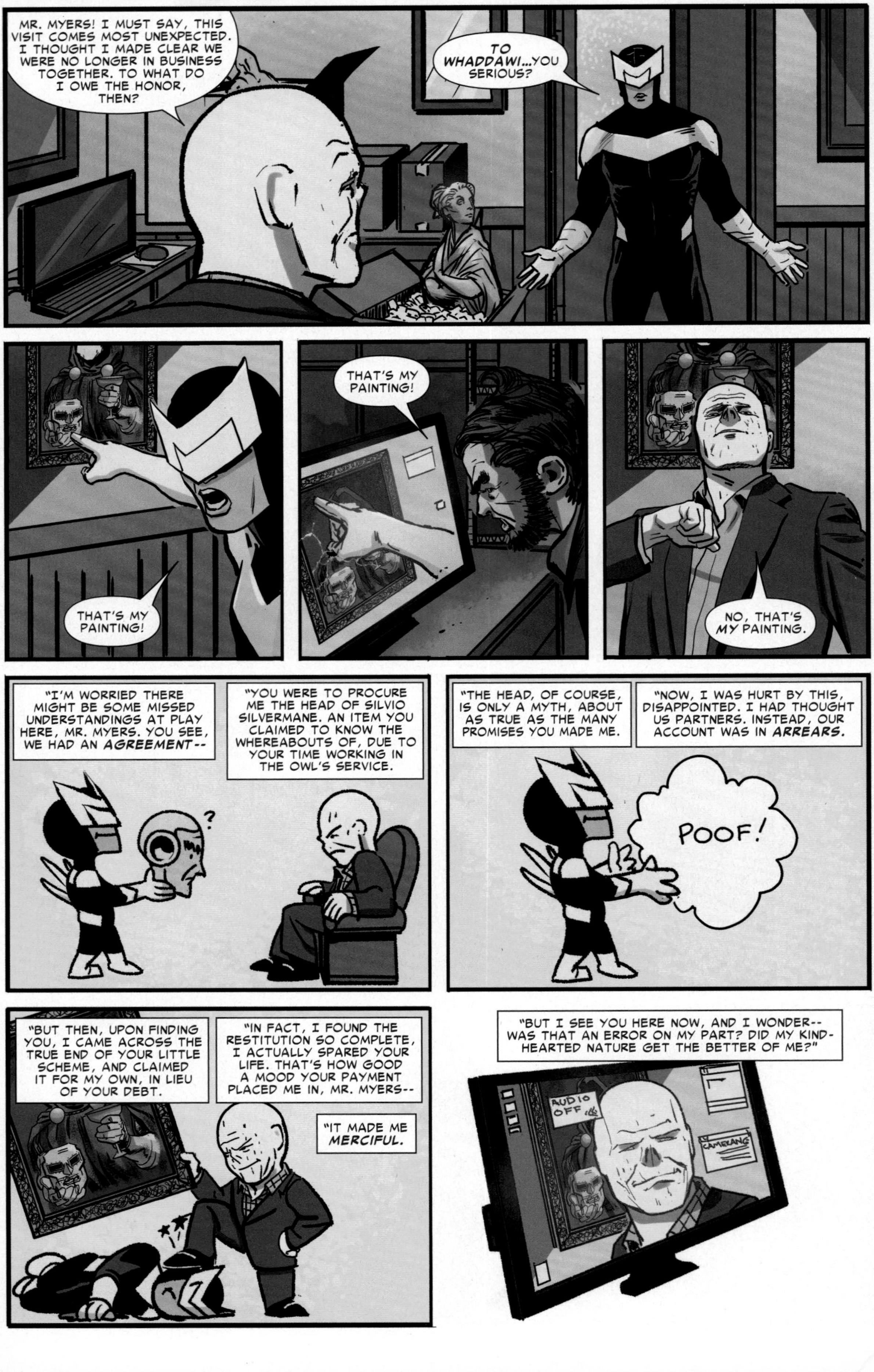
MR. MYERS! I MUST SAY, THIS VISIT COMES MOST UNEXPECTED. I THOUGHT I MADE CLEAR WE WERE NO LONGER IN BUSINESS TOGETHER. TO WHAT DO I OWE THE HONOR, THEN?
TO WHADDAWI...YOU SERIOUS?
THAT'S MY PAINTING!
THAT'S MY PAINTING!
NO, THAT'S MY PAINTING.
"I'M WORRIED THERE MIGHT BE SOME MISSED UNDERSTANDINGS AT PLAY HERE, MR. MYERS. YOU SEE, WE HAD AN AGREEMENT--
"YOU WERE TO PROCURE ME THE HEAD OF SILVIO SILVERMANE. AN ITEM YOU CLAIMED TO KNOW THE WHEREABOUTS OF, DUE TO YOUR TIME WORKING IN THE OWL'S SERVICE.
?
"THE HEAD, OF COURSE, IS ONLY A MYTH, ABOUT AS TRUE AS THE MANY PROMISES YOU MADE ME.
"NOW, I WAS HURT BY THIS, DISAPPOINTED. I HAD THOUGHT US PARTNERS. INSTEAD, OUR ACCOUNT WAS IN ARREARS.
POOF!
"BUT THEN, UPON FINDING YOU, I CAME ACROSS THE TRUE END OF YOUR LITTLE SCHEME, AND CLAIMED IT FOR MY OWN, IN LIEU OF YOUR DEBT.
"IN FACT, I FOUND THE RESTITUTION SO COMPLETE, I ACTUALLY SPARED YOUR LIFE. THAT'S HOW GOOD A MOOD YOUR PAYMENT PLACED ME IN, MR. MYERS--
"IT MADE ME MERCIFUL.
"BUT I SEE YOU HERE NOW, AND I WONDER-- WAS THAT AN ERROR ON MY PART? DID MY KIND-HEARTED NATURE GET THE BETTER OF ME?"
AUDIO OFF
CAMERA ON

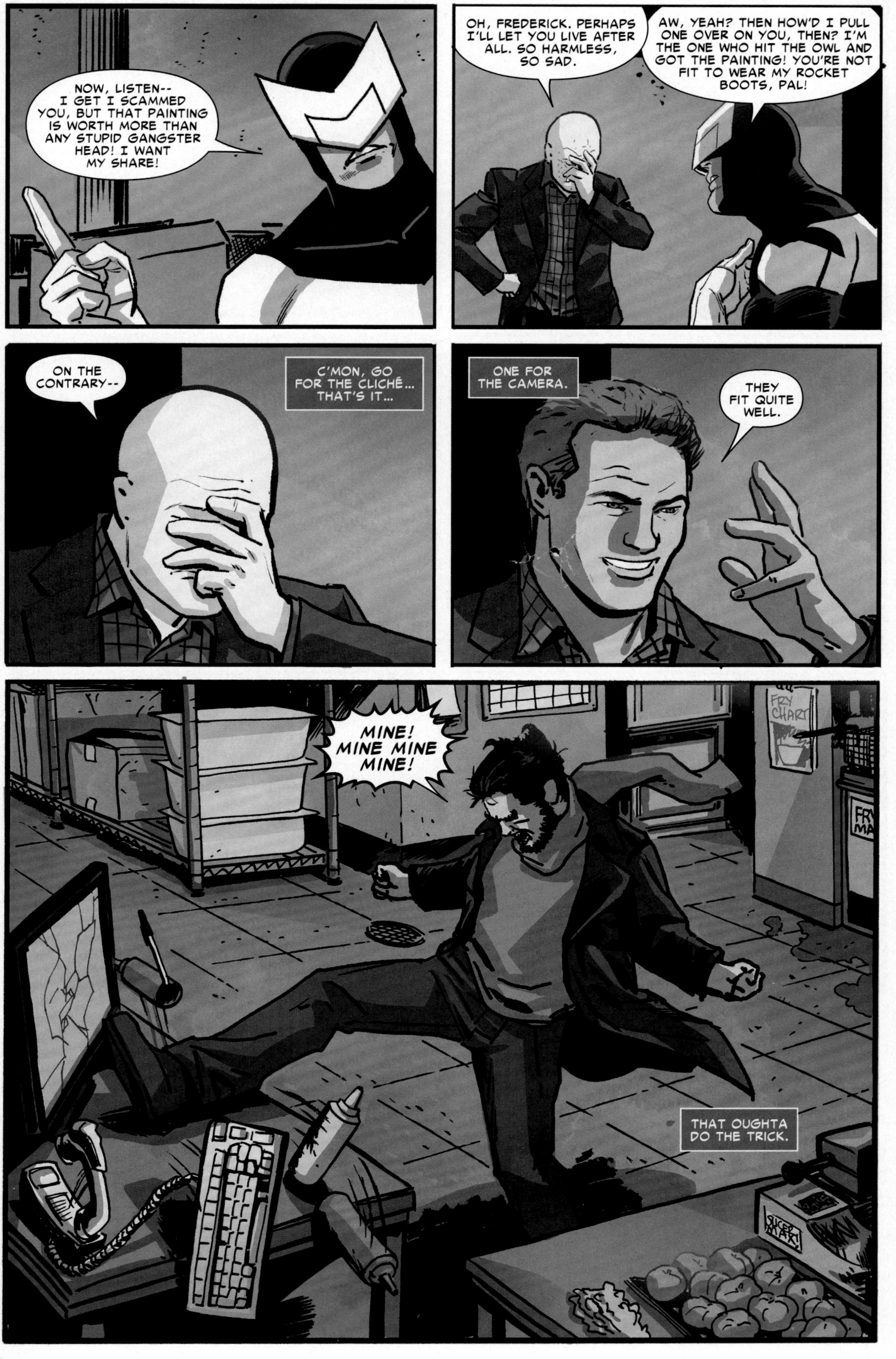
NOW, LISTEN-- I GET I SCAMMED YOU, BUT THAT PAINTING IS WORTH MORE THAN ANY STUPID GANGSTER HEAD! I WANT MY SHARE!
OH, FREDERICK. PERHAPS I'LL LET YOU LIVE AFTER ALL. SO HARMLESS, SO SAD.
AW, YEAH? THEN HOW'D I PULL ONE OVER ON YOU, THEN? I'M THE ONE WHO HIT THE OWL AND GOT THE PAINTING! YOU'RE NOT FIT TO WEAR MY ROCKET BOOTS, PAL!
ON THE CONTRARY--
C'MON, GO FOR THE CLICHÉ... THAT'S IT...
ONE FOR THE CAMERA.
THEY FIT QUITE WELL.
MINE! MINE MINE MINE!
FRY CHART
THAT OUGHTA DO THE TRICK.

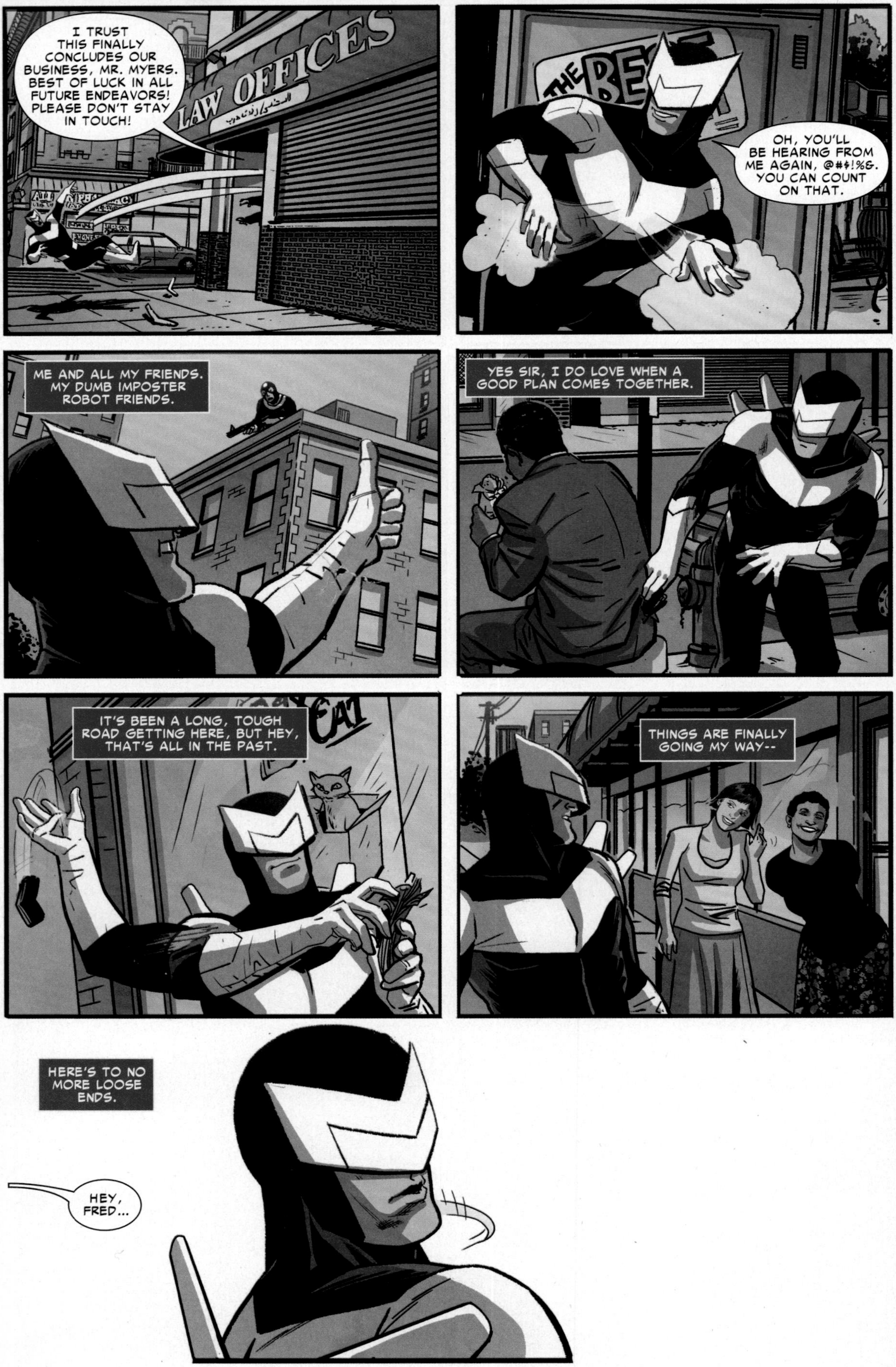
I TRUST THIS FINALLY CONCLUDES OUR BUSINESS, MR. MYERS. BEST OF LUCK IN ALL FUTURE ENDEAVORS! PLEASE DON'T STAY IN TOUCH!
LAW OFFICES
OH, YOU'LL BE HEARING FROM ME AGAIN, @#$!%&. YOU CAN COUNT ON THAT.
ME AND ALL MY FRIENDS. MY DUMB IMPOSTER ROBOT FRIENDS.
YES SIR, I DO LOVE WHEN A GOOD PLAN COMES TOGETHER.
IT'S BEEN A LONG, TOUGH ROAD GETTING HERE, BUT HEY, THAT'S ALL IN THE PAST.
THINGS ARE FINALLY GOING MY WAY--
HERE'S TO NO MORE LOOSE ENDS.
HEY, FRED...

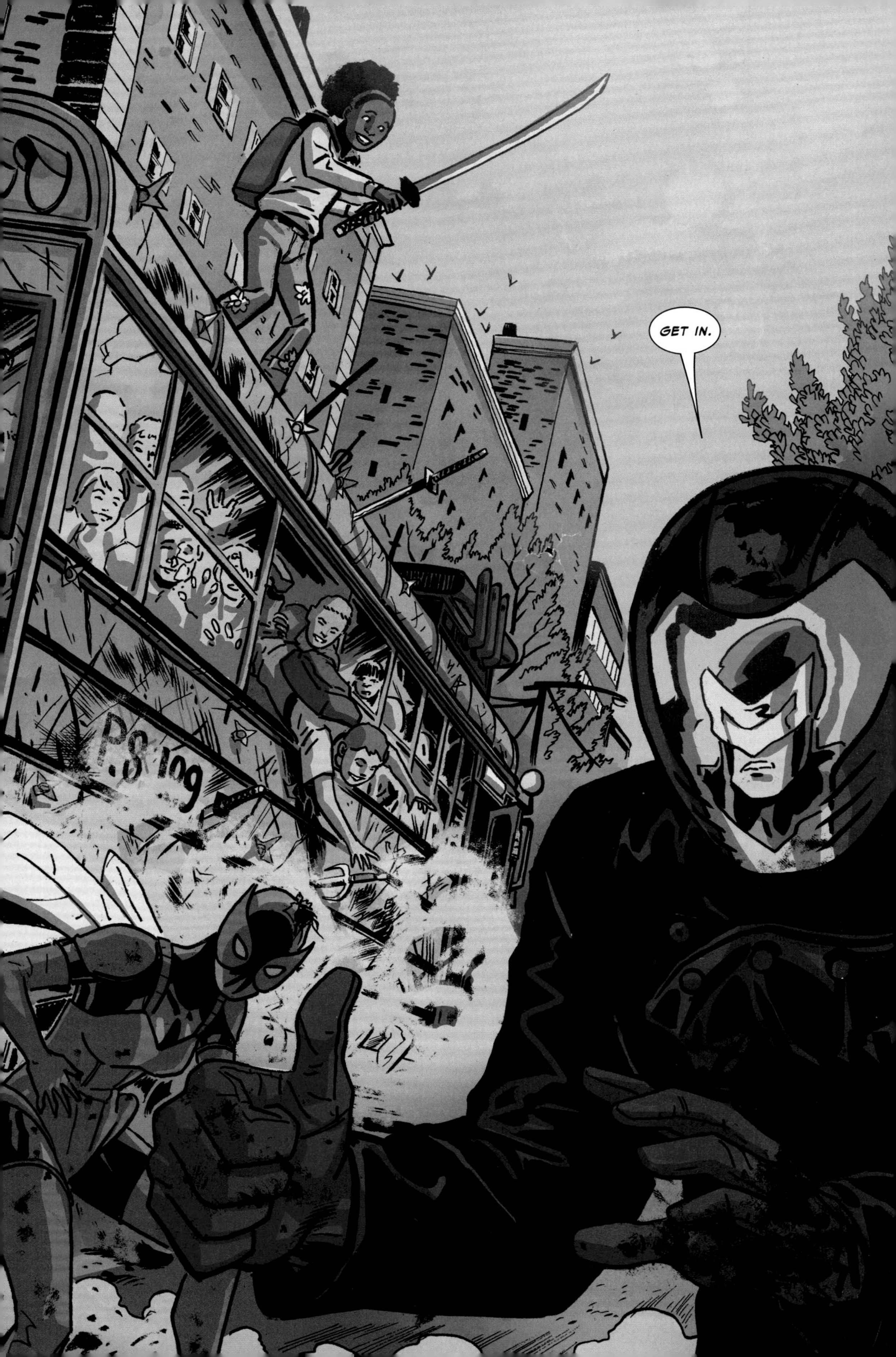
GET IN.
P.S 109

10

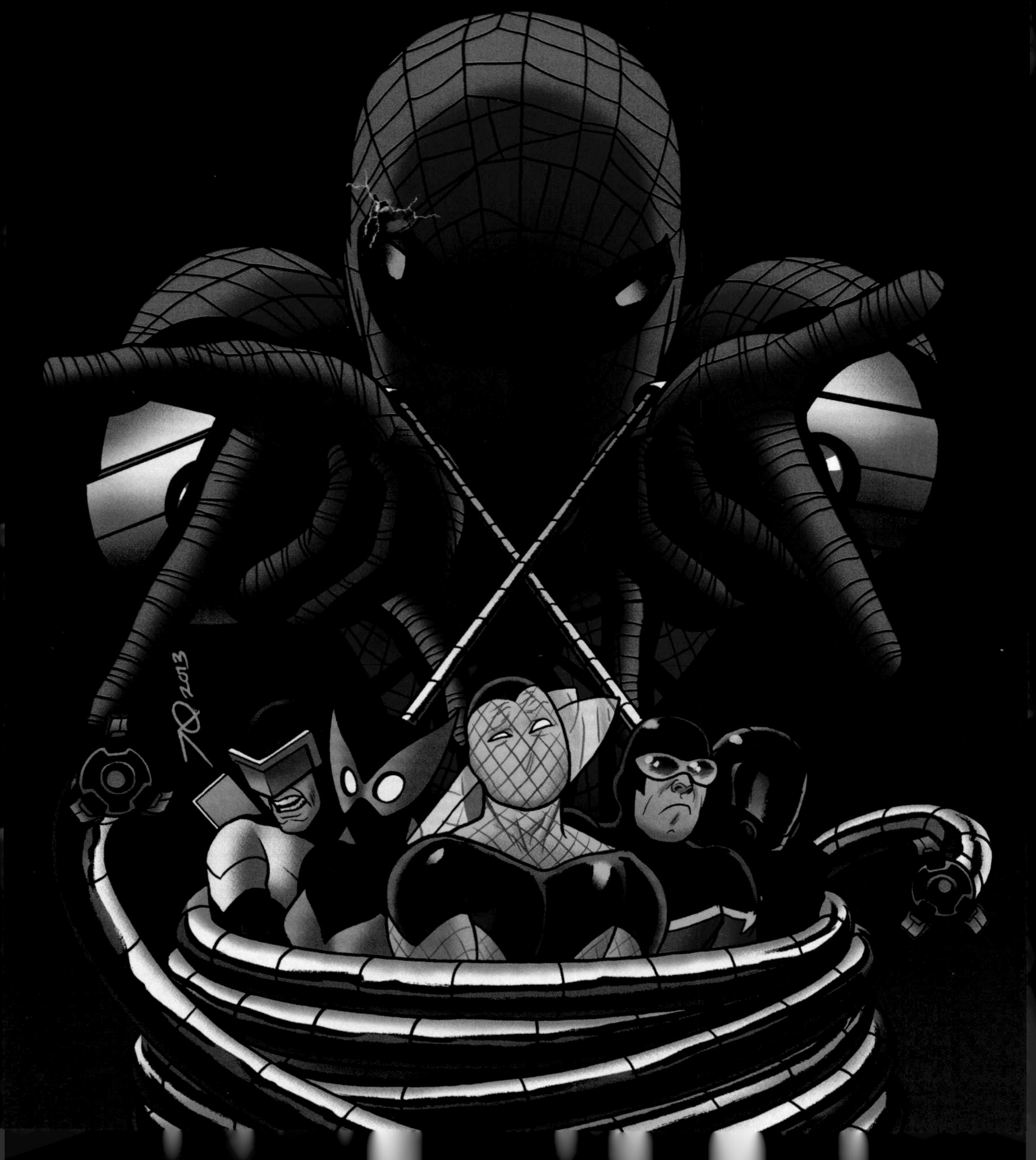

Who are the
Superior Foes of
Spider-Man?

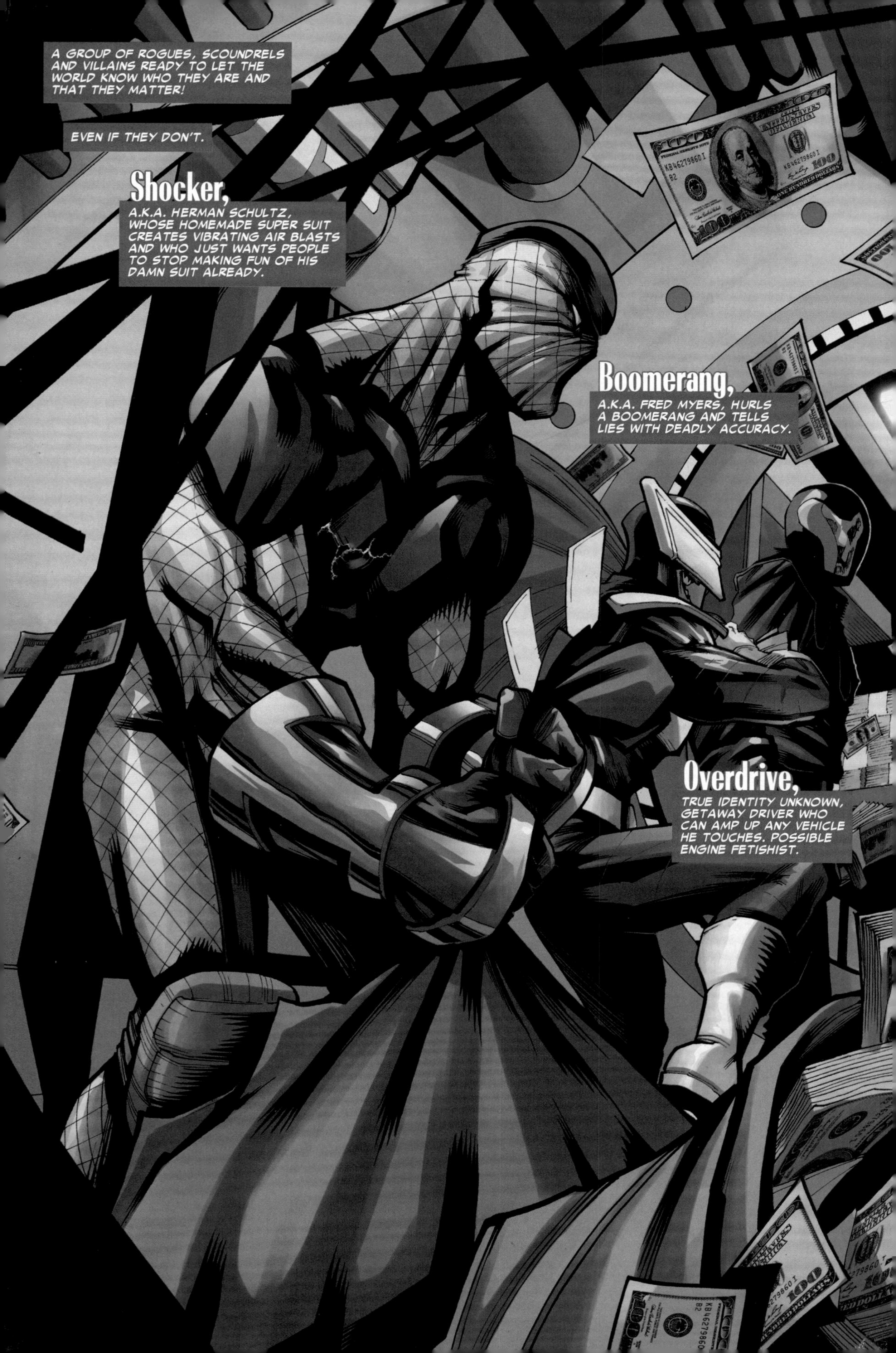
A GROUP OF ROGUES, SCOUNDRELS AND VILLAINS READY TO LET THE WORLD KNOW WHO THEY ARE AND THAT THEY MATTER!
EVEN IF THEY DON'T.
Shocker,
A.K.A. HERMAN SCHULTZ, WHOSE HOMEMADE SUPER SUIT CREATES VIBRATING AIR BLASTS AND WHO JUST WANTS PEOPLE TO STOP MAKING FUN OF HIS DAMN SUIT ALREADY.
Boomerang,
A.K.A. FRED MYERS, HURLS A BOOMERANG AND TELLS LIES WITH DEADLY ACCURACY.
Overdrive,
TRUE IDENTITY UNKNOWN, GETAWAY DRIVER WHO CAN AMP UP ANY VEHICLE HE TOUCHES. POSSIBLE ENGINE FETISHIST.

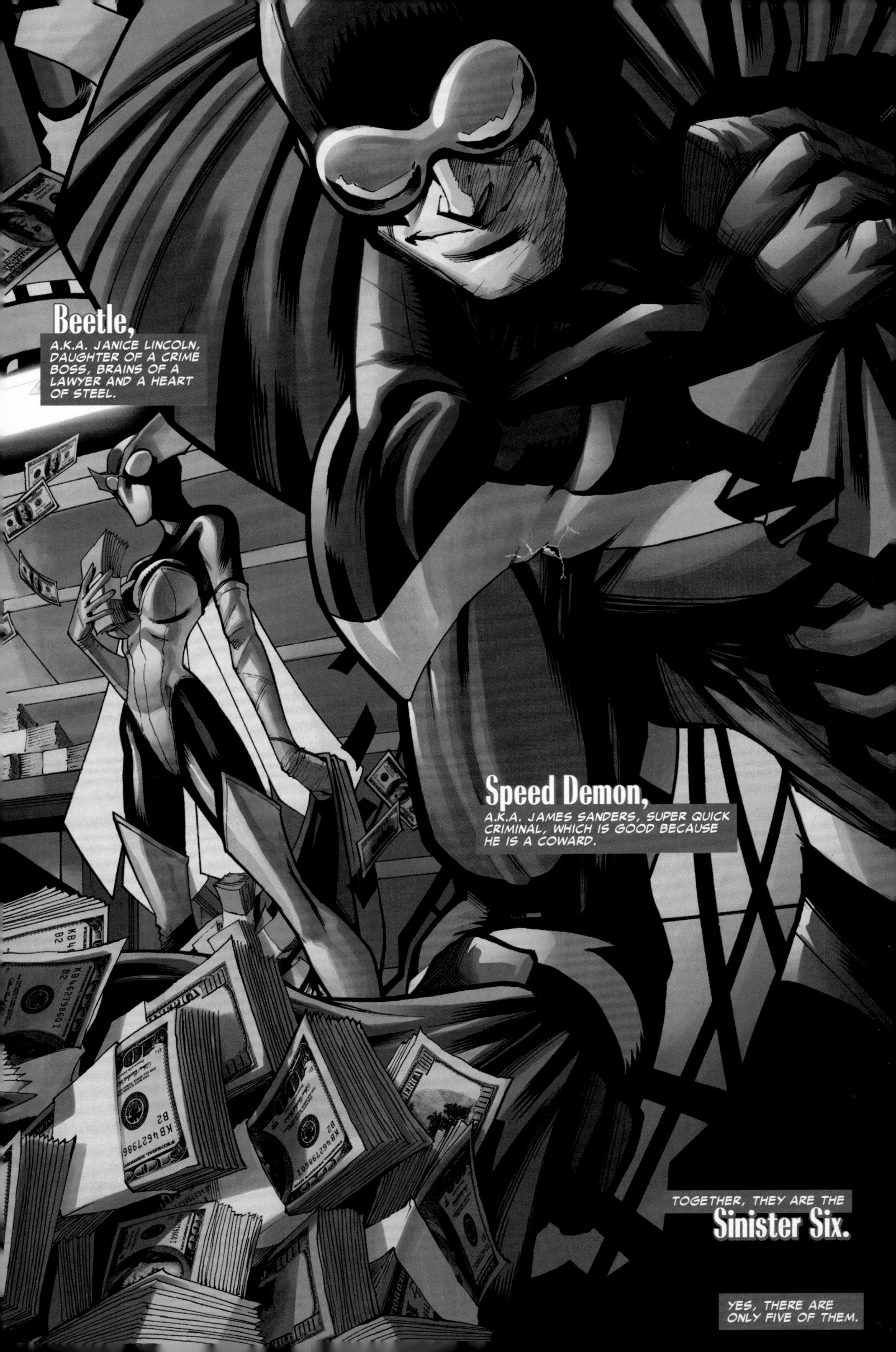
Beetle,
A.K.A. JANICE LINCOLN, DAUGHTER OF A CRIME BOSS, BRAINS OF A LAWYER AND A HEART OF STEEL.
Speed Demon,
A.K.A. JAMES SANDERS, SUPER QUICK CRIMINAL, WHICH IS GOOD BECAUSE HE IS A COWARD.
TOGETHER, THEY ARE THE
Sinister Six.
YES, THERE ARE ONLY FIVE OF THEM.

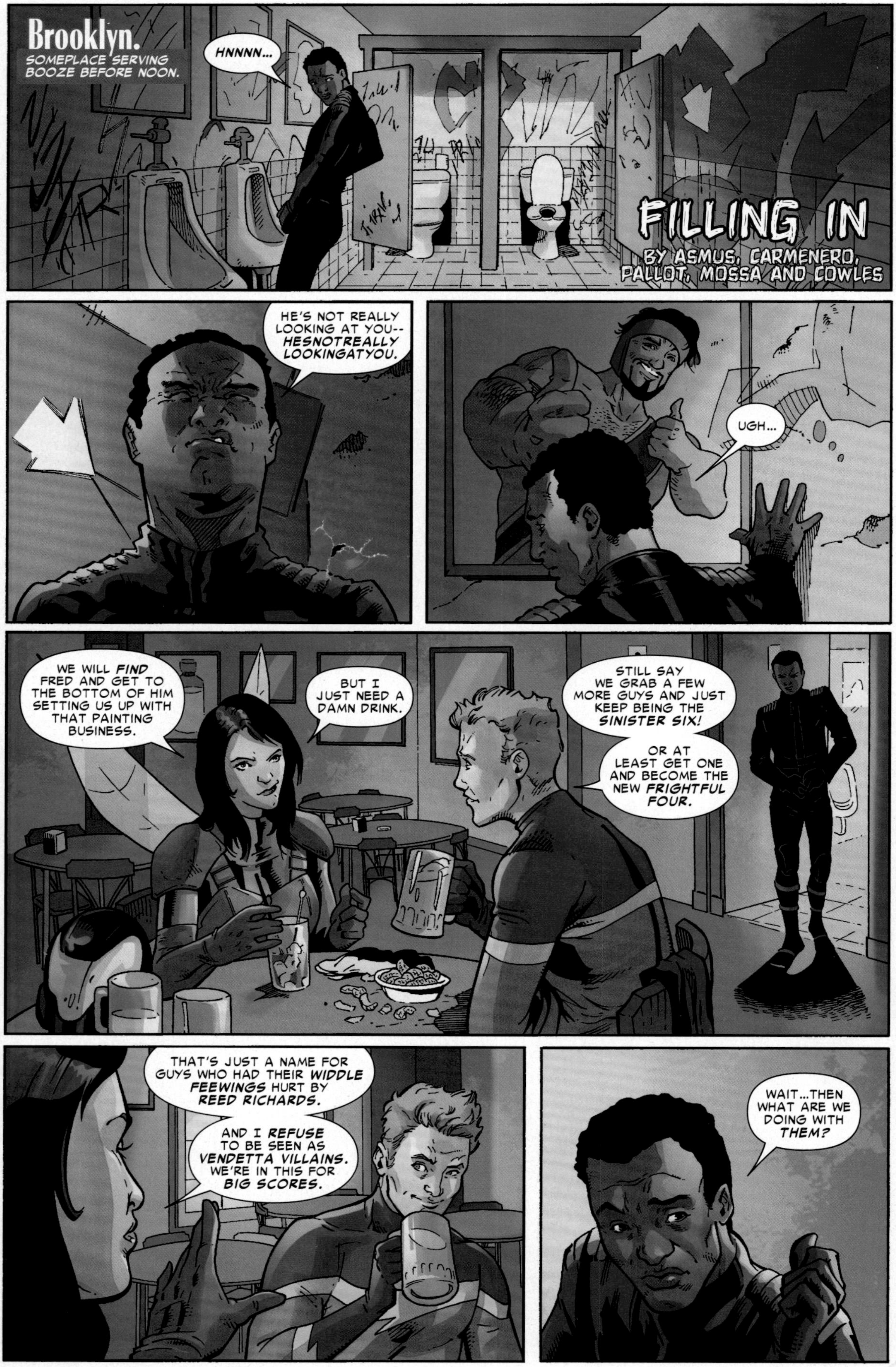

Brooklyn.
SOMEPLACE SERVING BOOZE BEFORE NOON.
HNNNN...
FILLING IN
BY ASMUS, CARMENERO, PALLOT, MOSSA AND COWLES
HE'S NOT REALLY LOOKING AT YOU-- HESNOTREALLY LOOKINGATYOU.
UGH...
WE WILL FIND FRED AND GET TO THE BOTTOM OF HIM SETTING US UP WITH THAT PAINTING BUSINESS.
BUT I JUST NEED A DAMN DRINK.
STILL SAY WE GRAB A FEW MORE GUYS AND JUST KEEP BEING THE SINISTER SIX!
OR AT LEAST GET ONE AND BECOME THE NEW FRIGHTFUL FOUR.
THAT'S JUST A NAME FOR GUYS WHO HAD THEIR WIDDLE FEEWINGS HURT BY REED RICHARDS.
AND I REFUSE TO BE SEEN AS VENDETTA VILLAINS. WE'RE IN THIS FOR BIG SCORES.
WAIT...THEN WHAT ARE WE DOING WITH THEM?

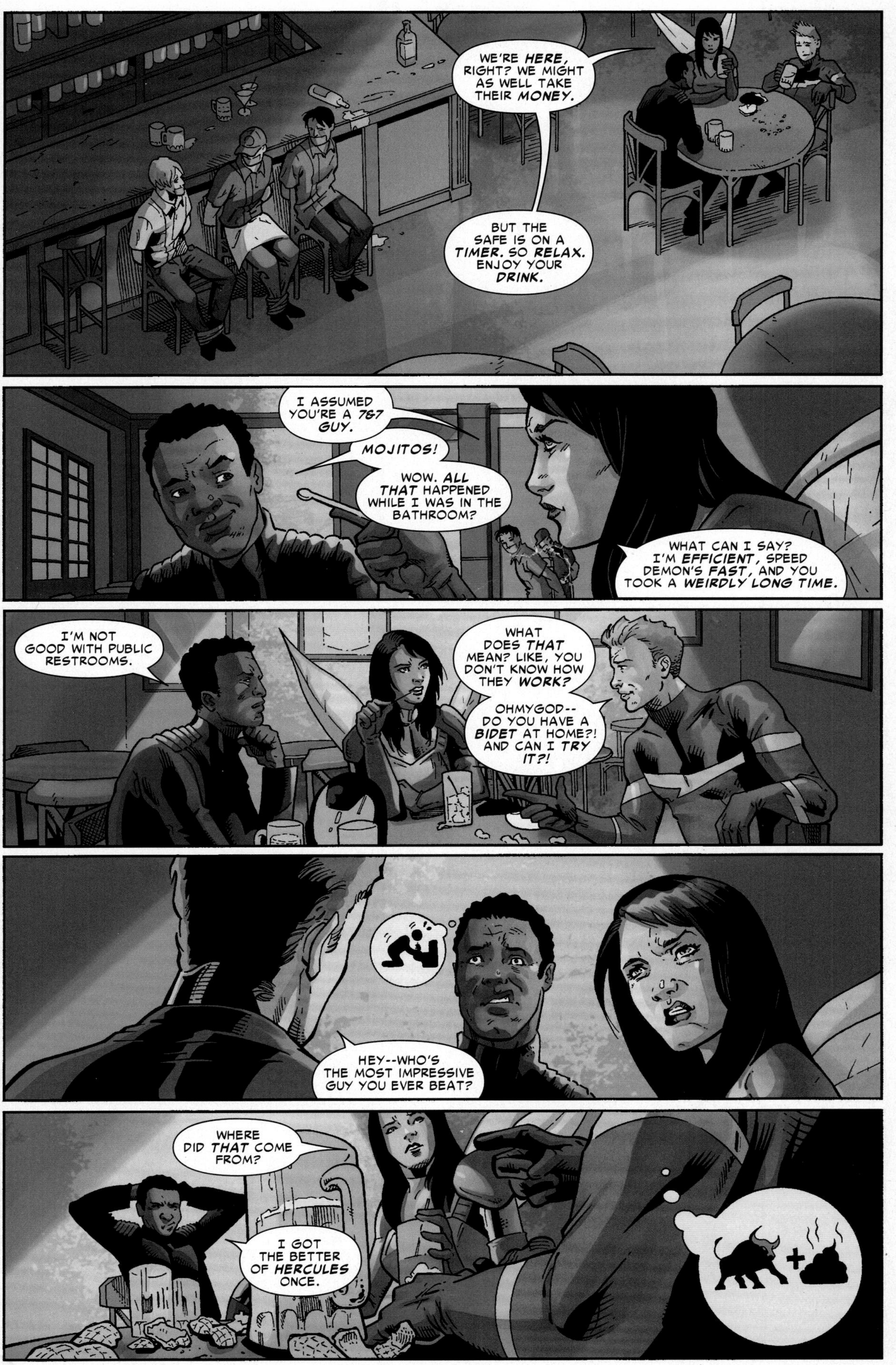
WE'RE HERE, RIGHT? WE MIGHT AS WELL TAKE THEIR MONEY.
BUT THE SAFE IS ON A TIMER. SO RELAX. ENJOY YOUR DRINK.
I ASSUMED YOU'RE A 7&7 GUY.
MOJITOS!
WOW. ALL THAT HAPPENED WHILE I WAS IN THE BATHROOM?
WHAT CAN I SAY? I'M EFFICIENT, SPEED DEMON'S FAST, AND YOU TOOK A WEIRDLY LONG TIME.
I'M NOT GOOD WITH PUBLIC RESTROOMS.
WHAT DOES THAT MEAN? LIKE, YOU DON'T KNOW HOW THEY WORK?
OHMYGOD-- DO YOU HAVE A BIDET AT HOME?! AND CAN I TRY IT?!
HEY--WHO'S THE MOST IMPRESSIVE GUY YOU EVER BEAT?
WHERE DID THAT COME FROM?
I GOT THE BETTER OF HERCULES ONCE.

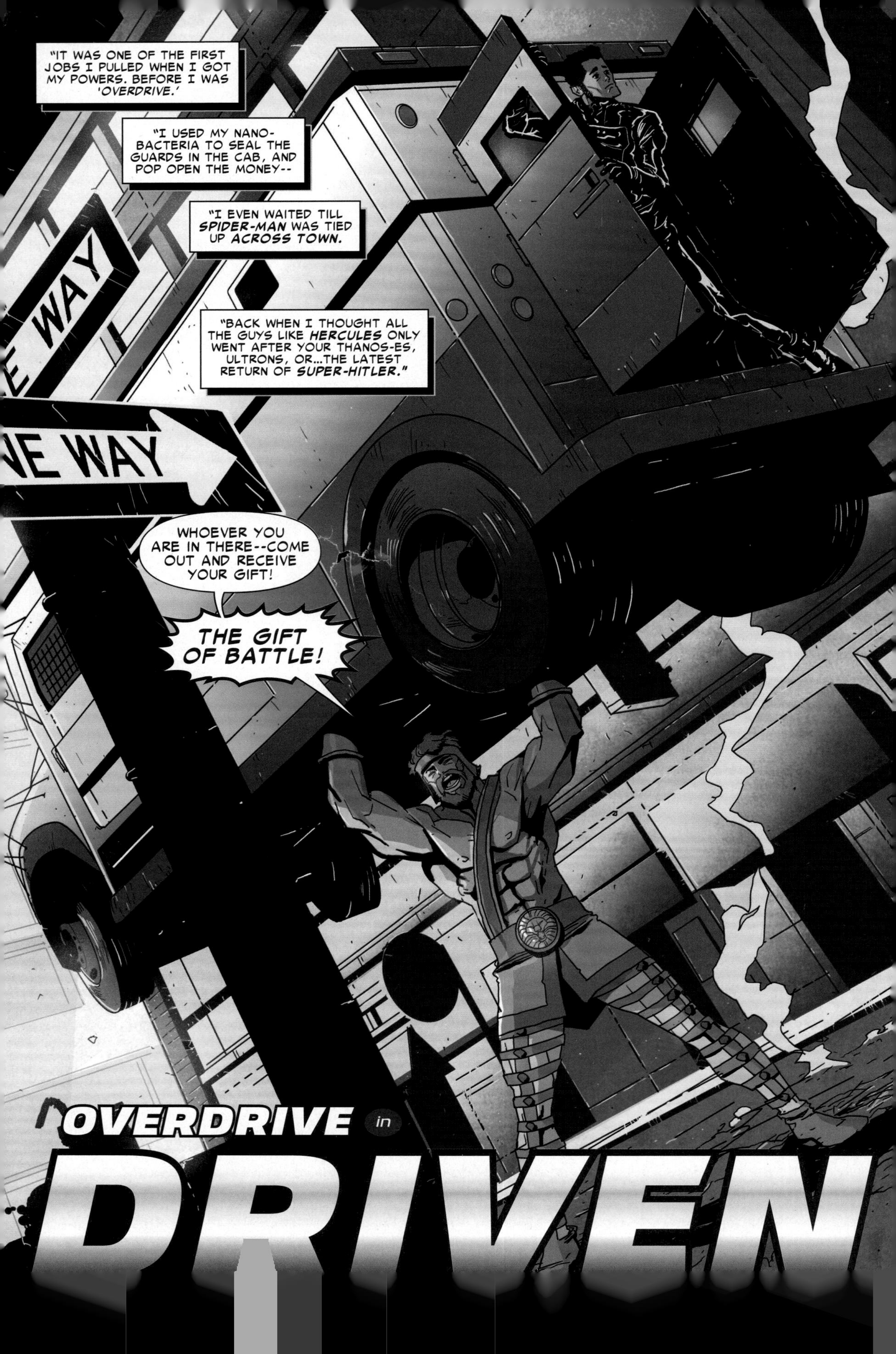
"IT WAS ONE OF THE FIRST JOBS I PULLED WHEN I GOT MY POWERS. BEFORE I WAS 'OVERDRIVE.'
"I USED MY NANO-BACTERIA TO SEAL THE GUARDS IN THE CAB, AND POP OPEN THE MONEY--
"I EVEN WAITED TILL SPIDER-MAN WAS TIED UP ACROSS TOWN.
"BACK WHEN I THOUGHT ALL THE GUYS LIKE HERCULES ONLY WENT AFTER YOUR THANOS-ES, ULTRONS, OR...THE LATEST RETURN OF SUPER-HITLER."
E WAY
NE WAY
WHOEVER YOU ARE IN THERE--COME OUT AND RECEIVE YOUR GIFT!
THE GIFT OF BATTLE!
OVERDRIVE in
DRIVEN

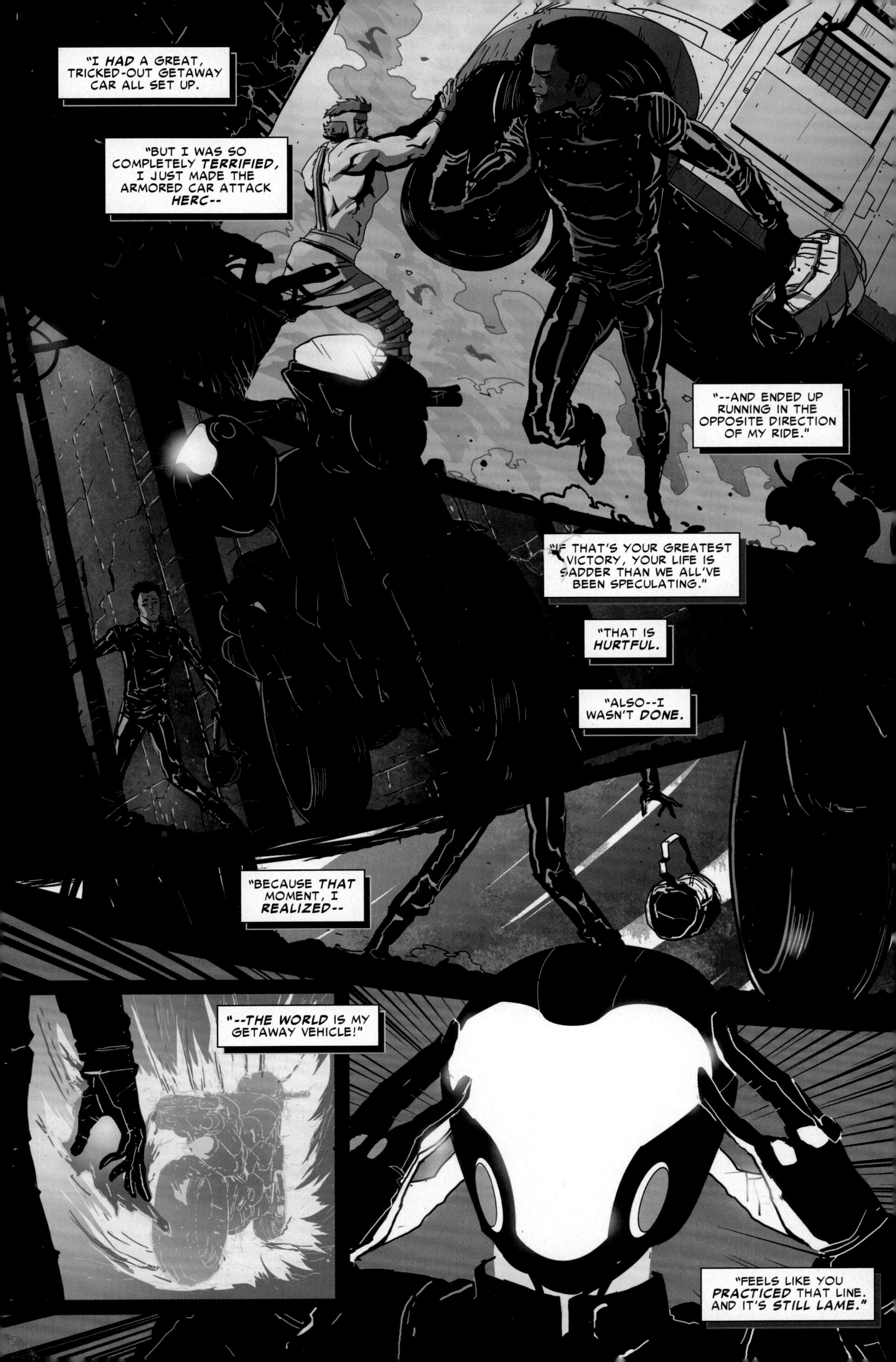
"I HAD A GREAT, TRICKED-OUT GETAWAY CAR ALL SET UP.
"BUT I WAS SO COMPLETELY TERRIFIED, I JUST MADE THE ARMORED CAR ATTACK HERC--
"--AND ENDED UP RUNNING IN THE OPPOSITE DIRECTION OF MY RIDE."
"IF THAT'S YOUR GREATEST VICTORY, YOUR LIFE IS SADDER THAN WE ALL'VE BEEN SPECULATING."
"THAT IS HURTFUL.
"ALSO--I WASN'T DONE.
"BECAUSE THAT MOMENT, I REALIZED--
"--THE WORLD IS MY GETAWAY VEHICLE!"
"FEELS LIKE YOU PRACTICED THAT LINE. AND IT'S STILL LAME."

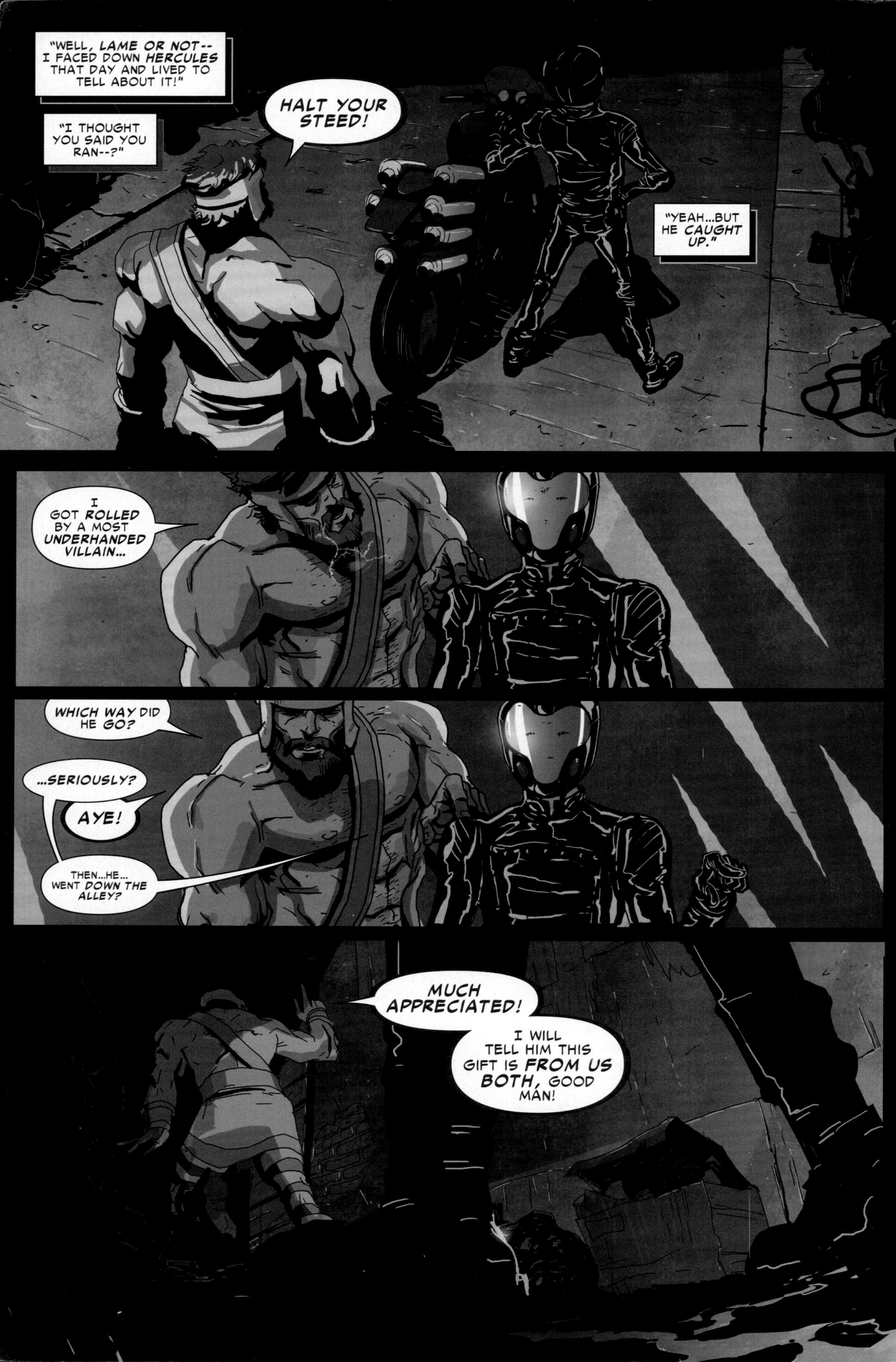
"WELL, LAME OR NOT-- I FACED DOWN HERCULES THAT DAY AND LIVED TO TELL ABOUT IT!"
"I THOUGHT YOU SAID YOU RAN--?"
HALT YOUR STEED!
"YEAH...BUT HE CAUGHT UP."
I GOT ROLLED BY A MOST UNDERHANDED VILLAIN...
WHICH WAY DID HE GO?
...SERIOUSLY?
AYE!
THEN...HE... WENT DOWN THE ALLEY?
MUCH APPRECIATED!
I WILL TELL HIM THIS GIFT IS FROM US BOTH, GOOD MAN!

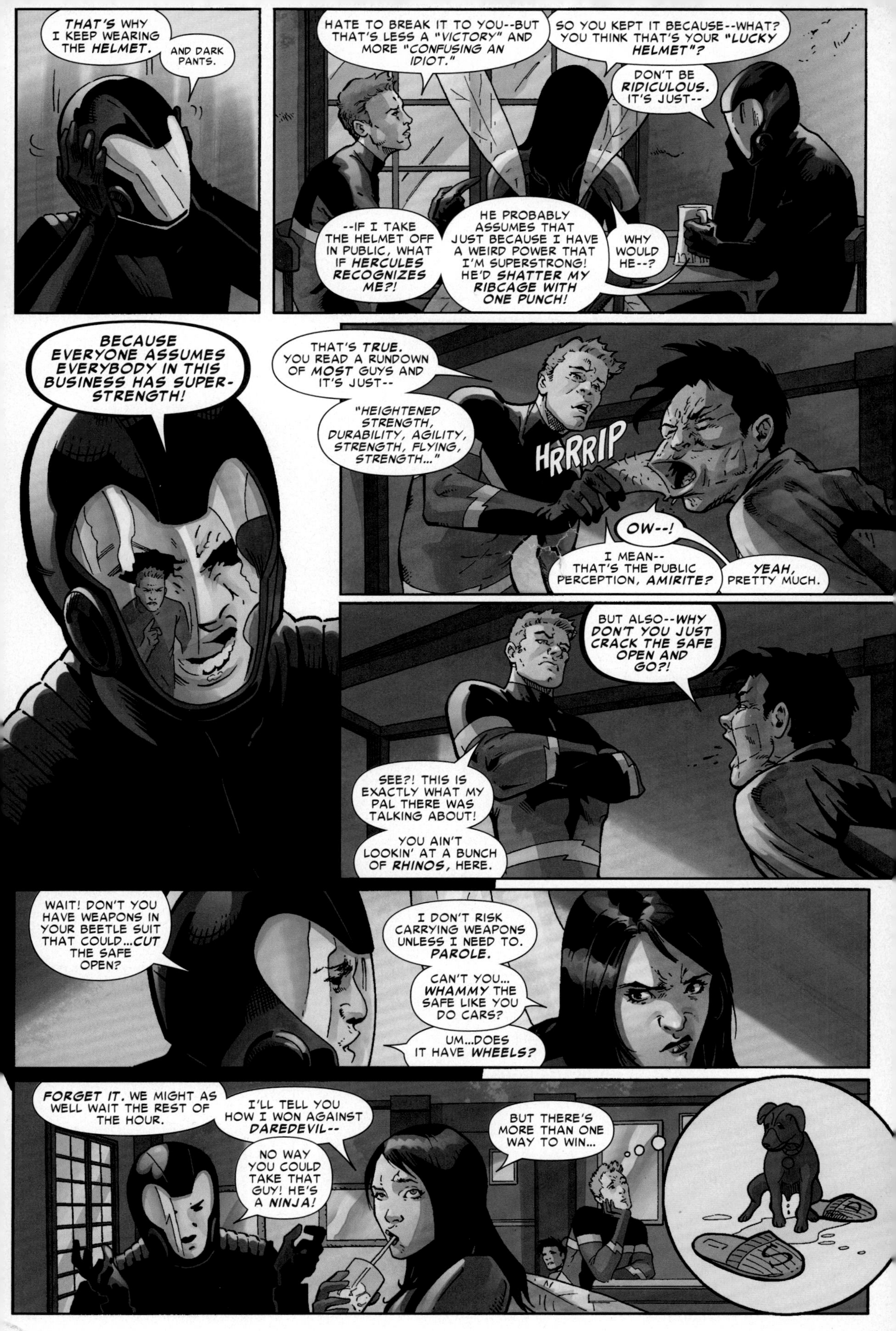
THAT'S WHY I KEEP WEARING THE HELMET.
AND DARK PANTS.
HATE TO BREAK IT TO YOU--BUT THAT'S LESS A "VICTORY" AND MORE "CONFUSING AN IDIOT."
SO YOU KEPT IT BECAUSE--WHAT? YOU THINK THAT'S YOUR "LUCKY HELMET"?
DON'T BE RIDICULOUS. IT'S JUST--
--IF I TAKE THE HELMET OFF IN PUBLIC, WHAT IF HERCULES RECOGNIZES ME?!
HE PROBABLY ASSUMES THAT JUST BECAUSE I HAVE A WEIRD POWER THAT I'M SUPERSTRONG! HE'D SHATTER MY RIBCAGE WITH ONE PUNCH!
WHY WOULD HE--?
BECAUSE EVERYONE ASSUMES EVERYBODY IN THIS BUSINESS HAS SUPER-STRENGTH!
THAT'S TRUE. YOU READ A RUNDOWN OF MOST GUYS AND IT'S JUST--
"HEIGHTENED STRENGTH, DURABILITY, AGILITY, STRENGTH, FLYING, STRENGTH..."
HRRRIP
OW--!
I MEAN-- THAT'S THE PUBLIC PERCEPTION, AMIRITE?
YEAH, PRETTY MUCH.
BUT ALSO--WHY DON'T YOU JUST CRACK THE SAFE OPEN AND GO?!
SEE?! THIS IS EXACTLY WHAT MY PAL THERE WAS TALKING ABOUT!
YOU AIN'T LOOKIN' AT A BUNCH OF RHINOS, HERE.
WAIT! DON'T YOU HAVE WEAPONS IN YOUR BEETLE SUIT THAT COULD...CUT THE SAFE OPEN?
I DON'T RISK CARRYING WEAPONS UNLESS I NEED TO. PAROLE.
CAN'T YOU... WHAMMY THE SAFE LIKE YOU DO CARS?
UM...DOES IT HAVE WHEELS?
FORGET IT. WE MIGHT AS WELL WAIT THE REST OF THE HOUR.
I'LL TELL YOU HOW I WON AGAINST DAREDEVIL--
NO WAY YOU COULD TAKE THAT GUY! HE'S A NINJA!
BUT THERE'S MORE THAN ONE WAY TO WIN...

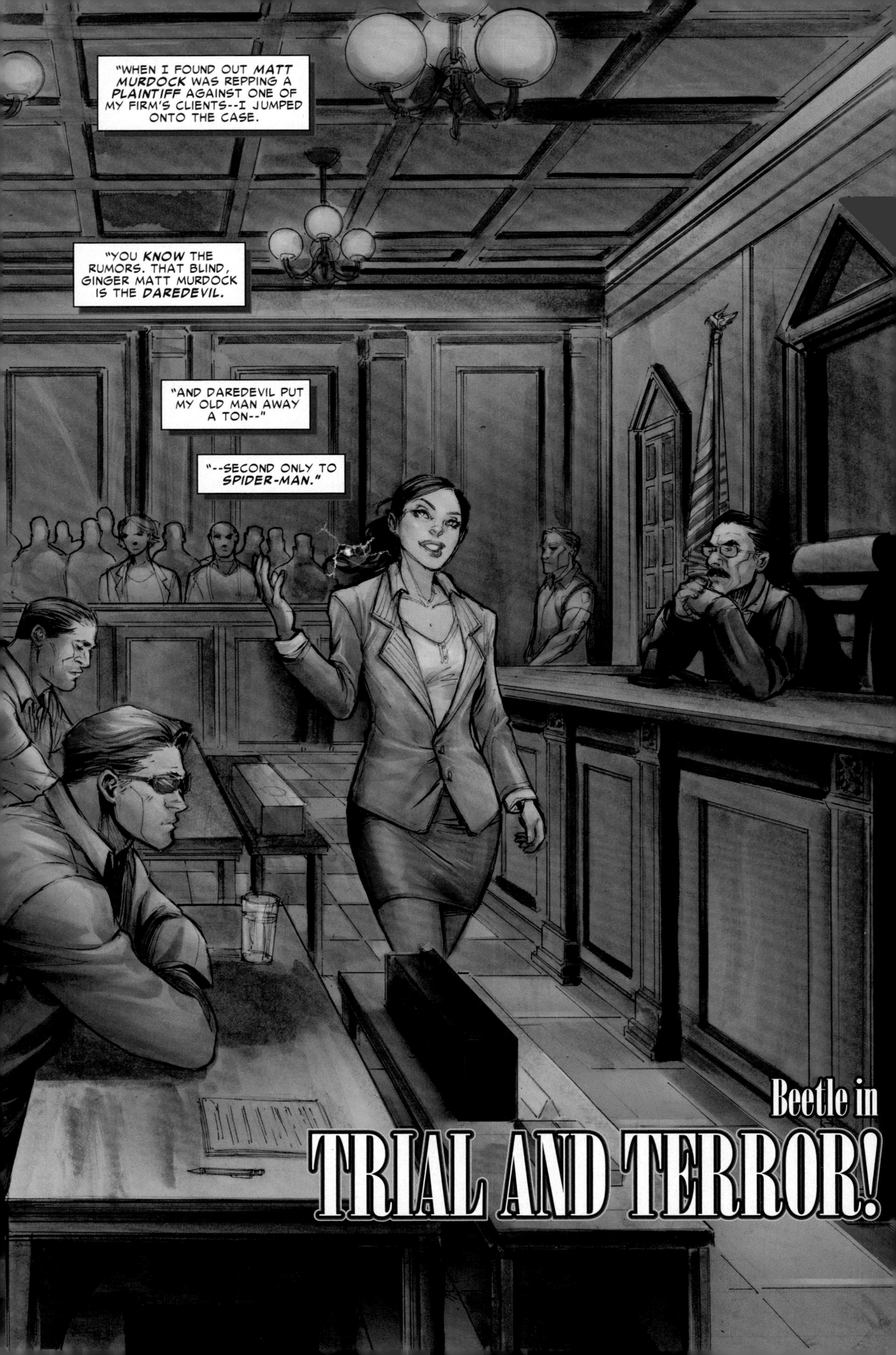
"WHEN I FOUND OUT MATT MURDOCK WAS REPPING A PLAINTIFF AGAINST ONE OF MY FIRM'S CLIENTS--I JUMPED ONTO THE CASE.
"YOU KNOW THE RUMORS. THAT BLIND, GINGER MATT MURDOCK IS THE DAREDEVIL.
"AND DAREDEVIL PUT MY OLD MAN AWAY A TON--"
"--SECOND ONLY TO SPIDER-MAN."
Beetle in
TRIAL AND TERROR!

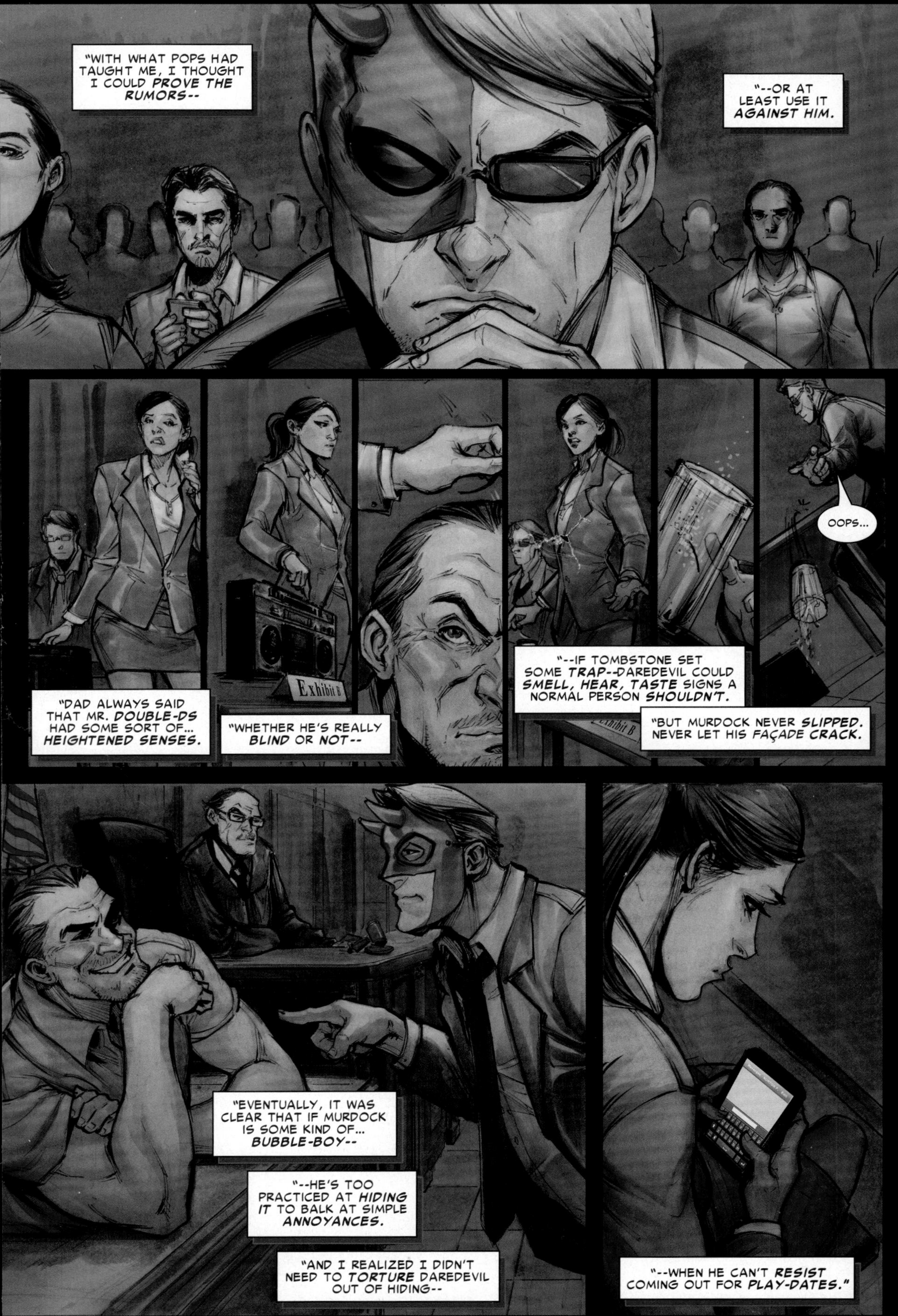
"WITH WHAT POPS HAD TAUGHT ME, I THOUGHT I COULD PROVE THE RUMORS--
"--OR AT LEAST USE IT AGAINST HIM.
"DAD ALWAYS SAID THAT MR. DOUBLE-DS HAD SOME SORT OF... HEIGHTENED SENSES.
Exhibit B
"WHETHER HE'S REALLY BLIND OR NOT--
"--IF TOMBSTONE SET SOME TRAP--DAREDEVIL COULD SMELL, HEAR, TASTE SIGNS A NORMAL PERSON SHOULDN'T.
Exhibit B
OOPS...
"BUT MURDOCK NEVER SLIPPED. NEVER LET HIS FAÇADE CRACK.
"EVENTUALLY, IT WAS CLEAR THAT IF MURDOCK IS SOME KIND OF... BUBBLE-BOY--
"--HE'S TOO PRACTICED AT HIDING IT TO BALK AT SIMPLE ANNOYANCES.
"AND I REALIZED I DIDN'T NEED TO TORTURE DAREDEVIL OUT OF HIDING--
"--WHEN HE CAN'T RESIST COMING OUT FOR PLAY-DATES."

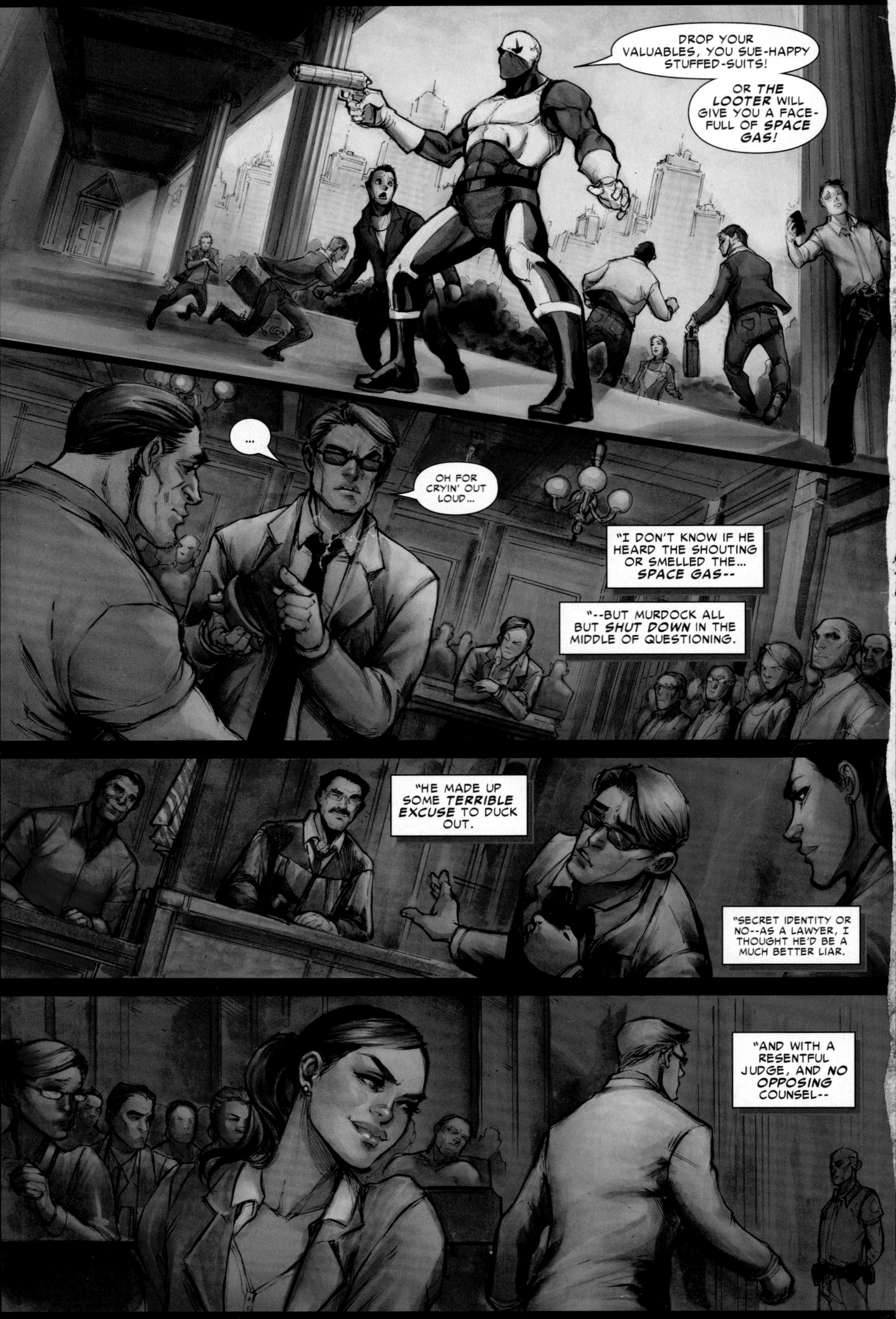
DROP YOUR VALUABLES, YOU SUE-HAPPY STUFFED-SUITS!
OR THE LOOTER WILL GIVE YOU A FACE-FULL OF SPACE GAS!
...
OH FOR CRYIN' OUT LOUD...
"I DON'T KNOW IF HE HEARD THE SHOUTING OR SMELLED THE... SPACE GAS--
"--BUT MURDOCK ALL BUT SHUT DOWN IN THE MIDDLE OF QUESTIONING.
"HE MADE UP SOME TERRIBLE EXCUSE TO DUCK OUT.
"SECRET IDENTITY OR NO--AS A LAWYER, I THOUGHT HE'D BE A MUCH BETTER LIAR.
"AND WITH A RESENTFUL JUDGE, AND NO OPPOSING COUNSEL--

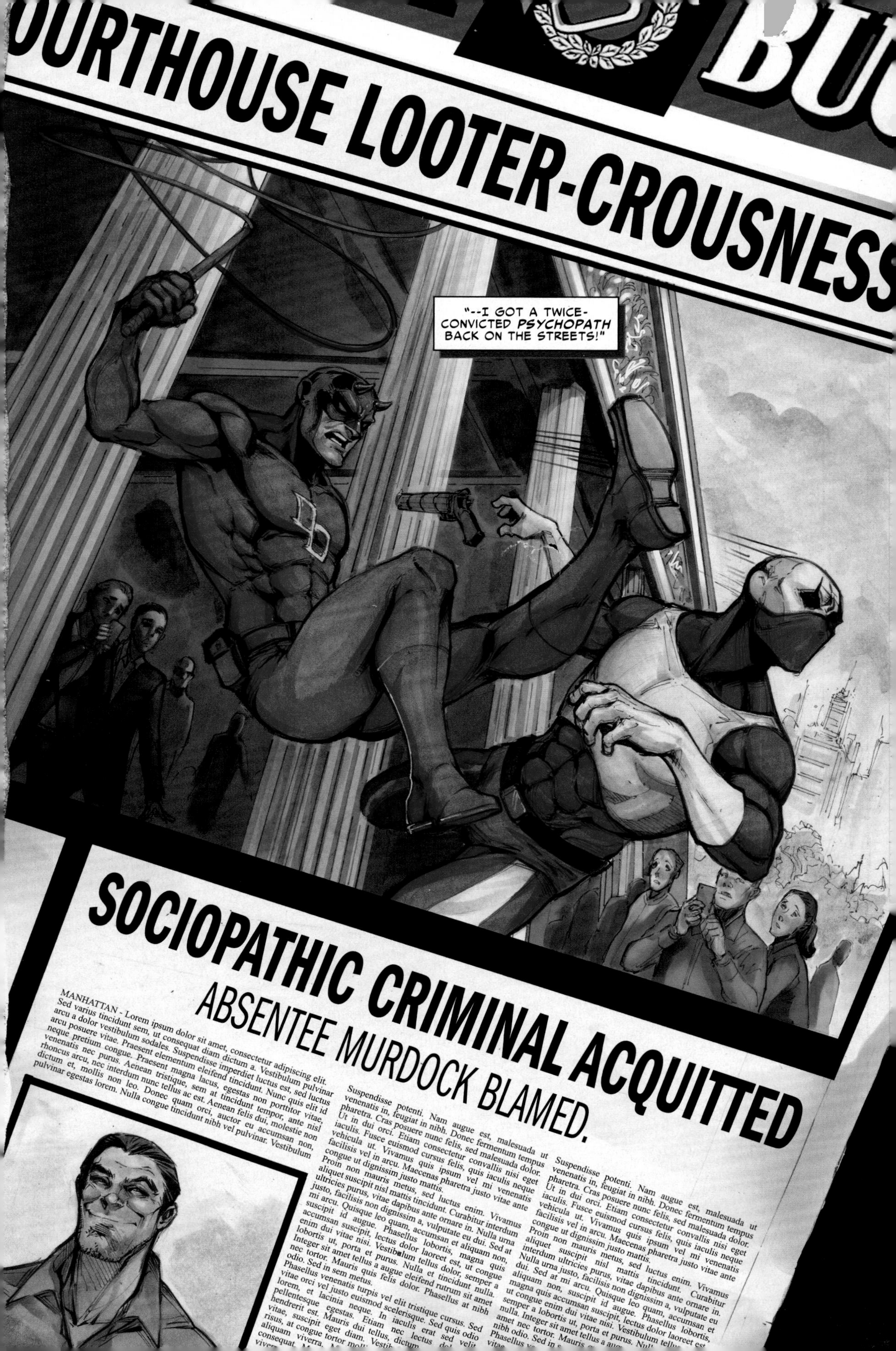
OURTHOUSE LOOTER-CROUSNESS
"--I GOT A TWICE-CONVICTED PSYCHOPATH BACK ON THE STREETS!"
SOCIOPATHIC CRIMINAL ACQUITTED
ABSENTEE MURDOCK BLAMED.
MANHATTAN - Lorem ipsum dolor sit amet, consectetur adipiscing elit. Sed varius tincidunt sem, ut consequat diam dictum a. Vestibulum pulvinar arcu a dolor vestibulum sodales. Suspendisse imperdiet luctus est, sed luctus arcu posuere vitae. Praesent elementum eleifend tincidunt. Nunc quis elit id neque pretium congue. Praesent magna lacus, egestas non porttitor vitae, venenatis nec purus. Aenean tristique, sem at tincidunt tempor, ante nisl rhoncus arcu, nec interdum nunc tellus ac est. Aenean felis dui, molestie non dictum et, mollis non leo. Donec quam orci, auctor eu accumsan non, pulvinar egestas lorem. Nulla congue tincidunt nibh vel pulvinar. Vestibulum

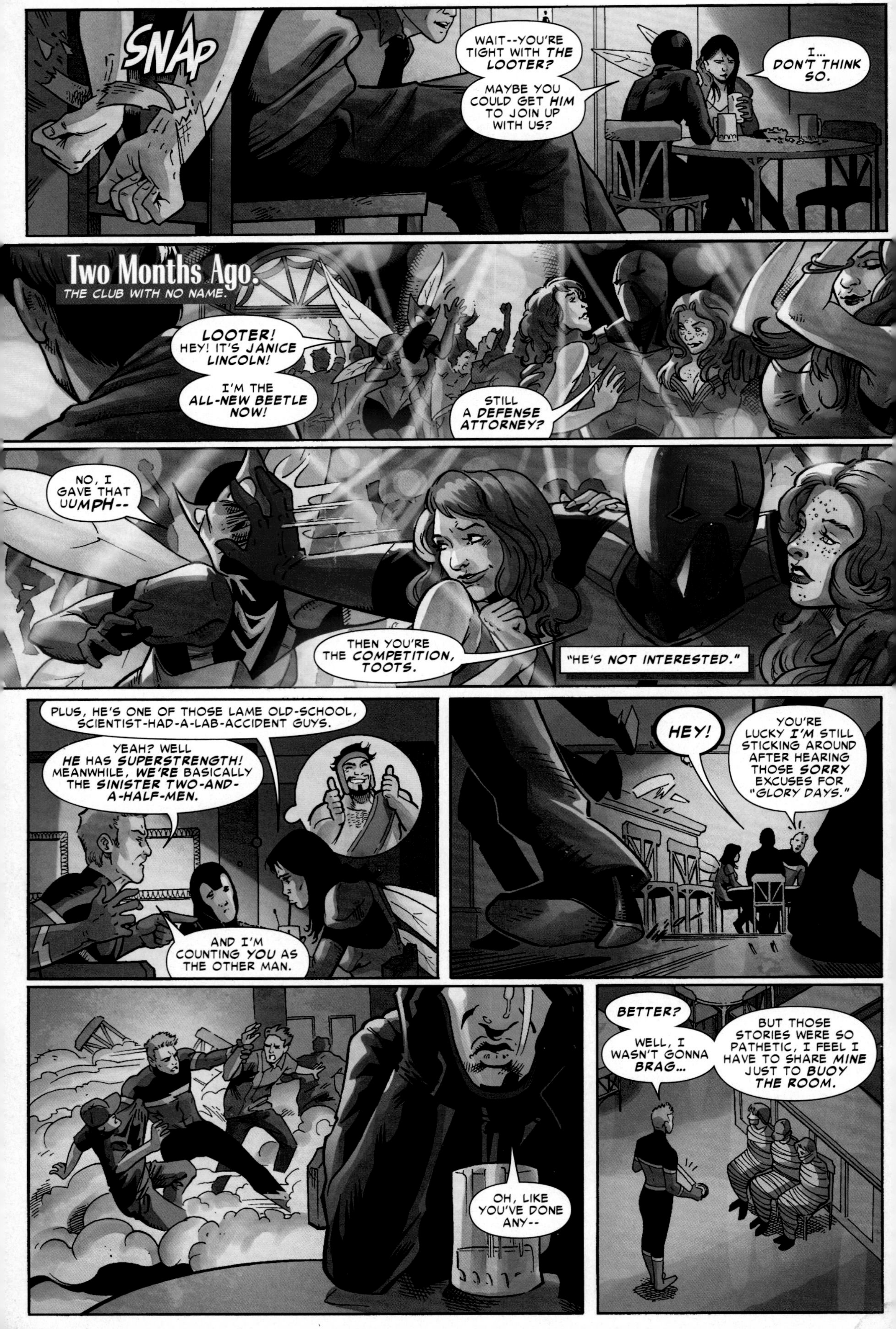
SNAP
WAIT--YOU'RE TIGHT WITH THE LOOTER?
MAYBE YOU COULD GET HIM TO JOIN UP WITH US?
I... DON'T THINK SO.
Two Months Ago.
THE CLUB WITH NO NAME.
LOOTER! HEY! IT'S JANICE LINCOLN!
I'M THE ALL-NEW BEETLE NOW!
STILL A DEFENSE ATTORNEY?
NO, I GAVE THAT UUMPH--
THEN YOU'RE THE COMPETITION, TOOTS.
"HE'S NOT INTERESTED."
PLUS, HE'S ONE OF THOSE LAME OLD-SCHOOL, SCIENTIST-HAD-A-LAB-ACCIDENT GUYS.
YEAH? WELL HE HAS SUPERSTRENGTH! MEANWHILE, WE'RE BASICALLY THE SINISTER TWO-AND-A-HALF-MEN.
AND I'M COUNTING YOU AS THE OTHER MAN.
HEY!
YOU'RE LUCKY I'M STILL STICKING AROUND AFTER HEARING THOSE SORRY EXCUSES FOR "GLORY DAYS."
OH, LIKE YOU'VE DONE ANY--
BETTER?
WELL, I WASN'T GONNA BRAG...
BUT THOSE STORIES WERE SO PATHETIC, I FEEL I HAVE TO SHARE MINE JUST TO BUOY THE ROOM.

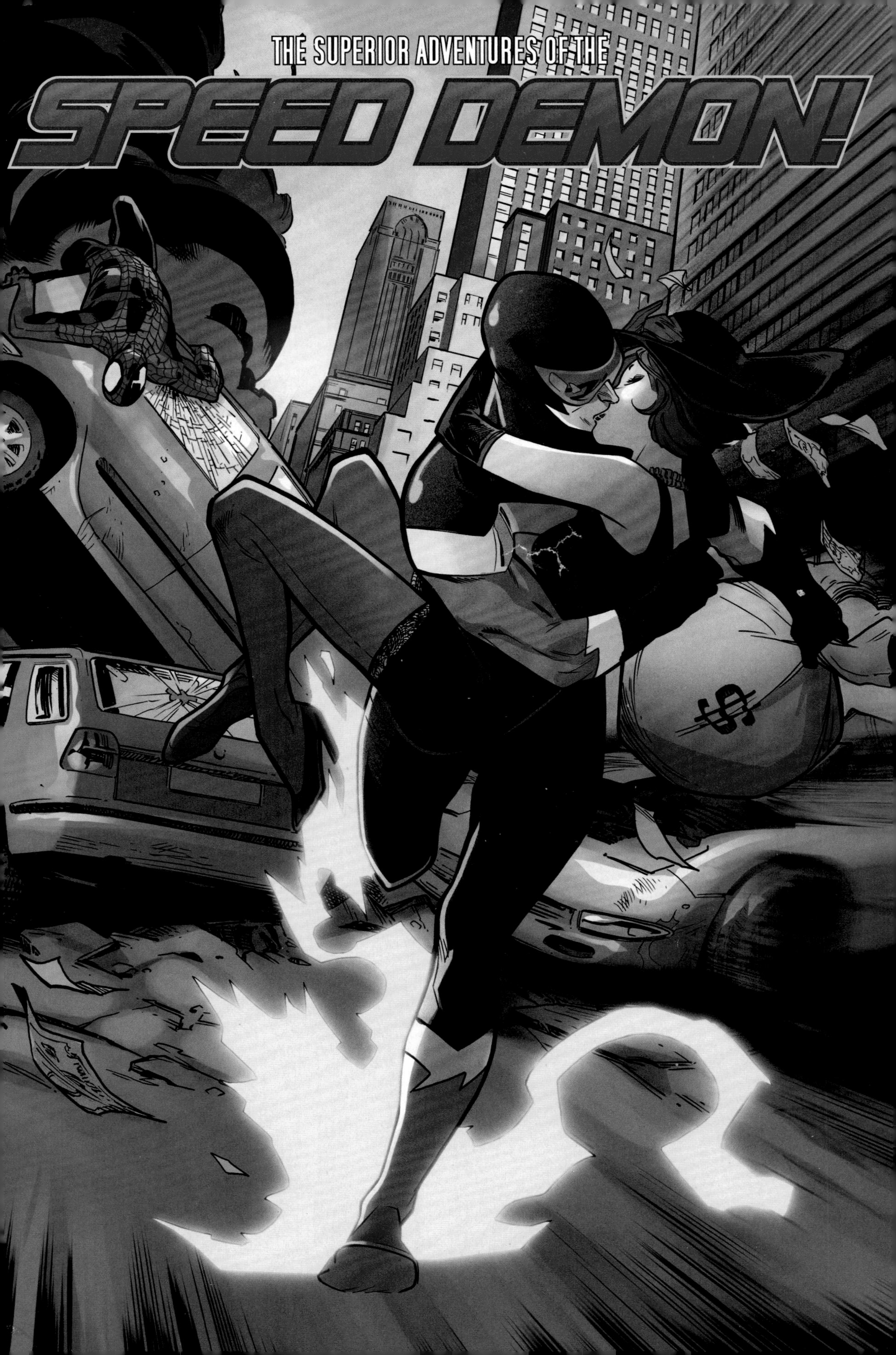
THE SUPERIOR ADVENTURES OF THE
SPEED DEMON!

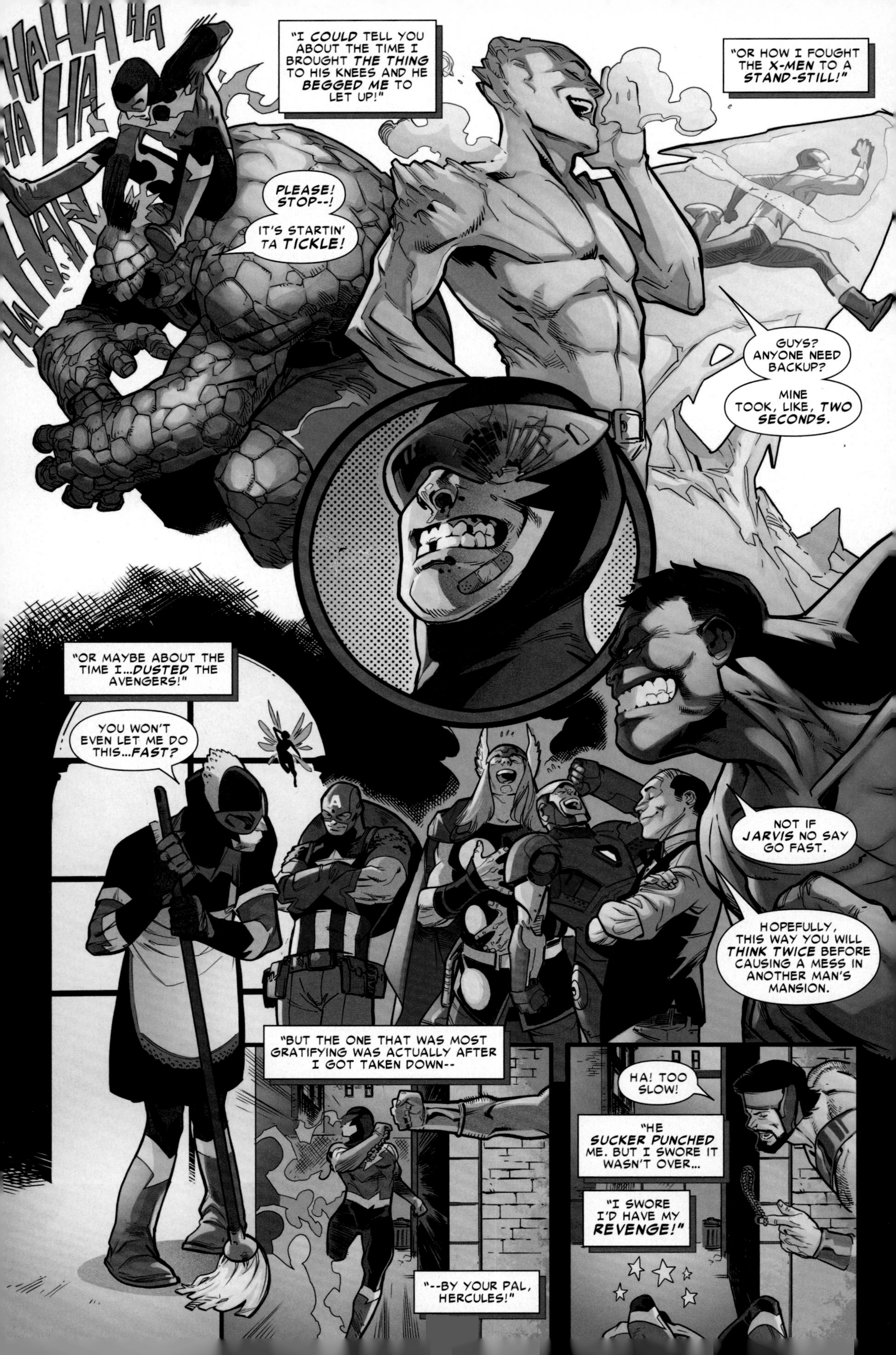

HA HA HA HA HA HA HA HA HA
"I COULD TELL YOU ABOUT THE TIME I BROUGHT THE THING TO HIS KNEES AND HE BEGGED ME TO LET UP!"
PLEASE! STOP--!
IT'S STARTIN' TA TICKLE!
"OR HOW I FOUGHT THE X-MEN TO A STAND-STILL!"
GUYS? ANYONE NEED BACKUP?
MINE TOOK, LIKE, TWO SECONDS.
"OR MAYBE ABOUT THE TIME I...DUSTED THE AVENGERS!"
YOU WON'T EVEN LET ME DO THIS...FAST?
NOT IF JARVIS NO SAY GO FAST.
HOPEFULLY, THIS WAY YOU WILL THINK TWICE BEFORE CAUSING A MESS IN ANOTHER MAN'S MANSION.
"BUT THE ONE THAT WAS MOST GRATIFYING WAS ACTUALLY AFTER I GOT TAKEN DOWN--
"--BY YOUR PAL, HERCULES!"
HA! TOO SLOW!
"HE SUCKER PUNCHED ME. BUT I SWORE IT WASN'T OVER...
"I SWORE I'D HAVE MY REVENGE!"

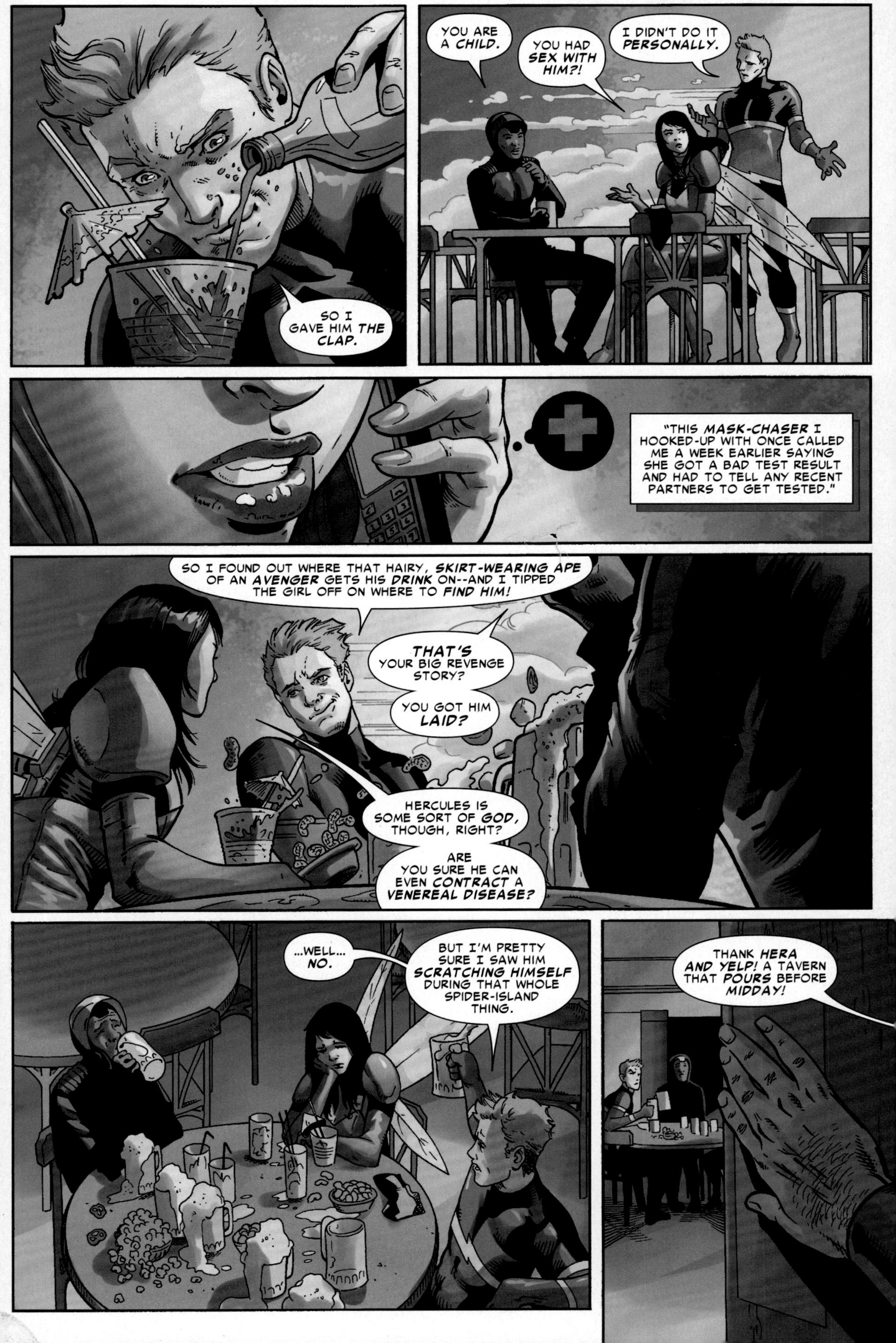
SO I GAVE HIM THE CLAP.
YOU ARE A CHILD.
YOU HAD SEX WITH HIM?!
I DIDN'T DO IT PERSONALLY.
"THIS MASK-CHASER I HOOKED-UP WITH ONCE CALLED ME A WEEK EARLIER SAYING SHE GOT A BAD TEST RESULT AND HAD TO TELL ANY RECENT PARTNERS TO GET TESTED."
SO I FOUND OUT WHERE THAT HAIRY, SKIRT-WEARING APE OF AN AVENGER GETS HIS DRINK ON--AND I TIPPED THE GIRL OFF ON WHERE TO FIND HIM!
THAT'S YOUR BIG REVENGE STORY?
YOU GOT HIM LAID?
HERCULES IS SOME SORT OF GOD, THOUGH, RIGHT?
ARE YOU SURE HE CAN EVEN CONTRACT A VENEREAL DISEASE?
...WELL... NO.
BUT I'M PRETTY SURE I SAW HIM SCRATCHING HIMSELF DURING THAT WHOLE SPIDER-ISLAND THING.
THANK HERA AND YELP! A TAVERN THAT POURS BEFORE MIDDAY!

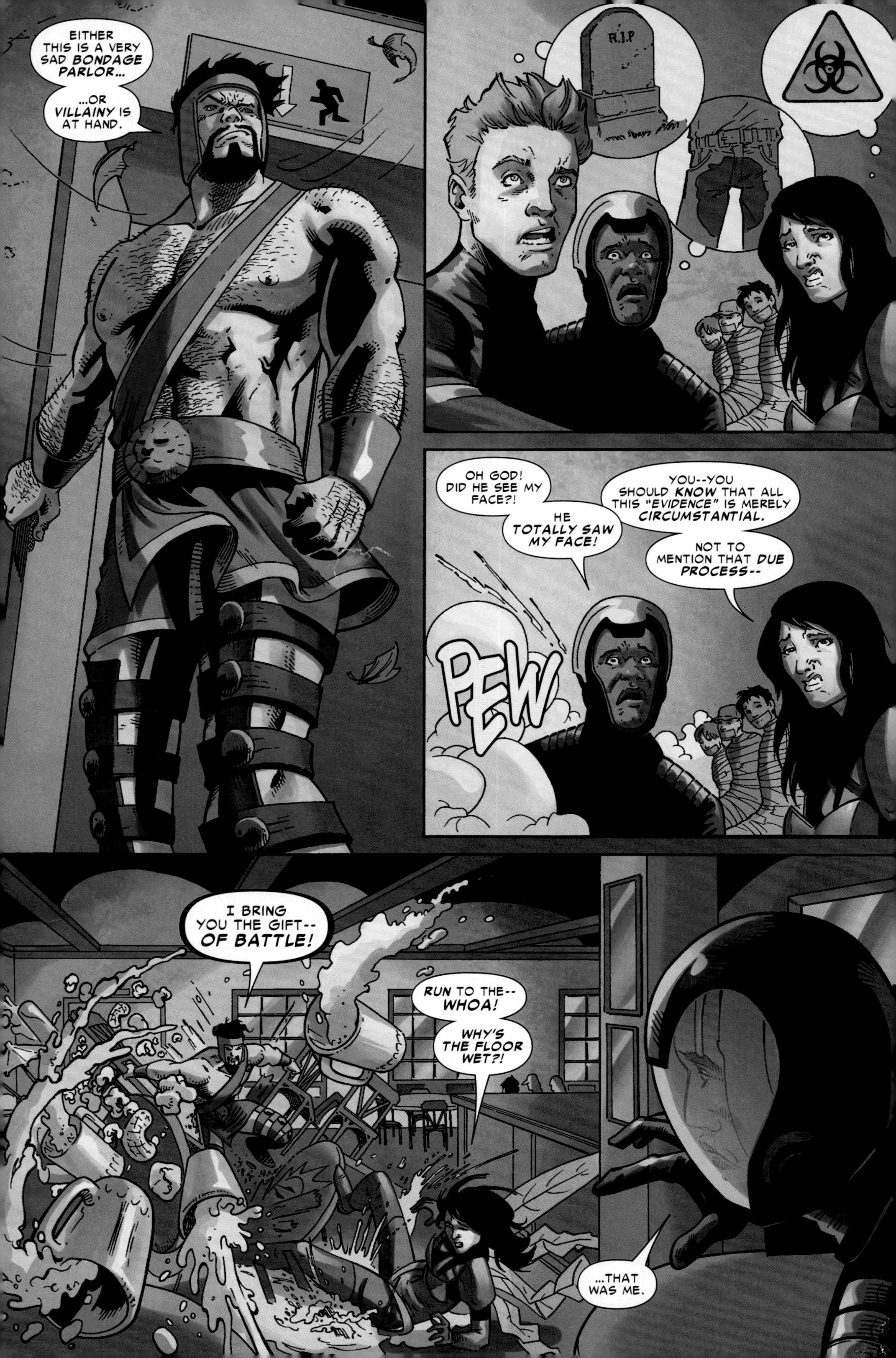
EITHER THIS IS A VERY SAD BONDAGE PARLOR...
...OR VILLAINY IS AT HAND.
R.I.P
OH GOD! DID HE SEE MY FACE?!
HE TOTALLY SAW MY FACE!
YOU--YOU SHOULD KNOW THAT ALL THIS "EVIDENCE" IS MERELY CIRCUMSTANTIAL.
NOT TO MENTION THAT DUE PROCESS--
PEW
I BRING YOU THE GIFT-- OF BATTLE!
RUN TO THE-- WHOA!
WHY'S THE FLOOR WET?!
...THAT WAS ME.

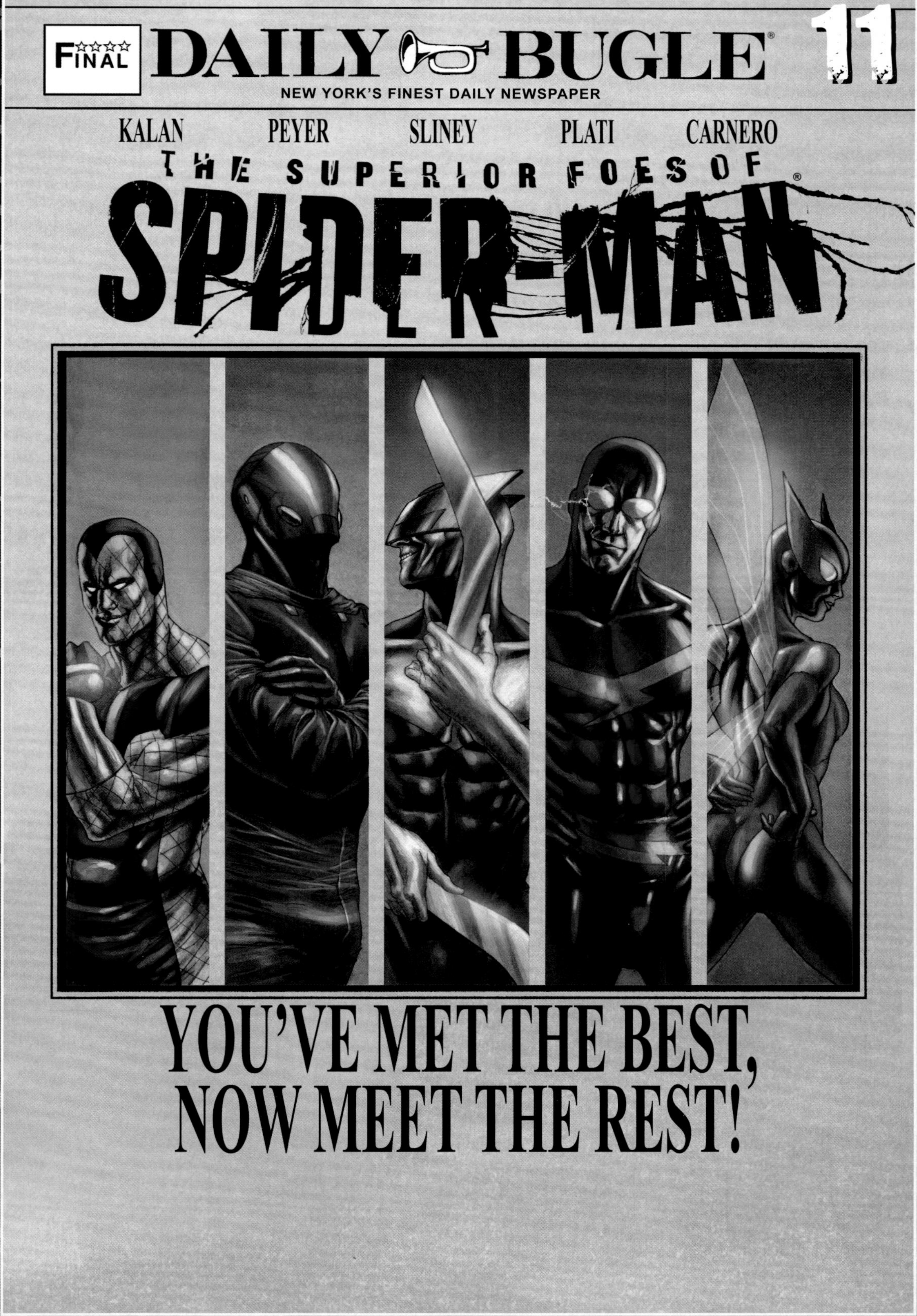

FINAL
DAILY BUGLE
NEW YORK'S FINEST DAILY NEWSPAPER
11
KALAN PEYER SLINEY PLATI CARNERO
THE SUPERIOR FOES OF
SPIDER-MAN
YOU'VE MET THE BEST, NOW MEET THE REST!

DON'T FEEL BAD,

YOU CAN BE GOOD!

YES!!! WE HAVE COFFEE & DONUTS!!!

THERE IS POWER IN NUMBERS.

JOIN SUPER VILLAINS ANONYMOUS TODAY!

Fridays in the St. Jude's Basement.

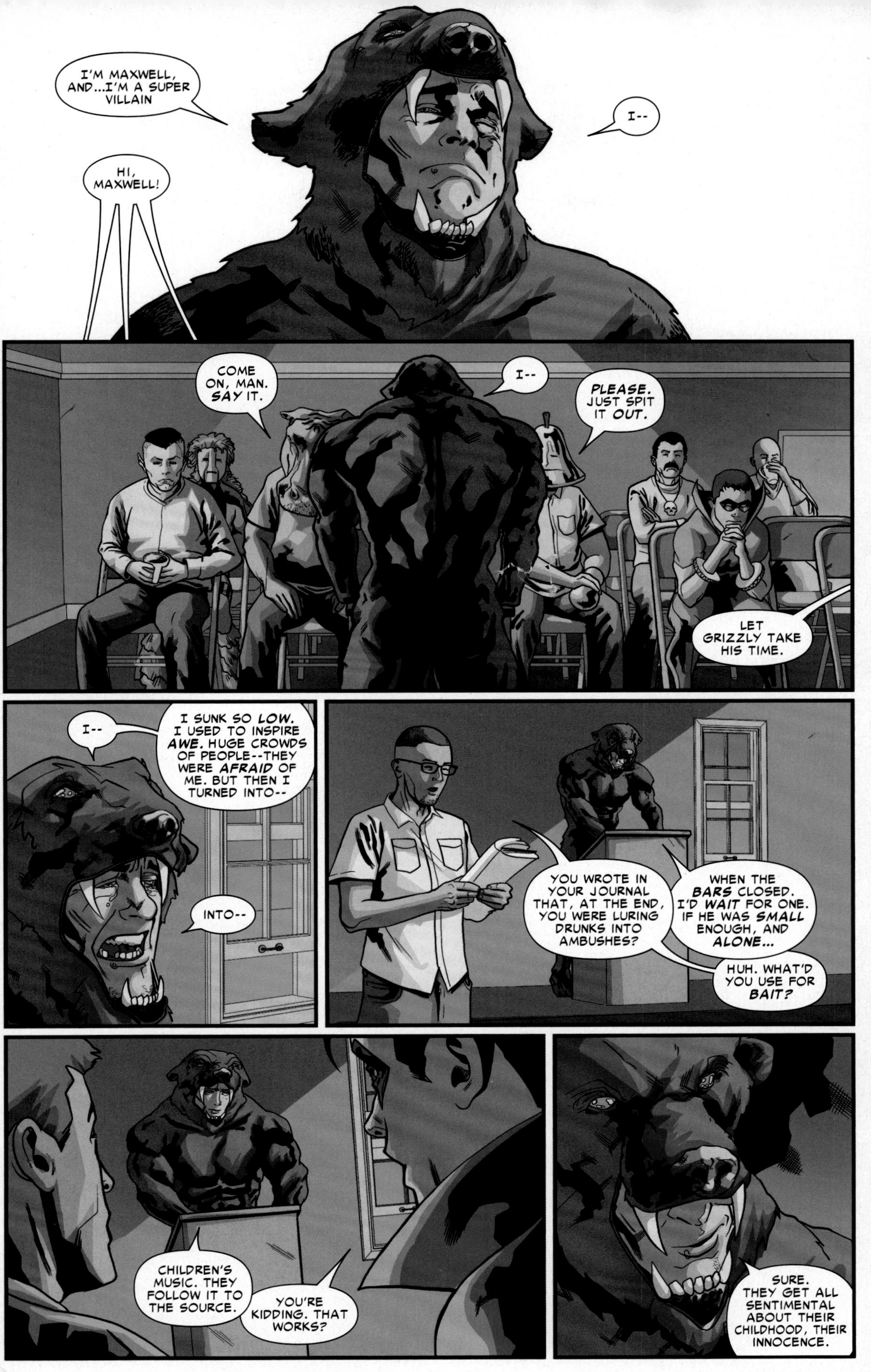
I'M MAXWELL, AND...I'M A SUPER VILLAIN
HI, MAXWELL!
I--
COME ON, MAN. SAY IT.
I--
PLEASE. JUST SPIT IT OUT.
LET GRIZZLY TAKE HIS TIME.
I--
I SUNK SO LOW. I USED TO INSPIRE AWE. HUGE CROWDS OF PEOPLE--THEY WERE AFRAID OF ME. BUT THEN I TURNED INTO--
INTO--
YOU WROTE IN YOUR JOURNAL THAT, AT THE END, YOU WERE LURING DRUNKS INTO AMBUSHES?
WHEN THE BARS CLOSED. I'D WAIT FOR ONE. IF HE WAS SMALL ENOUGH, AND ALONE...
HUH. WHAT'D YOU USE FOR BAIT?
CHILDREN'S MUSIC. THEY FOLLOW IT TO THE SOURCE.
YOU'RE KIDDING. THAT WORKS?
SURE. THEY GET ALL SENTIMENTAL ABOUT THEIR CHILDHOOD, THEIR INNOCENCE.

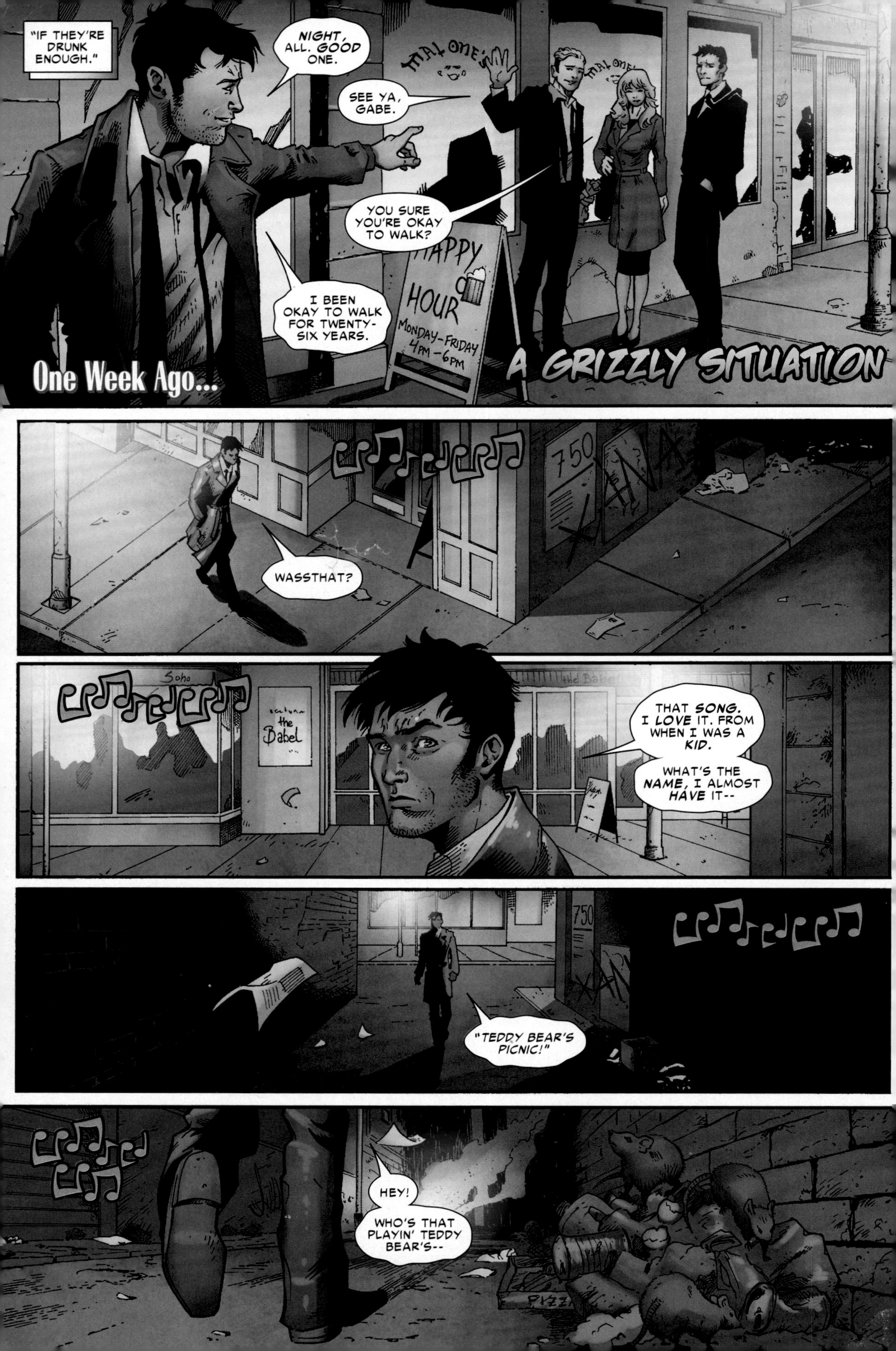
"IF THEY'RE DRUNK ENOUGH."
NIGHT, ALL. GOOD ONE.
SEE YA, GABE.
YOU SURE YOU'RE OKAY TO WALK?
I BEEN OKAY TO WALK FOR TWENTY-SIX YEARS.
MALONE'S
HAPPY HOUR
MONDAY-FRIDAY 4PM-6PM
One Week Ago...
A GRIZZLY SITUATION
WASSTHAT?
750
Soho
the Babel
THAT SONG. I LOVE IT. FROM WHEN I WAS A KID.
WHAT'S THE NAME, I ALMOST HAVE IT--
750
"TEDDY BEAR'S PICNIC!"
HEY!
WHO'S THAT PLAYIN' TEDDY BEAR'S--

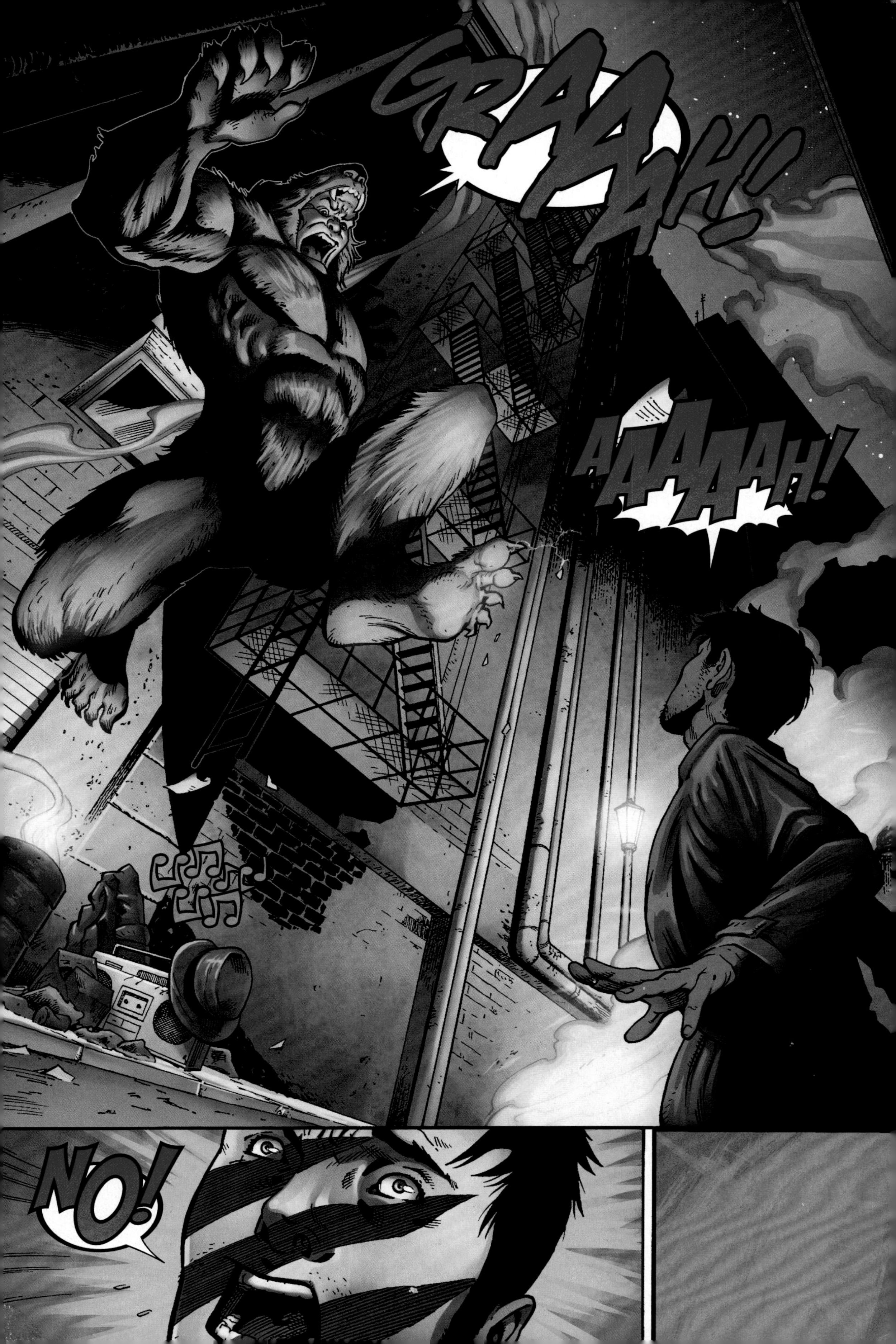
GRAAAAH!!
AAAAAAH!
NO!

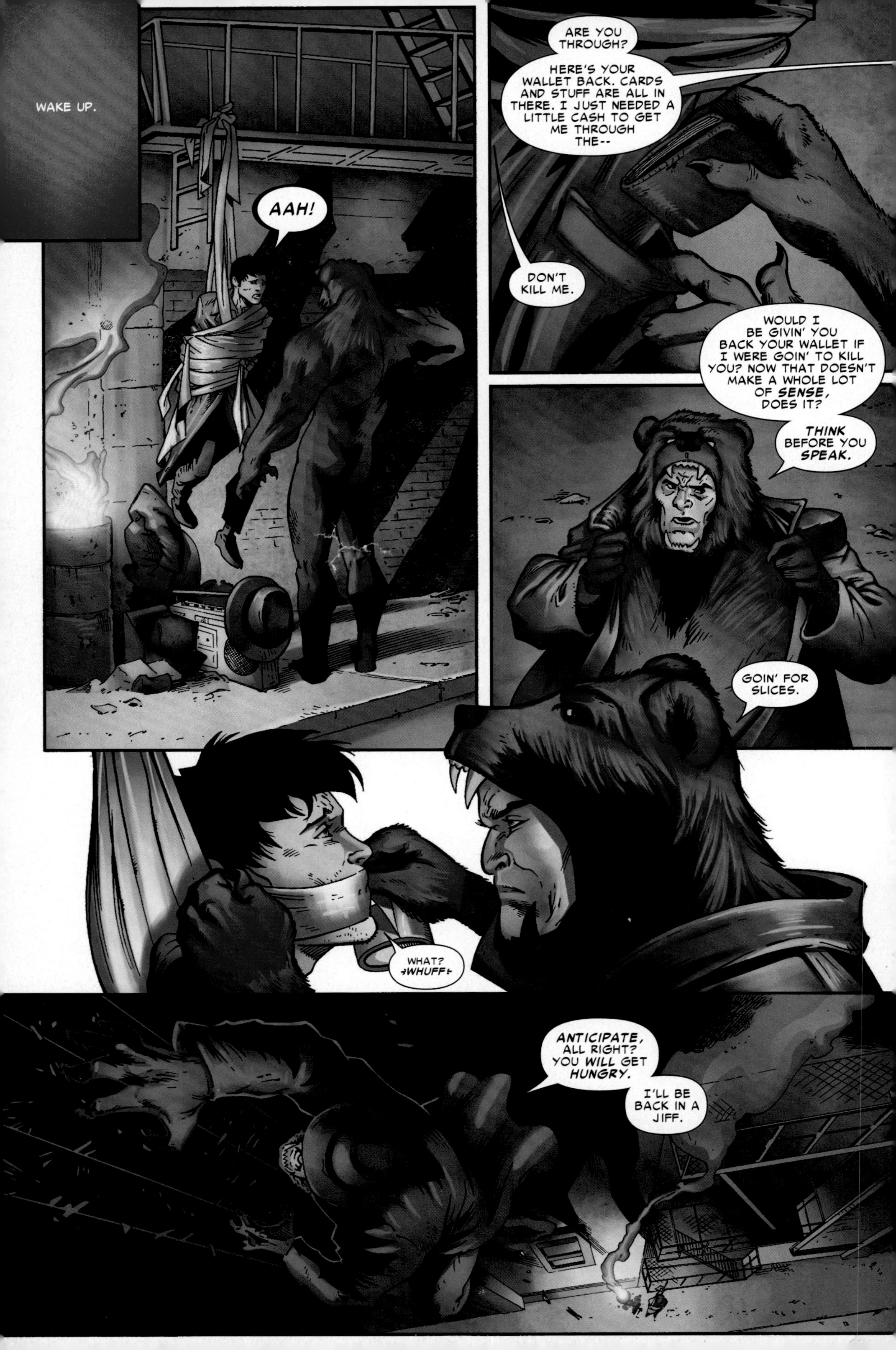
WAKE UP.
AAH!
ARE YOU THROUGH?
HERE'S YOUR WALLET BACK. CARDS AND STUFF ARE ALL IN THERE. I JUST NEEDED A LITTLE CASH TO GET ME THROUGH THE--
DON'T KILL ME.
WOULD I BE GIVIN' YOU BACK YOUR WALLET IF I WERE GOIN' TO KILL YOU? NOW THAT DOESN'T MAKE A WHOLE LOT OF SENSE, DOES IT?
THINK BEFORE YOU SPEAK.
GOIN' FOR SLICES.
WHAT? ~WHUFF~
ANTICIPATE, ALL RIGHT? YOU WILL GET HUNGRY.
I'LL BE BACK IN A JIFF.

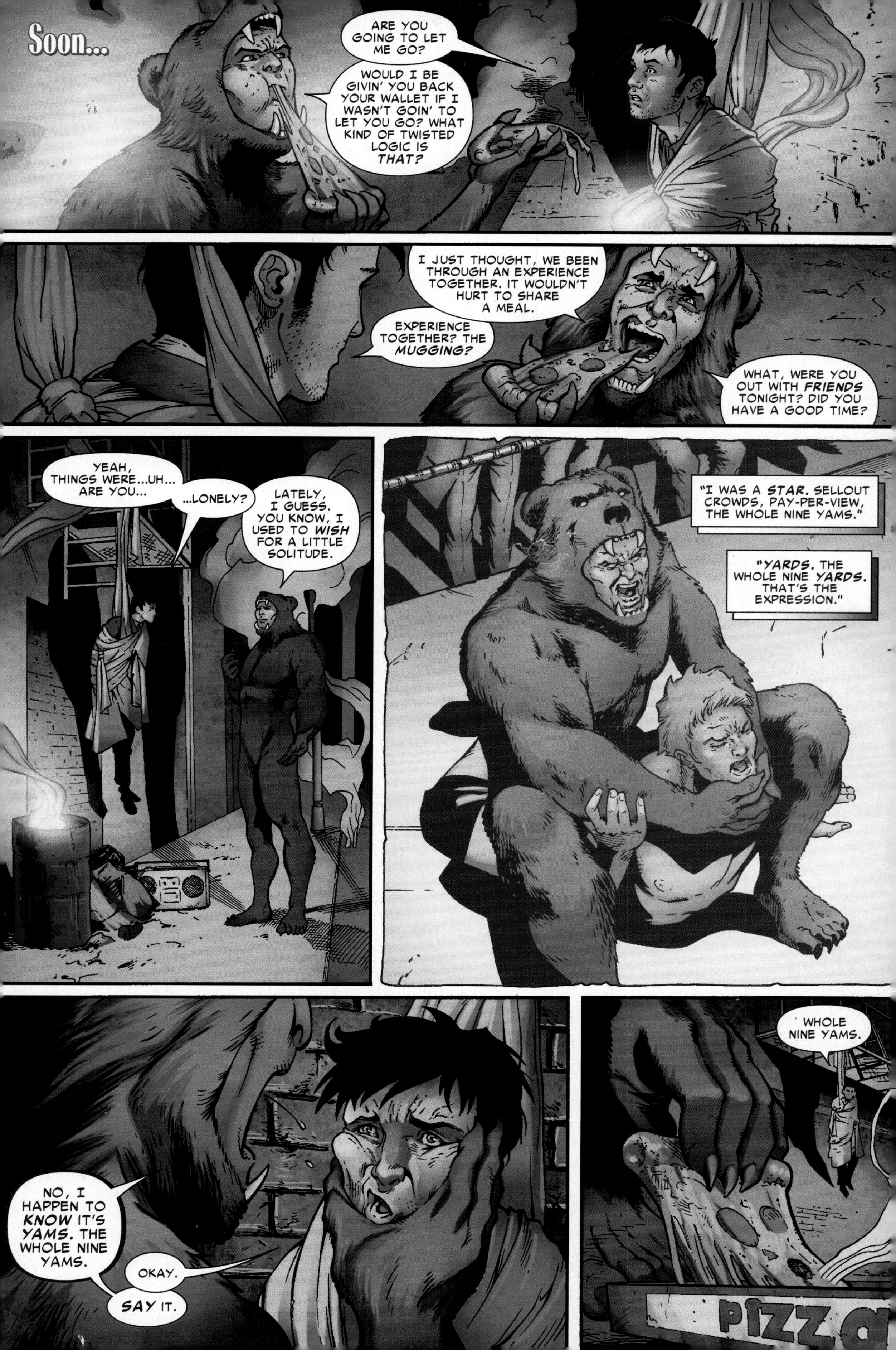
Soon...
ARE YOU GOING TO LET ME GO?
WOULD I BE GIVIN' YOU BACK YOUR WALLET IF I WASN'T GOIN' TO LET YOU GO? WHAT KIND OF TWISTED LOGIC IS *THAT?*
I JUST THOUGHT, WE BEEN THROUGH AN EXPERIENCE TOGETHER. IT WOULDN'T HURT TO SHARE A MEAL.
EXPERIENCE TOGETHER? THE *MUGGING?*
WHAT, WERE YOU OUT WITH *FRIENDS* TONIGHT? DID YOU HAVE A GOOD TIME?
YEAH, THINGS WERE...UH... ARE YOU...
...LONELY?
LATELY, I GUESS. YOU KNOW, I USED TO *WISH* FOR A LITTLE SOLITUDE.
"I WAS A *STAR.* SELLOUT CROWDS, PAY-PER-VIEW, THE WHOLE NINE YAMS."
"*YARDS.* THE WHOLE NINE *YARDS.* THAT'S THE EXPRESSION."
NO, I HAPPEN TO *KNOW* IT'S *YAMS.* THE WHOLE NINE YAMS.
OKAY.
SAY IT.
WHOLE NINE YAMS.
PIZZ

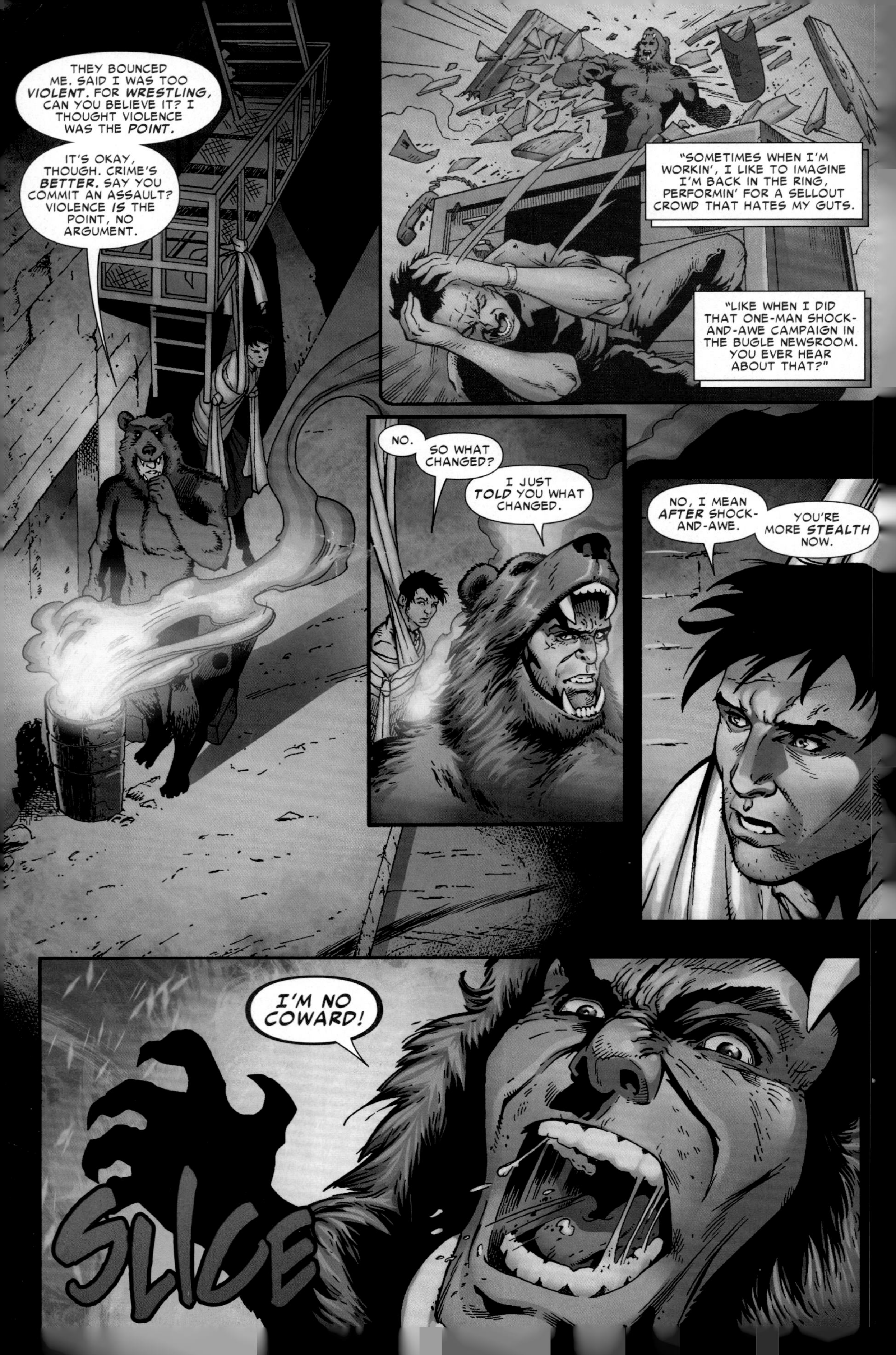
THEY BOUNCED ME. SAID I WAS TOO VIOLENT. FOR WRESTLING, CAN YOU BELIEVE IT? I THOUGHT VIOLENCE WAS THE POINT.
IT'S OKAY, THOUGH. CRIME'S BETTER. SAY YOU COMMIT AN ASSAULT? VIOLENCE IS THE POINT, NO ARGUMENT.
"SOMETIMES WHEN I'M WORKIN', I LIKE TO IMAGINE I'M BACK IN THE RING, PERFORMIN' FOR A SELLOUT CROWD THAT HATES MY GUTS.
"LIKE WHEN I DID THAT ONE-MAN SHOCK-AND-AWE CAMPAIGN IN THE BUGLE NEWSROOM. YOU EVER HEAR ABOUT THAT?"
NO.
SO WHAT CHANGED?
I JUST TOLD YOU WHAT CHANGED.
NO, I MEAN AFTER SHOCK-AND-AWE.
YOU'RE MORE STEALTH NOW.
I'M NO COWARD!
SLICE

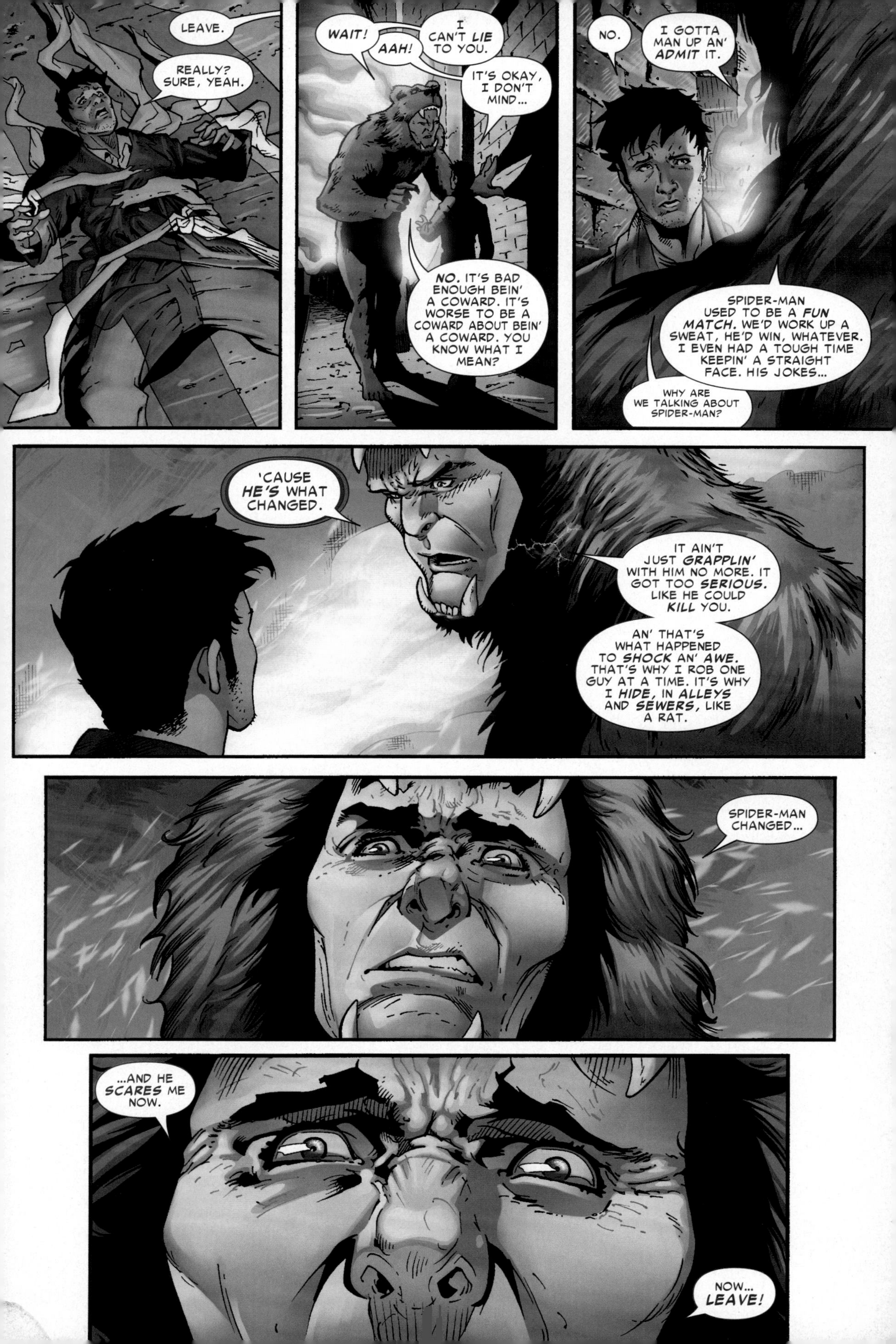
LEAVE.
REALLY? SURE, YEAH.
WAIT!
I CAN'T LIE TO YOU.
AAH!
IT'S OKAY, I DON'T MIND...
NO. IT'S BAD ENOUGH BEIN' A COWARD. IT'S WORSE TO BE A COWARD ABOUT BEIN' A COWARD. YOU KNOW WHAT I MEAN?
NO.
I GOTTA MAN UP AN' ADMIT IT.
SPIDER-MAN USED TO BE A FUN MATCH. WE'D WORK UP A SWEAT, HE'D WIN, WHATEVER. I EVEN HAD A TOUGH TIME KEEPIN' A STRAIGHT FACE. HIS JOKES...
WHY ARE WE TALKING ABOUT SPIDER-MAN?
'CAUSE HE'S WHAT CHANGED.
IT AIN'T JUST GRAPPLIN' WITH HIM NO MORE. IT GOT TOO SERIOUS. LIKE HE COULD KILL YOU.
AN' THAT'S WHAT HAPPENED TO SHOCK AN' AWE. THAT'S WHY I ROB ONE GUY AT A TIME. IT'S WHY I HIDE, IN ALLEYS AND SEWERS, LIKE A RAT.
SPIDER-MAN CHANGED...
...AND HE SCARES ME NOW.
NOW... LEAVE!

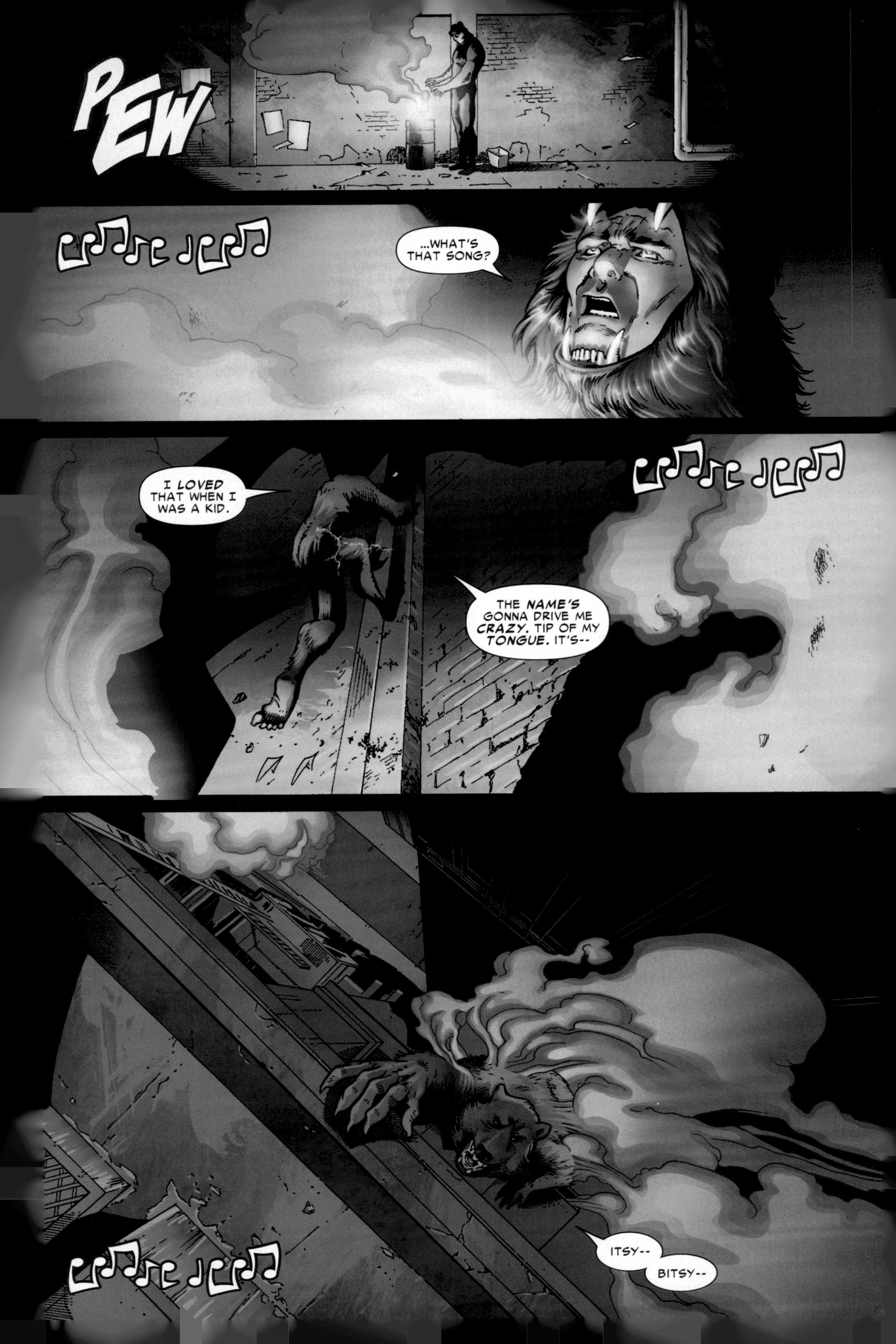
PEW
...WHAT'S THAT SONG?
I LOVED THAT WHEN I WAS A KID.
THE NAME'S GONNA DRIVE ME CRAZY. TIP OF MY TONGUE. IT'S--
ITSY--
BITSY--

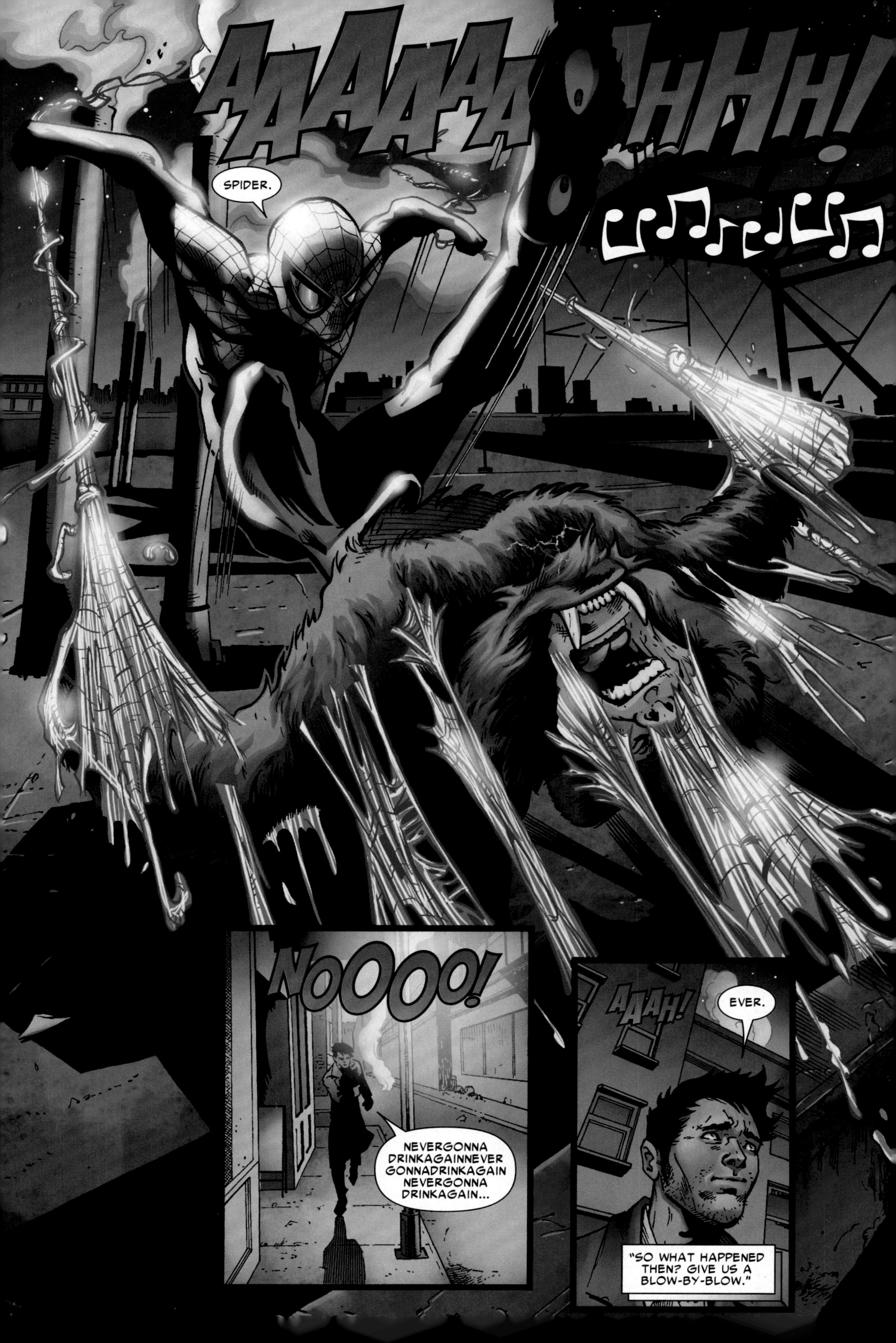
AAAAAAHHHH!
SPIDER.
NOOOO!
NEVERGONNA DRINKAGAINNEVER GONNADRINKAGAIN NEVERGONNA DRINKAGAIN...
AAAH!
EVER.
"SO WHAT HAPPENED THEN? GIVE US A BLOW-BY-BLOW."

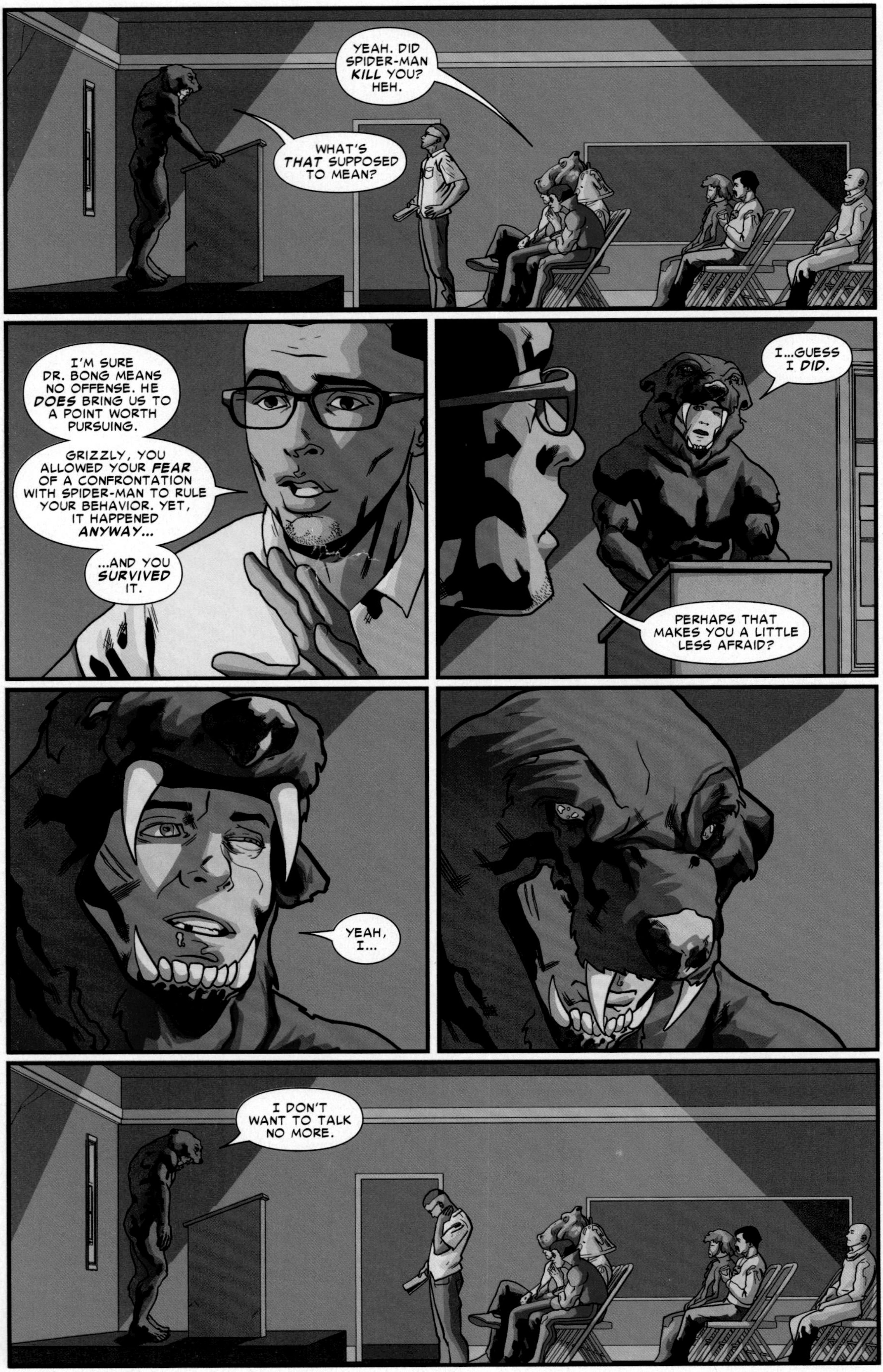
YEAH. DID SPIDER-MAN KILL YOU? HEH.
WHAT'S THAT SUPPOSED TO MEAN?
I'M SURE DR. BONG MEANS NO OFFENSE. HE DOES BRING US TO A POINT WORTH PURSUING.
GRIZZLY, YOU ALLOWED YOUR FEAR OF A CONFRONTATION WITH SPIDER-MAN TO RULE YOUR BEHAVIOR. YET, IT HAPPENED ANYWAY...
...AND YOU SURVIVED IT.
I...GUESS I DID.
PERHAPS THAT MAKES YOU A LITTLE LESS AFRAID?
YEAH, I...
I DON'T WANT TO TALK NO MORE.

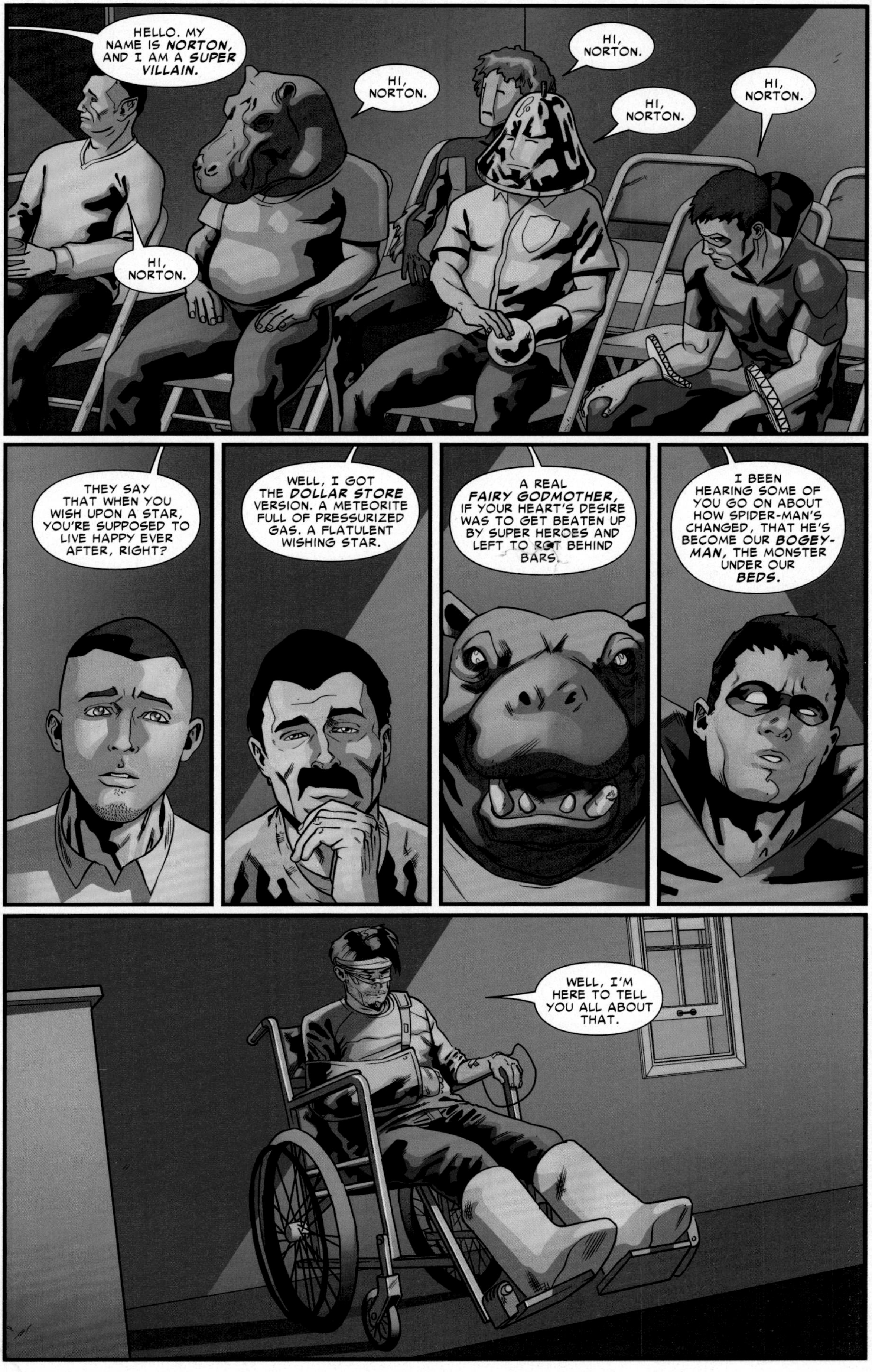
HELLO. MY NAME IS NORTON, AND I AM A SUPER VILLAIN.
HI, NORTON.
HI, NORTON.
HI, NORTON.
HI, NORTON.
HI, NORTON.
THEY SAY THAT WHEN YOU WISH UPON A STAR, YOU'RE SUPPOSED TO LIVE HAPPY EVER AFTER, RIGHT?
WELL, I GOT THE DOLLAR STORE VERSION. A METEORITE FULL OF PRESSURIZED GAS. A FLATULENT WISHING STAR.
A REAL FAIRY GODMOTHER, IF YOUR HEART'S DESIRE WAS TO GET BEATEN UP BY SUPER HEROES AND LEFT TO ROT BEHIND BARS.
I BEEN HEARING SOME OF YOU GO ON ABOUT HOW SPIDER-MAN'S CHANGED, THAT HE'S BECOME OUR BOGEYMAN, THE MONSTER UNDER OUR BEDS.
WELL, I'M HERE TO TELL YOU ALL ABOUT THAT.

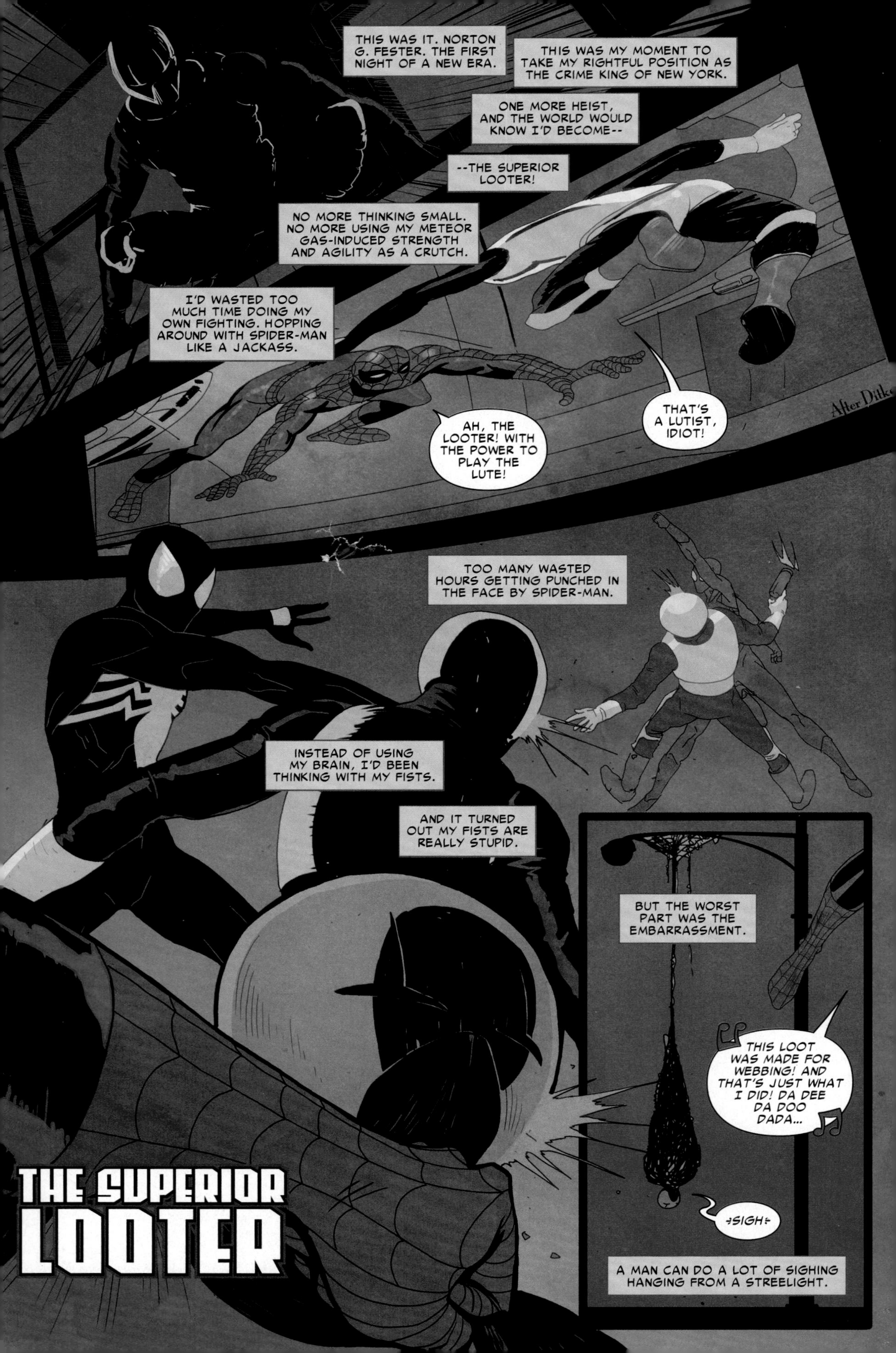
THIS WAS IT. NORTON G. FESTER. THE FIRST NIGHT OF A NEW ERA.
THIS WAS MY MOMENT TO TAKE MY RIGHTFUL POSITION AS THE CRIME KING OF NEW YORK.
ONE MORE HEIST, AND THE WORLD WOULD KNOW I'D BECOME--
--THE SUPERIOR LOOTER!
NO MORE THINKING SMALL. NO MORE USING MY METEOR GAS-INDUCED STRENGTH AND AGILITY AS A CRUTCH.
I'D WASTED TOO MUCH TIME DOING MY OWN FIGHTING. HOPPING AROUND WITH SPIDER-MAN LIKE A JACKASS.
AH, THE LOOTER! WITH THE POWER TO PLAY THE LUTE!
THAT'S A LUTIST, IDIOT!
After Ditko
TOO MANY WASTED HOURS GETTING PUNCHED IN THE FACE BY SPIDER-MAN.
INSTEAD OF USING MY BRAIN, I'D BEEN THINKING WITH MY FISTS.
AND IT TURNED OUT MY FISTS ARE REALLY STUPID.
BUT THE WORST PART WAS THE EMBARRASSMENT.
THIS LOOT WAS MADE FOR WEBBING! AND THAT'S JUST WHAT I DID! DA DEE DA DOO DADA...
÷SIGH÷
A MAN CAN DO A LOT OF SIGHING HANGING FROM A STREELIGHT.
THE SUPERIOR LOOTER

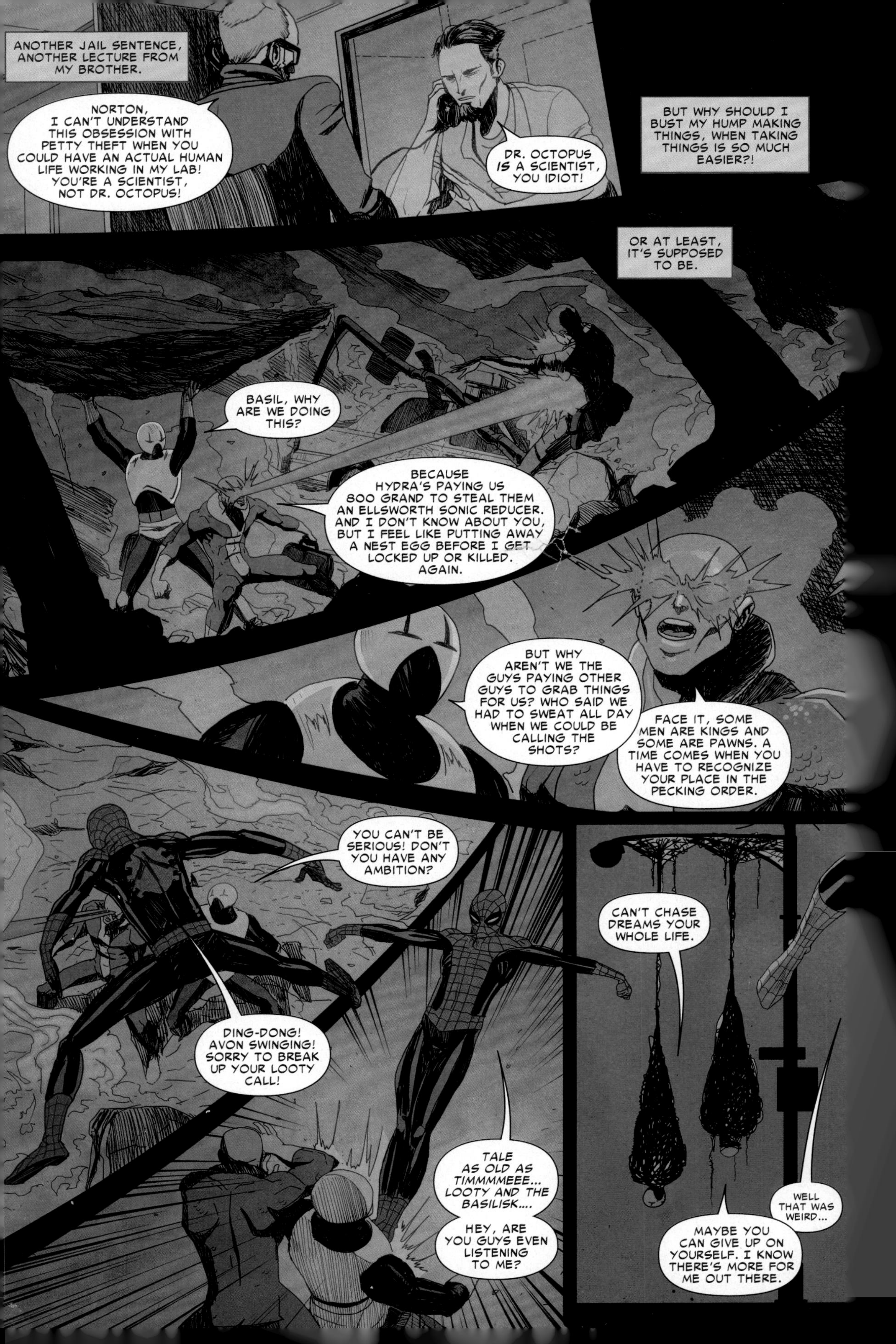
ANOTHER JAIL SENTENCE, ANOTHER LECTURE FROM MY BROTHER.
NORTON, I CAN'T UNDERSTAND THIS OBSESSION WITH PETTY THEFT WHEN YOU COULD HAVE AN ACTUAL HUMAN LIFE WORKING IN MY LAB! YOU'RE A SCIENTIST, NOT DR. OCTOPUS!
DR. OCTOPUS IS A SCIENTIST, YOU IDIOT!
BUT WHY SHOULD I BUST MY HUMP MAKING THINGS, WHEN TAKING THINGS IS SO MUCH EASIER?!
OR AT LEAST, IT'S SUPPOSED TO BE.
BASIL, WHY ARE WE DOING THIS?
BECAUSE HYDRA'S PAYING US 800 GRAND TO STEAL THEM AN ELLSWORTH SONIC REDUCER. AND I DON'T KNOW ABOUT YOU, BUT I FEEL LIKE PUTTING AWAY A NEST EGG BEFORE I GET LOCKED UP OR KILLED. AGAIN.
BUT WHY AREN'T WE THE GUYS PAYING OTHER GUYS TO GRAB THINGS FOR US? WHO SAID WE HAD TO SWEAT ALL DAY WHEN WE COULD BE CALLING THE SHOTS?
FACE IT, SOME MEN ARE KINGS AND SOME ARE PAWNS. A TIME COMES WHEN YOU HAVE TO RECOGNIZE YOUR PLACE IN THE PECKING ORDER.
YOU CAN'T BE SERIOUS! DON'T YOU HAVE ANY AMBITION?
DING-DONG! AVON SWINGING! SORRY TO BREAK UP YOUR LOOTY CALL!
TALE AS OLD AS TIMMMMEEE... LOOTY AND THE BASILISK....
HEY, ARE YOU GUYS EVEN LISTENING TO ME?
CAN'T CHASE DREAMS YOUR WHOLE LIFE.
MAYBE YOU CAN GIVE UP ON YOURSELF. I KNOW THERE'S MORE FOR ME OUT THERE.
WELL THAT WAS WEIRD...

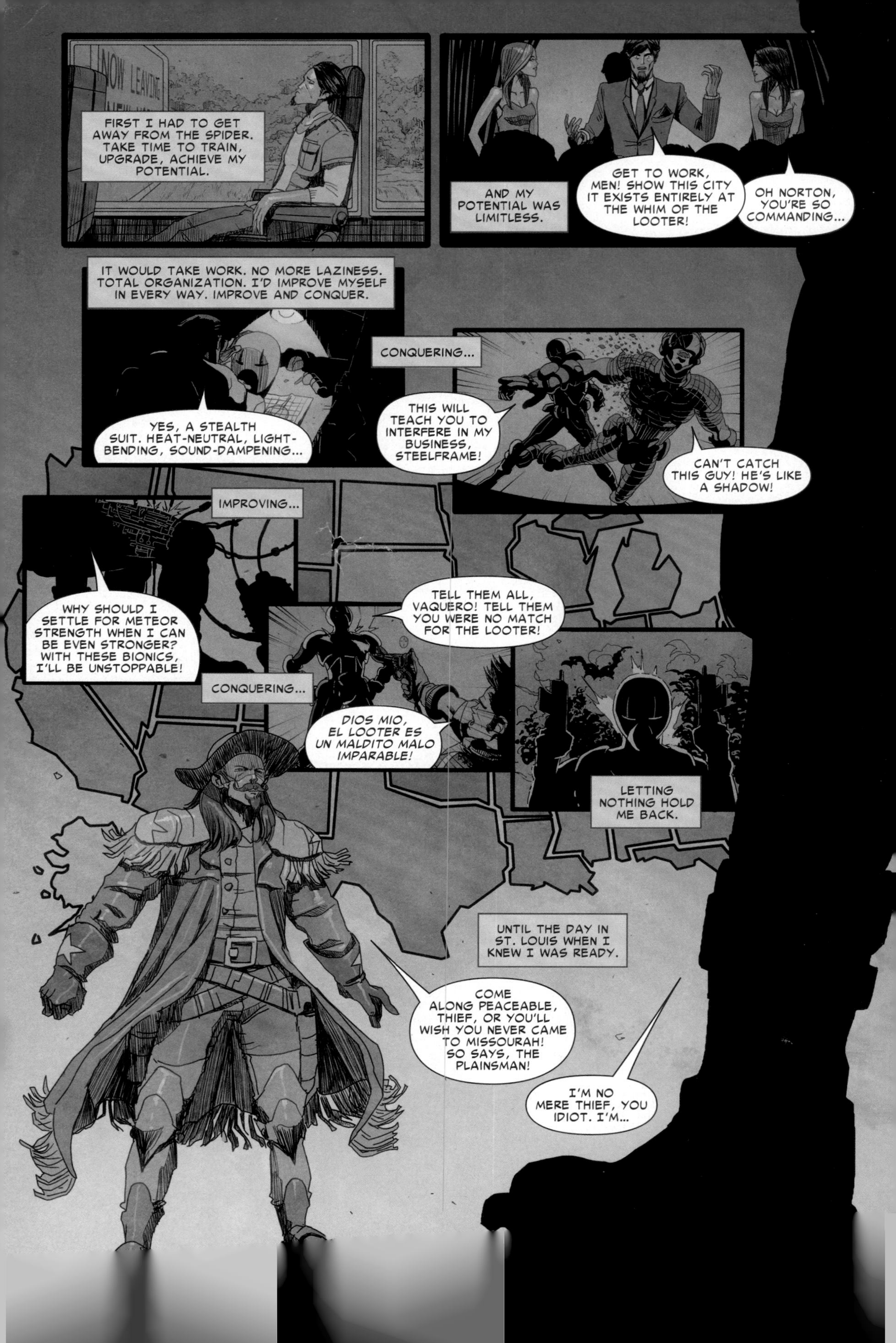
NOW LEAVING
FIRST I HAD TO GET AWAY FROM THE SPIDER. TAKE TIME TO TRAIN, UPGRADE, ACHIEVE MY POTENTIAL.
AND MY POTENTIAL WAS LIMITLESS.
GET TO WORK, MEN! SHOW THIS CITY IT EXISTS ENTIRELY AT THE WHIM OF THE LOOTER!
OH NORTON, YOU'RE SO COMMANDING...
IT WOULD TAKE WORK. NO MORE LAZINESS. TOTAL ORGANIZATION. I'D IMPROVE MYSELF IN EVERY WAY. IMPROVE AND CONQUER.
YES, A STEALTH SUIT. HEAT-NEUTRAL, LIGHT-BENDING, SOUND-DAMPENING...
CONQUERING...
THIS WILL TEACH YOU TO INTERFERE IN MY BUSINESS, STEELFRAME!
CAN'T CATCH THIS GUY! HE'S LIKE A SHADOW!
IMPROVING...
WHY SHOULD I SETTLE FOR METEOR STRENGTH WHEN I CAN BE EVEN STRONGER? WITH THESE BIONICS, I'LL BE UNSTOPPABLE!
CONQUERING...
TELL THEM ALL, VAQUERO! TELL THEM YOU WERE NO MATCH FOR THE LOOTER!
DIOS MIO, EL LOOTER ES UN MALDITO MALO IMPARABLE!
LETTING NOTHING HOLD ME BACK.
UNTIL THE DAY IN ST. LOUIS WHEN I KNEW I WAS READY.
COME ALONG PEACEABLE, THIEF, OR YOU'LL WISH YOU NEVER CAME TO MISSOURAH! SO SAYS, THE PLAINSMAN!
I'M NO MERE THIEF, YOU IDIOT. I'M...

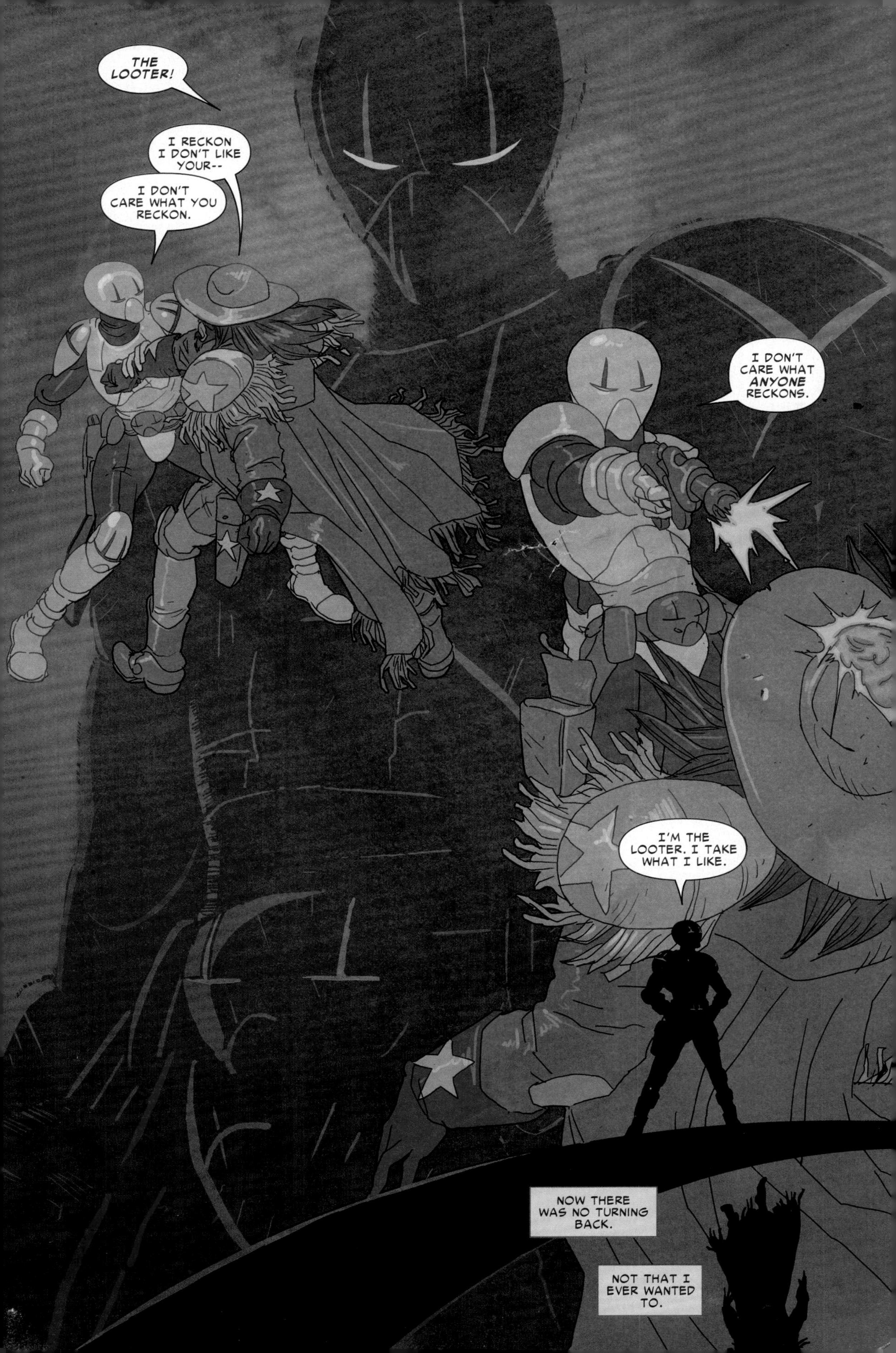
THE LOOTER!
I RECKON I DON'T LIKE YOUR--
I DON'T CARE WHAT YOU RECKON.
I DON'T CARE WHAT *ANYONE* RECKONS.
I'M THE LOOTER. I TAKE WHAT I LIKE.
NOW THERE WAS NO TURNING BACK.
NOT THAT I EVER WANTED TO.

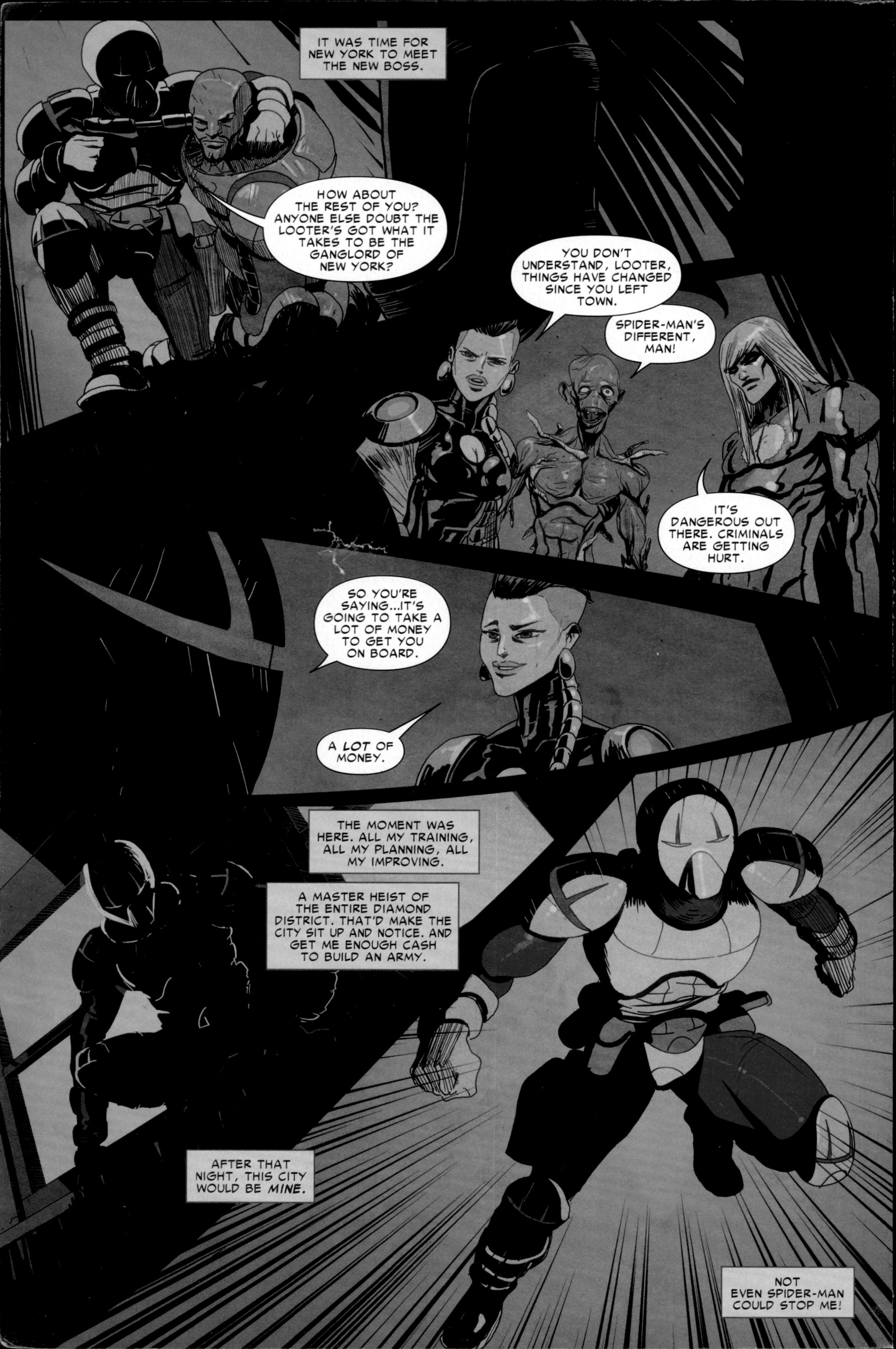
IT WAS TIME FOR NEW YORK TO MEET THE NEW BOSS.
HOW ABOUT THE REST OF YOU? ANYONE ELSE DOUBT THE LOOTER'S GOT WHAT IT TAKES TO BE THE GANGLORD OF NEW YORK?
YOU DON'T UNDERSTAND, LOOTER, THINGS HAVE CHANGED SINCE YOU LEFT TOWN.
SPIDER-MAN'S DIFFERENT, MAN!
IT'S DANGEROUS OUT THERE. CRIMINALS ARE GETTING HURT.
SO YOU'RE SAYING...IT'S GOING TO TAKE A LOT OF MONEY TO GET YOU ON BOARD.
A *LOT* OF MONEY.
THE MOMENT WAS HERE. ALL MY TRAINING, ALL MY PLANNING, ALL MY IMPROVING.
A MASTER HEIST OF THE ENTIRE DIAMOND DISTRICT. THAT'D MAKE THE CITY SIT UP AND NOTICE. AND GET ME ENOUGH CASH TO BUILD AN ARMY.
AFTER THAT NIGHT, THIS CITY WOULD BE *MINE*.
NOT EVEN SPIDER-MAN COULD STOP ME!

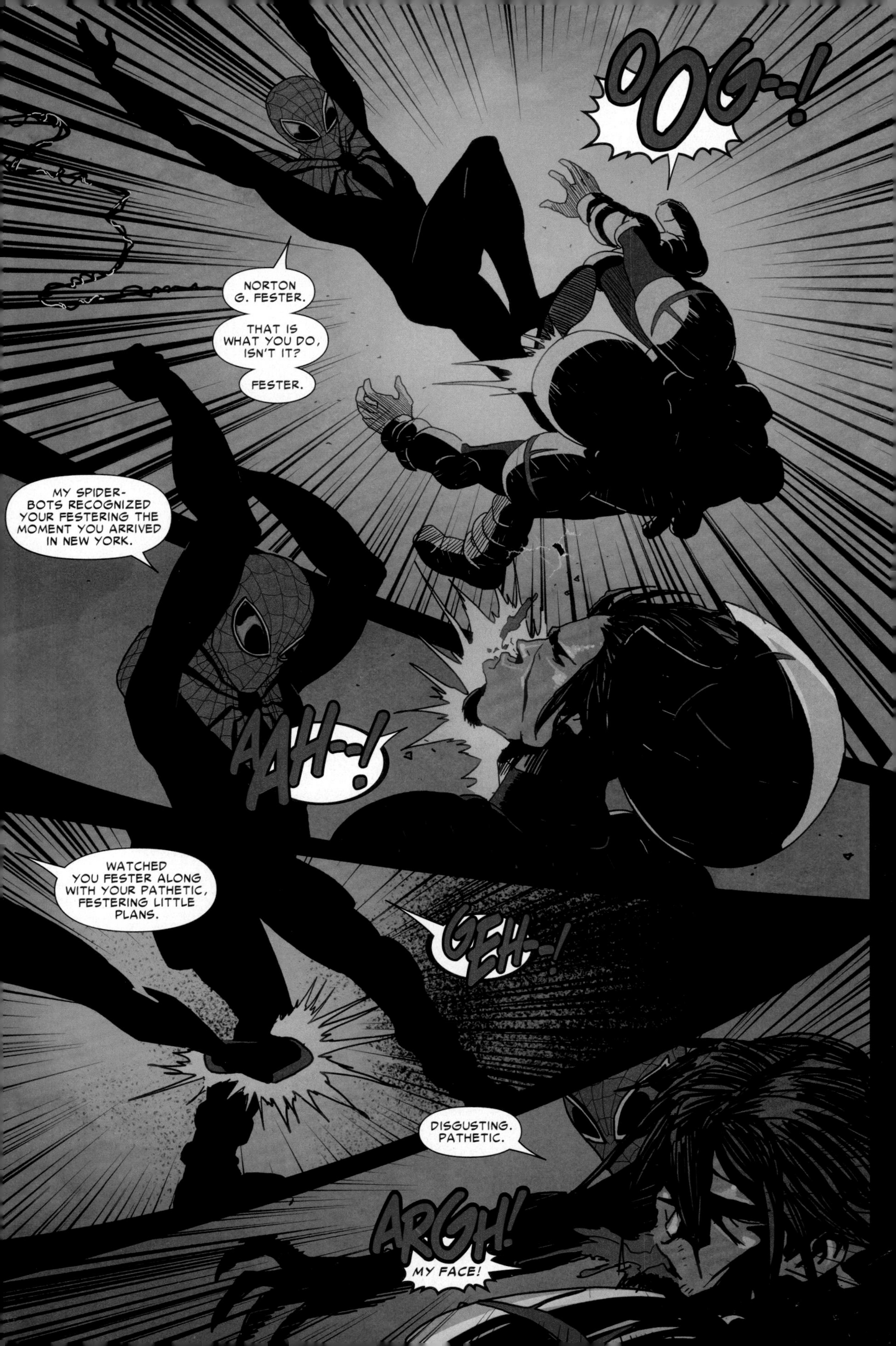

OOG--!
NORTON G. FESTER.
THAT IS WHAT YOU DO, ISN'T IT?
FESTER.
MY SPIDER-BOTS RECOGNIZED YOUR FESTERING THE MOMENT YOU ARRIVED IN NEW YORK.
AAH--!
WATCHED YOU FESTER ALONG WITH YOUR PATHETIC, FESTERING LITTLE PLANS.
GEH--!
DISGUSTING. PATHETIC.
ARGH!
MY FACE!

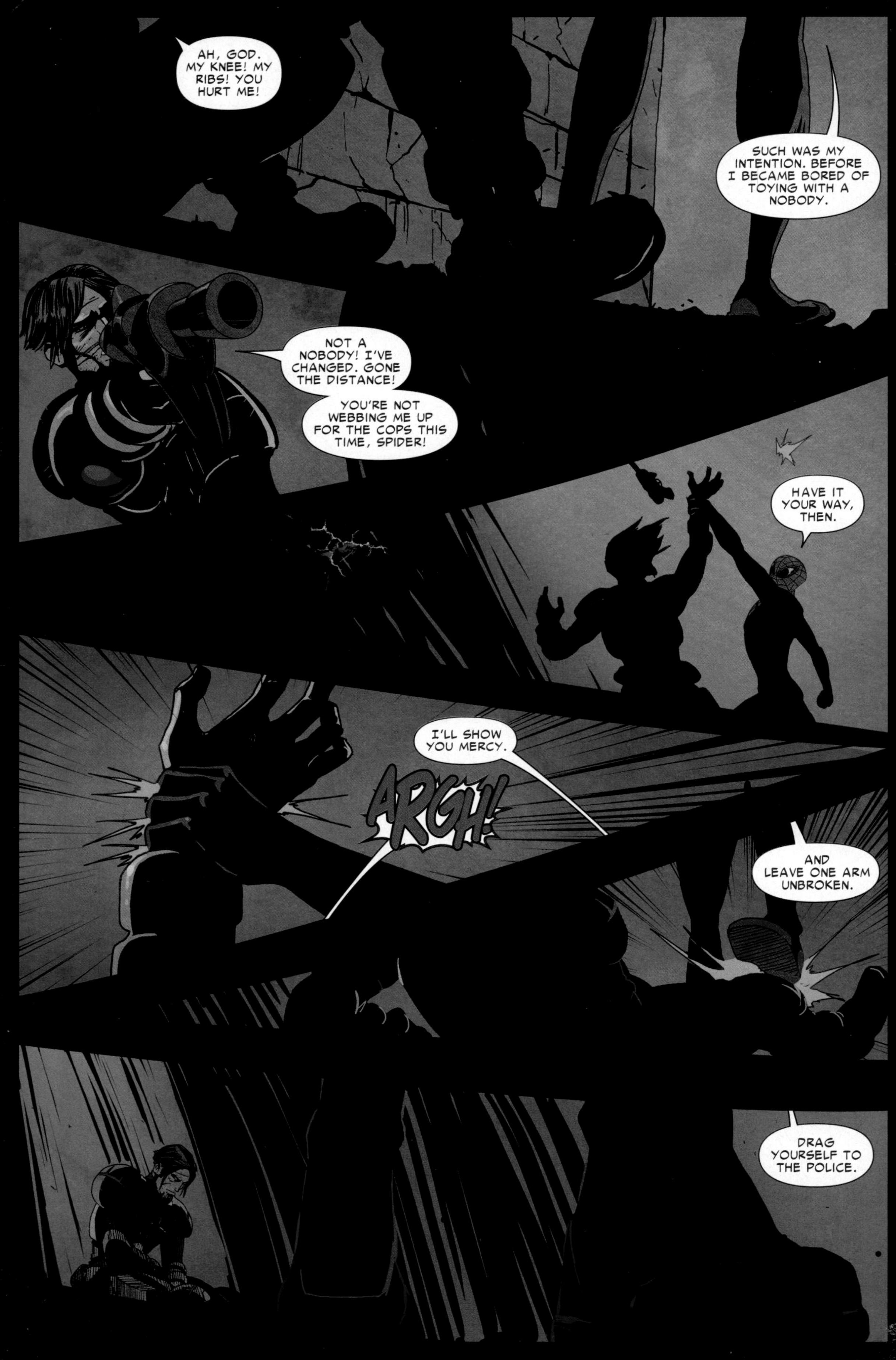
AH, GOD. MY KNEE! MY RIBS! YOU HURT ME!
SUCH WAS MY INTENTION. BEFORE I BECAME BORED OF TOYING WITH A NOBODY.
NOT A NOBODY! I'VE CHANGED. GONE THE DISTANCE!
YOU'RE NOT WEBBING ME UP FOR THE COPS THIS TIME, SPIDER!
HAVE IT YOUR WAY, THEN.
I'LL SHOW YOU MERCY.
ARGH!
AND LEAVE ONE ARM UNBROKEN.
AND DRAG YOURSELF TO THE POLICE.

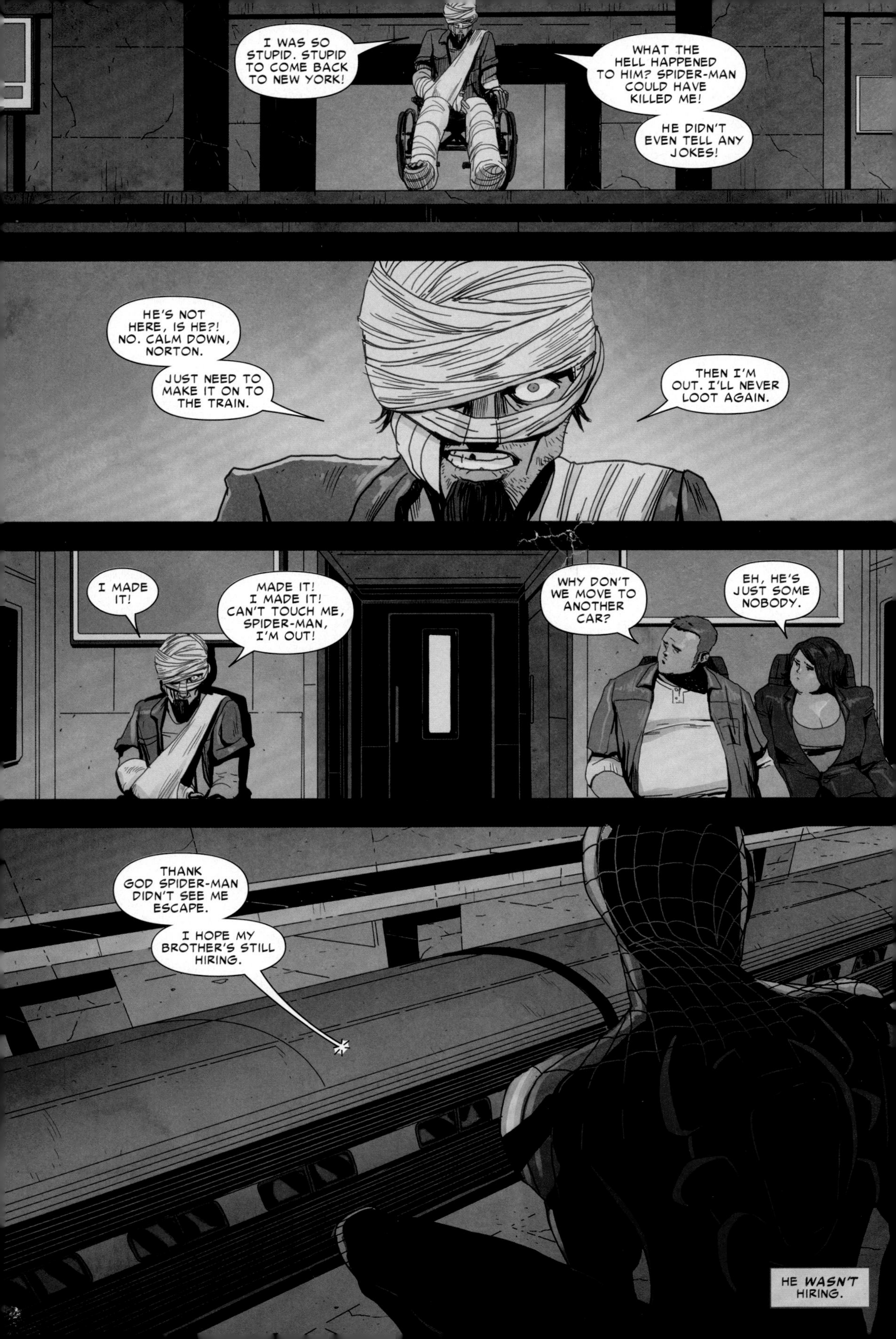
I WAS SO STUPID. STUPID TO COME BACK TO NEW YORK!
WHAT THE HELL HAPPENED TO HIM? SPIDER-MAN COULD HAVE KILLED ME!
HE DIDN'T EVEN TELL ANY JOKES!
HE'S NOT HERE, IS HE?! NO. CALM DOWN, NORTON.
JUST NEED TO MAKE IT ON TO THE TRAIN.
THEN I'M OUT. I'LL NEVER LOOT AGAIN.
I MADE IT!
MADE IT! I MADE IT! CAN'T TOUCH ME, SPIDER-MAN, I'M OUT!
WHY DON'T WE MOVE TO ANOTHER CAR?
EH, HE'S JUST SOME NOBODY.
THANK GOD SPIDER-MAN DIDN'T SEE ME ESCAPE.
I HOPE MY BROTHER'S STILL HIRING.
HE WASN'T HIRING.

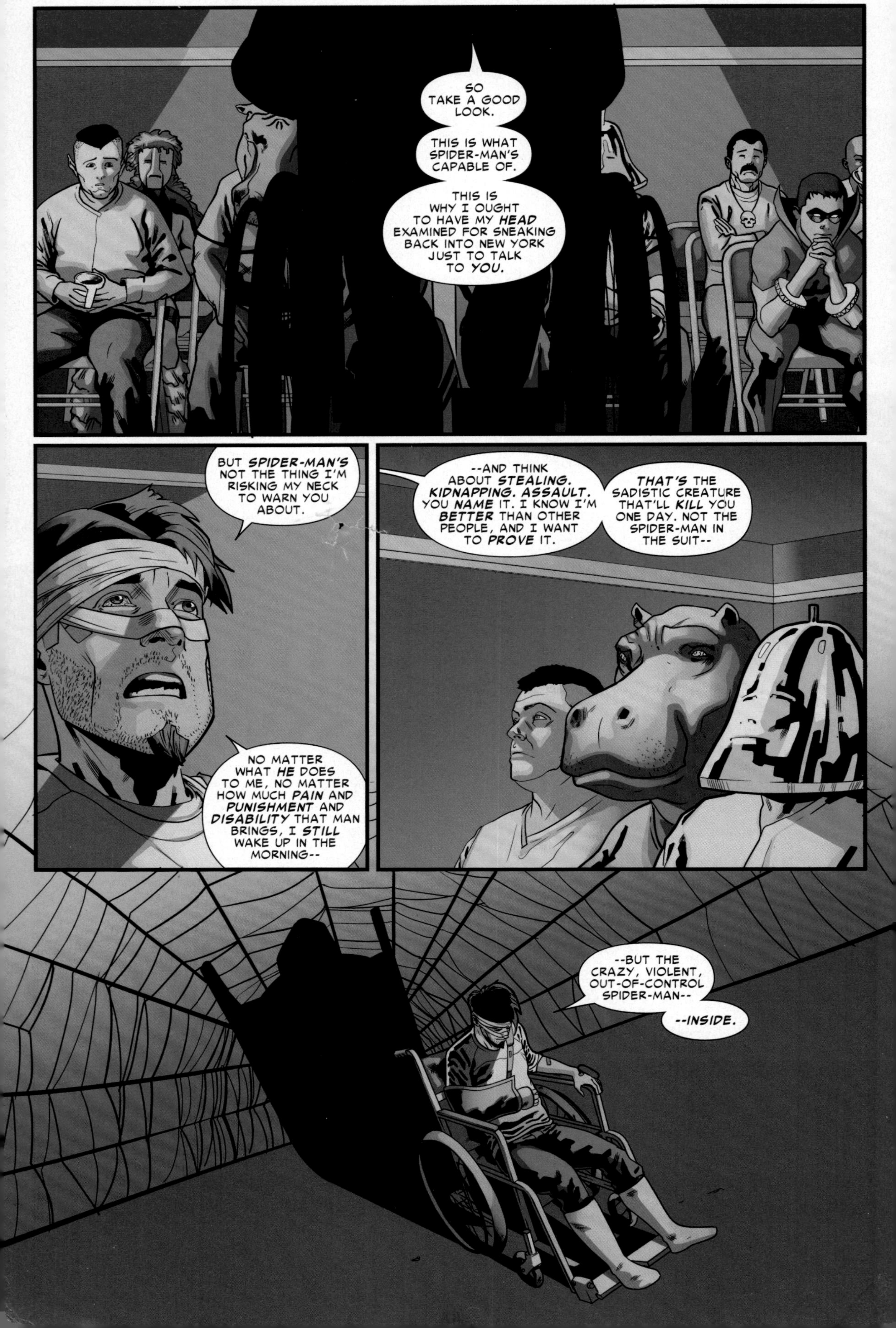
SO TAKE A GOOD LOOK.
THIS IS WHAT SPIDER-MAN'S CAPABLE OF.
THIS IS WHY I OUGHT TO HAVE MY HEAD EXAMINED FOR SNEAKING BACK INTO NEW YORK JUST TO TALK TO YOU.
BUT SPIDER-MAN'S NOT THE THING I'M RISKING MY NECK TO WARN YOU ABOUT.
NO MATTER WHAT HE DOES TO ME, NO MATTER HOW MUCH PAIN AND PUNISHMENT AND DISABILITY THAT MAN BRINGS, I STILL WAKE UP IN THE MORNING--
--AND THINK ABOUT STEALING. KIDNAPPING. ASSAULT. YOU NAME IT. I KNOW I'M BETTER THAN OTHER PEOPLE, AND I WANT TO PROVE IT.
THAT'S THE SADISTIC CREATURE THAT'LL KILL YOU ONE DAY. NOT THE SPIDER-MAN IN THE SUIT--
--BUT THE CRAZY, VIOLENT, OUT-OF-CONTROL SPIDER-MAN--
--INSIDE.

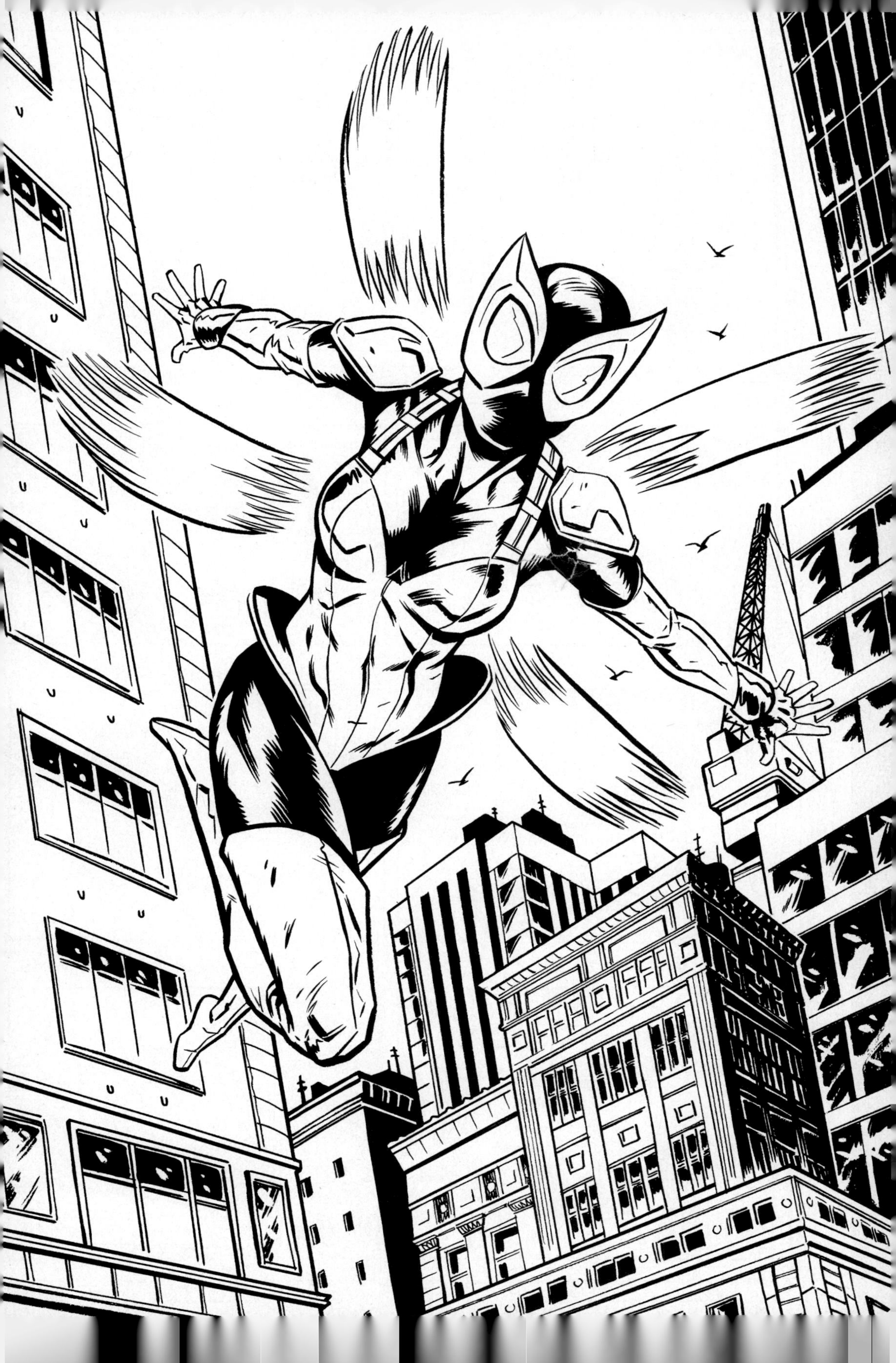

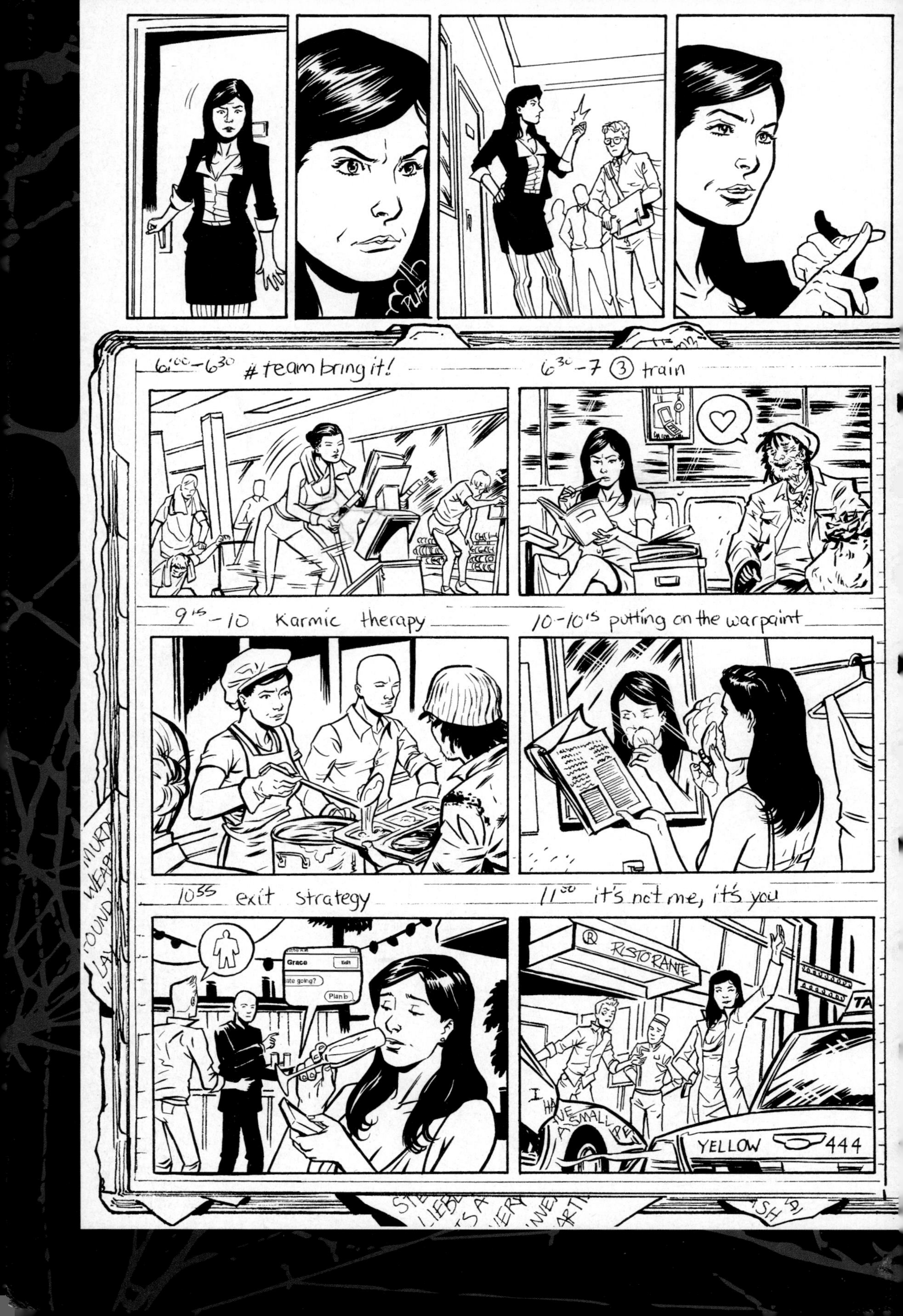

PUFF
$6^{00}-6^{30}$ #team bring it!
$6^{30}-7$ (3) train
$9^{15}-10$ Karmic therapy
$10-10^{15}$ putting on the warpaint
10^{55} exit strategy
Grace
Edit
date going?
Plan b
11^{00} it's not me, it's you
RISTORANTE
YELLOW
444

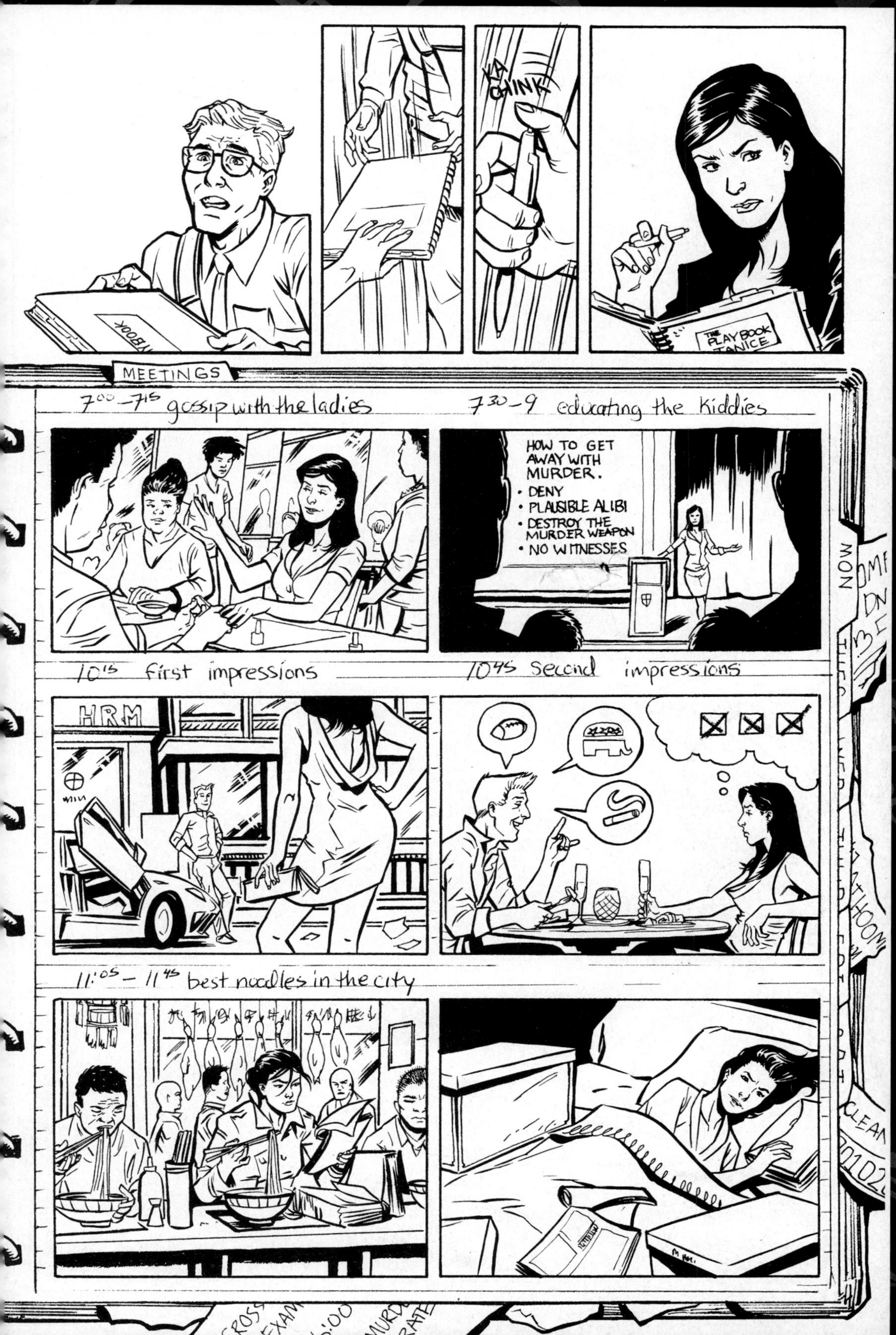
CHINK
THE PLAY BOOK JANICE
MEETINGS
7:00-7:15 gossip with the ladies
7:30-9 educating the kiddies
HOW TO GET AWAY WITH MURDER.
• DENY
• PLAUSIBLE ALIBI
• DESTROY THE MURDER WEAPON
• NO WITNESSES
MON
10:15 first impressions
10:45 second impressions
HRM
11:05 - 11:45 best noodles in the city
CLEAN

ISSUE #7, PAGES 11-12
ART BY RICH ELLIS

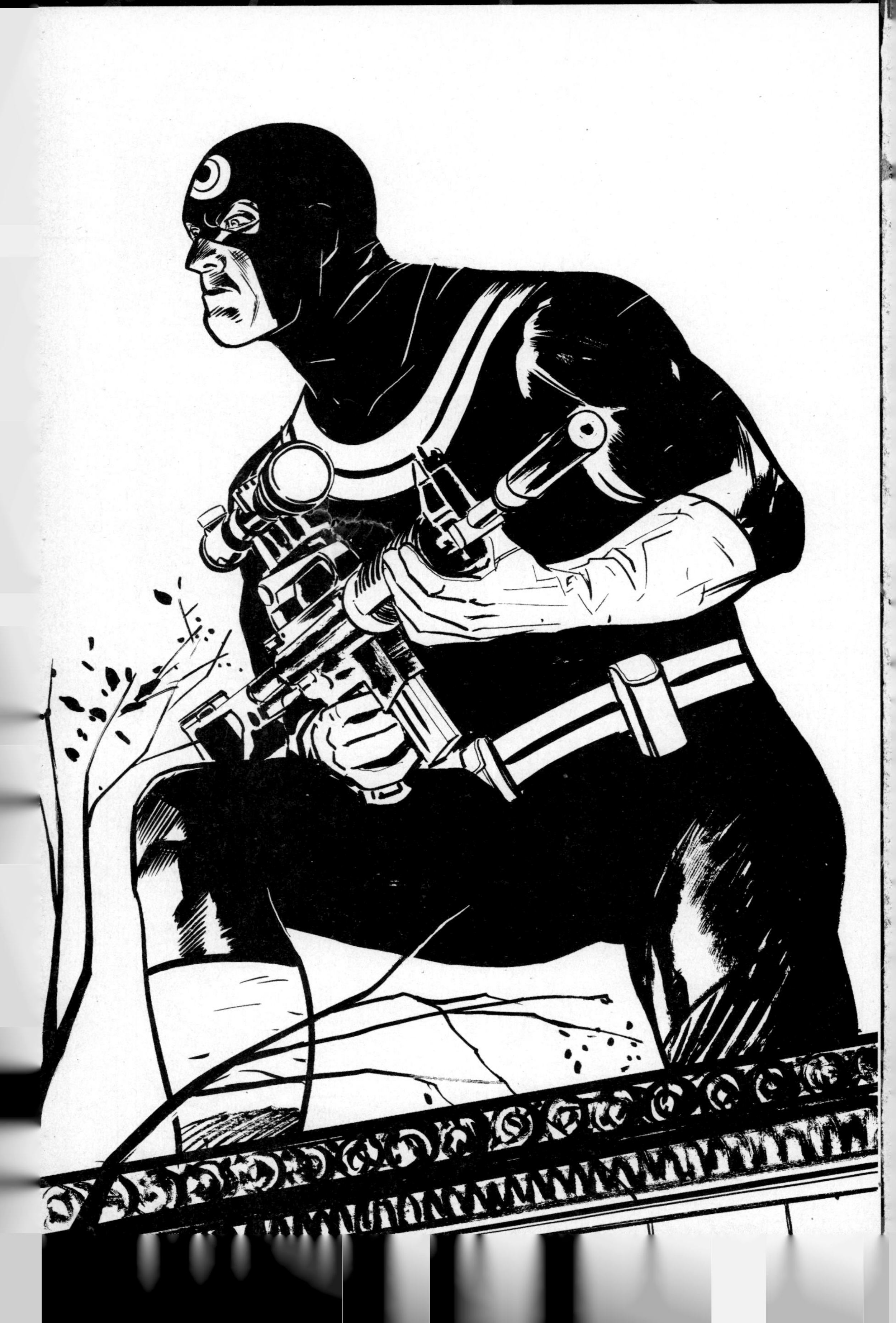